Migration and Wellbeing

This timely and comprehensive book delves into this complex and multi-faceted phenomenon of migration and illuminates its diverse facets and its profound influence on societies across the globe.

In an era marked by unprecedented global mobility, as people move across continents in search of better lives, it has never been more crucial to explore the intricate tapestry of human migration. This volume examines the social, economic, and cultural dimensions of migration, uncovering stories of migrants and the transformative potential and hardships their journeys often entail. The twelve chapters in this book demonstrate the scale of challenges and opportunities that lie ahead. The contributors examine policy, practice, research, and professional development across various international, European, and national settings, all viewed through the perspective of career guidance and counselling.

With a new chapter, conclusion, and a revised introduction, this book will be beneficial to students, researchers, teachers, policymakers, guidance and counselling practitioners who have an interest in migration, human psychology, social science, youth work, mental health, counselling, education, and community development. The other chapters were originally published in the *British Journal of Guidance and Counselling.*

Deirdre Hughes is Associate Professor at the University of Warwick, Institute for Employment Research (IER) in Coventry, England. She is an international careers practitioner, researcher, trainer, and senior policy adviser. For seven years, she led and co-edited an international series of Special Issue Journals on behalf of the *British Journal for Guidance and Counselling.* In 2012, she was awarded a Queen's Honorary Medal (2012) for her services to lifelong guidance.

Füsun Akkök, Emerita Professor of Psychology, Middle East Technical University, Ankara, Türkiye, has more than 40 years of academic and practical experience in guidance and counselling. She is a prolific trainer, writer, and lifelong guidance international expert working for international organisations, including Cedefop (CareersNet Country Expert), The International Organisation for Migration (IOM), the European Training Foundation (ETF), International Labour Organisation (ILO), and the World Bank.

Gideon Arulmani is a Clinical Psychologist with an M.Phil., in medical and social psychology and a doctoral degree in career psychology from the University of Portsmouth, UK. He is the Founder and Managing Trustee of The Promise Foundation, Bangalore, India. His interests lie in the interdisciplinary understanding the human potential. He has developed the Cultural Preparation Process Model of Career Development and formulated comprehensive culture-resonant systems of career counselling for India and other countries.

Migration and Wellbeing

Towards a More Inclusive World

Edited by

Deirdre Hughes, Füsun Akkök and Gideon Arulmani

Routledge
Taylor & Francis Group
LONDON AND NEW YORK

First published 2024
by Routledge
4 Park Square, Milton Park, Abingdon, Oxon OX14 4RN

and by Routledge
605 Third Avenue, New York, NY 10158

Routledge is an imprint of the Taylor & Francis Group, an informa business

British Library Cataloguing in Publication Data
A catalogue record for this book is available from the British Library

ISBN13: 978-1-032-63344-2 (hbk)
ISBN13: 978-1-032-63348-0 (pbk)
ISBN13: 978-1-032-63350-3 (ebk)

DOI: 10.4324/9781032633503

Typeset in Myriad Pro
by Newgen Publishing UK

Publisher's Note
The publisher accepts responsibility for any inconsistencies that may have arisen during the conversion of this book from journal articles to book chapters, namely the inclusion of journal terminology.

Disclaimer
Every effort has been made to contact copyright holders for their permission to reprint material in this book. The publishers would be grateful to hear from any copyright holder who is not here acknowledged and will undertake to rectify any errors or omissions in future editions of this book.

Contents

Citation Information

The following chapters were originally published in the *British Journal of Guidance and Counselling*, volume 47, issue 1 (2019). When citing this material, please use the original page numbering for each article, as follows:

Chapter 1

The effect of a career development programme based on the Hope-Action Theory: Hope to Work for refugees in British Columbia
Hyung Joon Yoon, Natasha Bailey, Norman Amundson and Spencer Niles
British Journal of Guidance and Counselling, volume 47, issue 1 (2019), pp. 6–19

Chapter 2

The cultural preparedness model of aspiration and engagement: understanding the dynamics of integration
Gideon Arulmani
British Journal of Guidance and Counselling, volume 47, issue 1 (2019), pp. 20–34

Chapter 3

Where are you from?' Identity as a key to parenting by 1.5 generation Korean-New Zealand migrants and implications for counselling
Hyeeun Kim and Margaret Nelson Agee
British Journal of Guidance and Counselling, volume 47, issue 1 (2019), pp. 35–49

Chapter 4

Considering boundaries when doing therapeutic work with people who are seeking asylum: a reflective case study
Megan Cowles and Mary Griggs
British Journal of Guidance and Counselling, volume 47, issue 1 (2019), pp. 50–64

Chapter 6

Factors that impact the sociocultural adjustment and well-being of Syrian refugees in Stuttgart, Germany
Samar Jean El Khoury
British Journal of Guidance and Counselling, volume 47, issue 1 (2019), pp. 65–80

Chapter 7

A job-seeking competency model for North Korean defectors who are college students in South Korea
Hyung Joon Yoon, Sungsik Ahn and Eun Hee Kang
British Journal of Guidance and Counselling, volume 47, issue 1 (2019), pp. 81–95

Chapter 8

Families left behind at the source of migration: implications for career guidance practitioners
Sachin Kumar
British Journal of Guidance and Counselling, volume 47, issue 1 (2019), pp. 96–108

Chapter 9

Learning engagement as a target for interventions: a qualitative study of first-generation migrant adolescents in Finnish secondary education
Linda Molin-Karakoc and Minna Ikola
British Journal of Guidance and Counselling, volume 47, issue 1 (2019), pp. 109–122

Chapter 10

A comparison of mental health literacy, attitudes, and help-seeking intentions among domestic and international tertiary students
Bonnie A. Clough, Sonia M. Nazareth, Jamin J. Day and Leanne M. Casey
British Journal of Guidance and Counselling, volume 47, issue 1 (2019), pp. 123–135

Notes on Contributors

Margaret Nelson Agee, Faculty of Education and Social Work, University of Auckland, Auckland, New Zealand.

Sungsik Ahn, Keimyung University, Republic of Korea.

Füsun Akkök, Middle East Technical University, Ankara, Türkiye.

Norman Amundson, Department of Educational and Counselling Psychology, and Special Education, The University of British Columbia, British Columbia, Canada.

Gideon Arulmani, The Promise Foundation, Bangalore, India.

Natasha Bailey, Independent Researcher, British Columbia, Canada.

Leanne M. Casey, School of Applied Psychology, Griffith University, Queensland, Australia.

Bonnie A. Clough, School of Applied Psychology, Griffith University, Menzies Health Institute Queensland, Nathan, Queensland, Australia.

Megan Cowles, Avon & Wiltshire Mental Health Partnership Trust, Complex Psychological Interventions, Petherton Resource Centre, Bristol, UK.

Jamin J. Day, Family Action Centre, University of Newcastle, Callaghan, New South Wales, Australia.

Samar Jean El Khoury, Faculty of Social and Behavioral Sciences, Haigazian University, Beirut, Lebanon.

Mary Griggs, Specialised Deaf Service & Traumatic Stress Service, NHS, Bristol, UK.

Daniel Hailemariam, Hailemariam Consulting, Sweden.

Deirdre Hughes, Institute for Employment Research, University of Warwick, Coventry, UK.

Minna Ikola, Harjuniitty School, School District of Nokia, Nokia, Finland.

Eun Hee Kang, Career Development Center, Korea University, Seoul, Republic of Korea.

Hyeeun Kim, School of Clinical Science, Auckland University of Technology, New Zealand.

Sachin Kumar, WRS Government College, Dehri, Kangra, Himachal Pradesh, India.

Linda Molin-Karakoc, Institute of Education, University College London, UK.

Sonia M. Nazareth, School of Applied Psychology, Griffith University, Queensland, Australia.

Spencer Niles, School of Education, William & Mary, Williamsburg, Virginia, USA.

Hyung Joon Yoon, Department of Learning and Performance Systems, The Pennsylvania State University, University Park, Pennsylvania, USA.

Acknowledgements

We dedicate this book to our dear colleague and friend Helmut Zelloth who worked closely with us bringing academics, policymakers, and practitioners together to explore this topic. Helmut tragically and unexpectedly passed away on the 17th of July 2020. We miss his wisdom and intellect.

Huge affection and gratitude also to Prof. Metin Akkök, late husband of Prof. Füsun Akkök for his grace, valuable guidance, and continuous support.

We are hugely indebted to career guidance and counselling practitioners from around the world for their inspirational work on migration issues deep in local communities, regional and national organisations. Your work changes people's lives for the better, offering them respect, hope, opportunity and, most importantly, dignity.

Finally, we would like to thank all the authors who participated in the creation of the "Migration: Theory, research and practice in guidance and counselling" Special Issue that have become this book and who have expressed their enthusiastic support for the project. We also thank the reviewers, patient co-editors, and production editors at the *British Journal of Guidance and Counselling*. We also thank our Routledge editor Anveshi Gupta.

Introduction—Migration: towards a more inclusive society

Deirdre Hughes, Füsun Akkök and Gideon Arulmani

Introduction

Migration is as old as the history of humanity. Today all over the world many people make one of the most challenging decisions in their lives: to leave their homes and townships in search of a safer or better life. Migration is a term that encompasses a wide variety of movements and situations that involve people of all walks of life and backgrounds. More than ever before, migration touches many countries and people in an era of deepening globalisation (Bimrose & McNair, 2011; International Organisation for Migration [IOM], 2017, 2022). This phenomenon is embedded in trade and cultural exchange and has offered opportunities for millions of people worldwide to forge safe and meaningful lives abroad (Organisation for Economic Co-operation and Development [OECD], 2018). Migration can result in the transfer of skills, knowledge and technology that have considerable positive impacts on productivity and economic growth (Carling & Schewel, 2018; Gelb & Krishnan, 2018; Näsholm, 2012).

This is driven by both pull and push factors. There are immigrants who have voluntarily or willing of their own accord moved home to a new country, others who have been placed temporarily on foreign shores by their employers and live their lives as expatriates and still others who have chosen the work lifestyle of the global worker, following opportunities from one country to another (Stahl, Chua, Caligiuri, Cerdin, & Taniguchi, 2009). On the other hand, various push factors such as war, political instability, climate calamities have left people with no other option than to seek refuge (perhaps involuntarily), in another country. Migration may have positive or sometimes negative impacts on the lives of the individuals concerned, depending on a considerable number of factors.

Focus

This book explores the interconnections within the concept of migration and discusses 'the art of the possible' in moving towards more inclusive societies. By putting the spotlight on this topic, we seek to outline the complexities of contemporary socio-economic, environmental and political challenges related to this specific theme. When individuals migrate across borders, they inevitably weave a global web of connections. Through their migration experience, they link the contacts they establish in their destination countries with those in their places of origin. From this perspective, their journey need not be about leaving one nation and entering another; it could serve as a bridge between the two. This holds significance because the flow of capital, knowledge and values become multi-dimensional.

By examining the complexities, challenges and opportunities for change, the synergies and interdependencies become apparent as outlined in this book. The authors in each chapter underscore the importance of a personalised and holistic approach to supporting young people and adults at a time in their lives when everything may have changed for them and their families. The role of intermediaries and what constitutes skilful practice is also considered within a guidance and counselling context.

Definitions

The terms 'refugee', 'asylum-seeker' and 'migrant' are often used to describe people who are on the move, who have left their countries and have crossed borders. The terms 'migrant' and 'refugee' are often used interchangeably but it is important to distinguish between them as there is a legal difference (Amnesty International, 2018a). There are negative perceptions of migrants in many societies. This is often framed in popular notions of 'us' and 'them', presenting economic challenges, or perhaps being seen as raising security concerns or creating ambivalence in cultural and political spheres, all of which have affected how migrants are perceived by host societies (McKinsey, 2016; Özer, 2014). Whilst there have been many European and international programmes and studies in response to the call for greater support mechanisms for migrants, this emergent focus is not without its issues. For example, there are several misconceptions about migrants when it comes to their contribution to society which draw on negative connotations such as cheap labour, 'stealing' jobs or being under-educated to name but a few. At the heart of the politics of migration is a notion that immigrants, especially those that are unskilled, depress wages. In Britain, Cable (2017) has argued that while at first sight this seems plausible and undeniably there is low wage competition in some places it is a politically charged perspective, with no data-driven evidence that it is a general problem.

Rhetoric and reality

The growing rhetoric of building a wall, creating a new border force, establishing a camp, stopping the boats or restricting access has political, social and humanitarian consequences. Many millions of people have been forced to leave their homes. For example, the Rohingya refugee crisis has caused close to a million people to flee from their homes to save their lives (United Nations, 2017). The recent mass movement of people from Central America towards the US border involves people fleeing from poverty and violence (Amnesty International, 2018b) and highlights that some people leave home to get a job or an education. Others are forced to flee persecution or human rights violations such as torture. Millions seek to escape from armed conflicts or other crises or violence. Some no longer feel safe due to being targeted just because of who they are or what they do or believe – for example, for their ethnicity, religion, sexuality or political opinions.

The current global estimate is that there were around 281 million international migrants in the world in 2020, which equates to 3.6 per cent of the global population. Overall, the estimated number of international migrants has increased over the past five decades. The total estimated 281 million people living in a country other than their countries of birth in 2020 was 128 million more than in 1990 and over three times the estimated number in 1970 (IOM, 2022). Further, the total number of people estimated to have been displaced globally is the highest on record (op. cit., p. 2). It is important to acknowledge that behind these cold numbers, for every migration statistic, there are individuals, children and families starting a new life in a new place. The acculturation of immigrants, asylum seekers and refugees does not take place in a social vacuum.

Identity, guidance and counselling

The integration of migrants can be a difficult process for all involved. It requires migrants to yield to the reality of their new lives and to agree to taking their lives forward in ways that may not have been their choice. It requires receiving communities and governments to accept new arrivals, to accommodate their presence with material and spiritual generosity and to be open to the possibility of enrichment (Gallagher, 2018, p. 2). Finding suitable housing, education, training and/or work is critical to successful integration. Local support mechanisms for individuals and families to adjust and make successful transitions into new communities are essential.

Guidance and counselling can support individual paths to self-sufficiency, better well-being and provide stability by addressing trauma, displacement, mental health, transitional readjustment, or simply opening up access to opportunities, and creating new ones. These services each provide a place and space for individuals and/or groups to find their own identity and to gain a sense of hope and optimism for a better future.

Academic interest in identity transformation (Vassilieva, 2016) and professional identity transformation (Brown & Bimrose, 2018) is increasing; yet, there is insufficient empirical research on migrants' identity transformation and their lived experiences in new community settings. We need to better understand what works, how and in what circumstances. Fundamentally, wrong assumptions, inequalities and bias have to be challenged by guidance and counselling professionals, underpinned by a strong evidence-base. This can then have a positive effect in influencing the public perception of migrants and the policymakers' stance.

Theory building and anchor points

Migration research is informed by different strands of theory building and is often anchored in epistemological, ontological and methodological frameworks. Research interest in this global phenomenon has amplified in recent years. This is evidenced in the multiplicity of journal articles and books published, as well as the various actors engaged, including academia, think tanks and intergovernmental organisations. But within guidance and counselling this topic is largely under-researched (Newman, Bimrose, Nielsen, & Zacher, 2018). There is a growing need for analytical tools and approaches that allow us to deal with the complex, contradictory and contested nature of migration. This is a political, cultural and social phenomenon that requires greater understanding of contemporary dynamics and their manifold implications. Those working in these professional fields need to be inspired by good and interesting theories, methods and innovative practice from around the world and develop knowledge, skills and competences for guiding and counselling people from varied ethnicities who are making a home within the same political-economic context (Arulmani & Kumar, 2023).

The collection

Migration poses challenges to migrants, the countries of their origin and the destination countries. This collection of ten chapters on *Migration: Towards a more inclusive society* comes at a critical juncture. Finding resources and sustainable methods to tackle the migrant crisis, displacement, discrimination and inequalities is vital to the wellbeing of societies. The contributors bring complementary theoretical and practical perspectives from their own research and analysis of issues in Canada, England, Finland, Germany, India, Norway, South Korea, New Zealand and Sweden.

As we delve into the complexities of migration, let us remember that each individual's story is a thread in the rich tapestry of human existence, deserving empathy and shared understanding. We engaged with this project because of a fundamental commitment to values that define our shared humanity: dignity, respect and strong beliefs in cultural integration and inclusion. Hopefully, the content of this book makes some contribution towards making the world a more tolerant and compassionate place.

Deirdre Hughes has woven these principles into her scholarly work, teaching and career guidance and counselling practice. This is not only to gain a deeper understanding of migration but also to contribute to a world where all individuals, regardless of their migration status, can live with dignity, receive respect, and most importantly to find the support they need to lead fulfilling lives. In doing so, this fulfils a shared responsibility to be culturally aware, and treat people with kindness as we would expect to be treated ourselves. She grew up in Northern Ireland during the Troubles from 1960 to 1981 and witnessed first-hand of the effects of individuals and families having to flee from the impact of terrorism and the psychological scarring effects of divisions in society.

Füsun Akkök has extensive experience of advising NGOs, researching and training managers and practitioners on migration issues in Turkey and further afield. The social, political, economic, psychological and humanitarian impact of migration should not be underestimated. Migration and displacement pose some of the biggest humanitarian challenges of our time. As a psychologist and a career development specialist, she wants politicians and others to reframe narratives on migration, especially for those in vulnerable situations by creating opportunities for migrants to share their own stories and perspectives, allowing them to reclaim their narratives and challenge negative portrayals. By doing so, societies can move closer to creating communities that treat people with dignity and enhancing social integration, tolerance and cohesion.

Gideon Arulmani has applied his cultural preparedness approach in his work with counsellors in Sweden and Norway over the last 10 years, who are working with people from varied cultures and ethnicities. This has led to the development of various counsellor training courses and tools designed to sharpen counsellors' knowledge, competencies and skills to work with migrant families. His work aims to bring counsellors closer to their own countries' policy developments that address the issues that surround cultural integration. Overall, Gideon's work aims at developing theory-driven skills training that could contribute to helping migrants develop a new cultural equilibrium as they attempt to make a home away from their original homes.

Our experiences and awareness of the importance of migration and working towards a more inclusive society, and the application of guidance and counselling policies and practice led us to undertake further work on this topic. The chapters you see here were originally articles published in 2021 as Volume 47. Issue 1, 2019 of the 'Migration: Theory, research and practice in guidance and counselling' symposium Special Issue within the *British Journal of Guidance and Counselling* .

We are extremely grateful to our dear colleague and friend Helmut Zelloth who provided earlier inspiration and input to the Special Issue. He worked closely with us bringing academics, researchers and practitioners together to explore this topic. Helmut tragically and unexpectedly passed away on the 17th of July 2020. We miss his wisdom and intellect.

Chapters: brief overview

The first chapter begins Yoon, Bailey, Admundson and Niles presenting a Hope-Action Theory applied in the context of working with Syrian refugees in British Columbia. They assess the proximal and distal outcomes of a career development training programme for refugees using a two-way mixed effects analysis of covariance and a serial mediation analysis. The authors discuss the need to create the conditions and chances for refugee newcomers to tell their unique stories during training.

In the second chapter, Arulmani draws upon his travelogue of 17 years capturing interviews with immigrants and refugees in different parts of the world. He describes two studies to understand the disturbance of cultural equilibrium as individuals try to find their way in a host country. Drawing upon his research, he presents the cultural preparation status model of aspiration and engagement as a framework that guidance and counselling workers might use to help immigrants optimise their engagement with the systems of the host country.

Next Kim and Agee consider identity as a major theme in chapter three. This qualitative study of the experiences of 1.5 generation Korean New Zealanders as parents considers their identity-related experiences as migrants. The term 1.5 generation refers to people who immigrated as children, old enough to remember the native country and retain its culture, yet young enough to adapt naturally to the new country and its culture. Reflecting on the challenges of their migration and identity journeys enabled them to recognise their vulnerabilities and their advantages, and the multiple ways in which identity-related cultural conflicts and confusion influenced their parenting of their children. The implications for further research and for counselling practice are identified.

Chapter 4 by Cowles and Griggs puts the spotlight on the challenges and dilemmas practitioners face in trauma-focused work. They focus on people who are seeking asylum who often have lived experience of their personal boundaries and human rights being violated. They provide a case study of work with a woman with a severe trauma history who was seeking asylum in England. Some perceived boundary crossings in the therapeutic relationship are examined, alongside considerations for other clinicians working with asylum seekers.

In Chapter 5, Hailemariam explores the nuances of intercultural counselling within a multifaceted and dynamic cultural landscape. He delves into practitioner challenges and opportunities presented by multiculturalism, emphasising the importance of culturally competent career guidance approaches. The discussion focuses on understanding the role of professional careers practitioners as bridges between different cultural contexts and the strategies and skills necessary for fostering meaningful cross-cultural relationships. Ethical considerations, potential pitfalls and possible solutions are discussed.

This is followed by El Khoury who investigates the impact of age, gender, language and acculturation choice on the socio-cultural adjustment and well-being of Syrian refugees in Stuttgart, Germany. Correlation analyses and t-tests were used to examine the relationships between different variables drawn from a demographics questionnaire, the Acculturation Attitudes Scale (AAS-16), the Revised Sociocultural Adjustment Scale (R-SCAS) and the Mental Health Inventory (MHI-18). The results indicate a wide range of factors at work affecting refugees' well-being. A case is made for coaching designed for refugees in socio-cultural adjustment and cross-cultural stressors.

In Chapter 7, Yoon, Ahn and Kang reflect on a job-seeking competency model for North Korean defectors who are college students in South Korea. They adopt the Delphi method with a panel of 17 experts and, through three Delphi rounds, 18 job-seeking competencies were identified. In addition, the preliminary utility of the competency model is examined. Implications of the study results and future directions for enhancing the validity and utility of the competency model are discussed.

Next, Kumar offers a fresh perspective on occupational identity, describing left-behind families of pine resin tappers in India. A review of the literature reveals that there is more focus on international migration compared to internal migration. Further, there is more emphasis on issues related to the migration destination rather than those at the source of migration. The left-behind families of pine resin tappers in the Changar region of the Indian Himalayas are presented as a case study to draw the attention of career guidance and counselling professionals to this unattended population.

Chapter 9, by Molin-Karakoc and Ikola considers findings from a qualitative study of first-generation migrant adolescents in Finnish secondary schools. They shed light on the multi-faceted construct of school engagement among migrant students. They highlight the implications of students' lived experiences for their integration, socialisation, development and well-being. Participant interviews and observations were conducted. The results indicate a need for reshaping support services to consider the cultural capital, multi-lingual literacies and the quality of existing social, in and out-of-school relationships of students in order to offer effective teaching, guidance and mentoring services.

In Chapter 10, Clough, Nazareth, Day and Casey underscore the relative neglect in examining distress or help-seeking knowledge and attitudes among international students in the literature. Their aim was to examine psychological distress, mental health literacy (MHL), and help-seeking attitudes and intentions among a sample of domestic and international tertiary students. International student status was predictive of lower scores for MHL, help-seeking attitudes and help-seeking intentions for suicidal ideation. Student group was not predictive of help-seeking intentions for emotional problems or psychological distress, but international students had lower help-seeking intentions for suicidal ideation.

References

Amnesty International. (2018a). Definitions: What exactly is a refugee, an asylum-seeker and a migrant? Retrieved from: www.amnesty.org/en/what-we-do/refugees-asylum-seekers-and-migrants/ [Google Scholar].

Amnesty International. (2018b). Key facts about the migrant and refugee caravans making their way to the USA. Retrieved from www.amnesty.org/en/latest/news/2018/11/key-facts-about-the-migrant-and-refugee-caravans-making-their-way-to-the-usa/ [Google Scholar].

Arulmani, G., & Kumar S. (2023). Livelihood thinking for career development: Rethinking work from alternative perspectives. In D. L. Blustein, & L. Y Flores (Eds.), *Rethinking Work: Essays on Building a Better Workplace* (pp. 15–19). New York: Routledge.

Bimrose, J., & McNair, S. (2011). Career support for migrants: Transformation or adaptation? *Journal Of Vocational Behavior*, *78*(3), 321–392. doi: 10.1016/j.jvb.2011.03.012, [Web of Science ®], [Google Scholar].

Brown, A., & Bimrose, J. (2018). Learning and identity development at work. In M. Milana, S. Webb, J. Holford, R. Waller, & P. Jarvis (Eds.), *The Palgrave International Handbook on Adult and Lifelong Education and Learning* (pp. 245–265). London: Palgrave Macmillan, [Google Scholar].

Cable, V. (2017). *The Tory fallacy: That migrants are taking British jobs and driving down wages*. London: *The Guardian*. September 8, 2017. Retrieved from www.theguardian.com/commentisfree/2017/sep/08/tory-fallacy-migrants-british-jobs-wages-brexit [Google Scholar].

Carling, J., & Schewel, K. (2018). Revisiting aspiration and ability in international migration. *Journal of Ethnic and Migration Studies*, *44*(6), 945–963. doi: 10.1080/1369183X.2017.1384146 [Taylor & Francis Online], [Web of Science ®], [Google Scholar].

Crawley, H., Duvell, F., Jones, K., Mcmahon, S., & Sigona, N. (2017). *Unravelling Europe's 'Migration Crisis'. Journeys over Land and Sea*. Bristol: University of Bristol, Policy Press. [Google Scholar].

Gallagher, A. (2018). *We Need to Talk about Integration after Migration*. Davos: World Economic Forum. Retrieved from www.weforum.org/agenda/2018/10/we-need-to-talk-about-integration-after-migration [Google Scholar].

Gelb, S., & Krishnan, A. (2018). *Technology, Migration and the 2030 Agenda for Sustainable Development. Briefing Note*. Switzerland: Federal Department for Foreign Affairs, Swiss Agency for Development and Co-operation, SDC. Retrieved from www.odi.org/sites/odi.org.uk/files/resource-documents/12395.pdf [Google Scholar].

International Organisation of Migration. (2017). *Executive Summary on Migrant Vulnerabilities and Integration Needs in Central Asia 2017: Assessing Migrants' and Community Needs and Managing Risks*. Geneva, Switzerland: IOM, The UN Migration Agency. Retrieved from www.iom.kz/images/books/2017-DAR-executive-summary-eng.pdf [Google Scholar].

International Organisation of Migration. (2022). *World Migration Report 2022*. Geneva, Switzerland: IOM, The UN Migration Agency. Retrieved from https://worldmigrationreport.iom.int/wmr-2022-interactive/ [Google Scholar].

McKinsey. (2016). *People on the Move: Global Migration's Impact and Opportunity*. McKinsey Global Institute Migration Policy Institute Europe. Retrieved from www.mckinsey.com/ca/~/media/mckinsey/industries/public%20and%20social%20sector/our%20insights/global%20migrations%20impact%20and%20opportunity/mgi-people-on-the-move-full-report.pdf [Google Scholar].

Näsholm, M. H. (2012). Global careerists' identity construction. *International Journal of Managing Projects in Business*, *5*(4), 804–812. doi: 10.1108/17538371211269068, [Google Scholar].

Newman, A., Bimrose, J., Nielsen, I., & Zacher, H. (2018). Vocational behavior of refugees: How do refugees seek employment, overcome work-related challenges, and navigate their careers? *Journal of Vocational Behavior*, *105*, 1–5. doi: 10.1016/j.jvb.2018.01.007, [Web of Science ®], [Google Scholar].

OECD. (2018). *International Migration Outlook* (42nd ed.). Paris: Organisation for Economic Cooperation and Development Publishing. [Google Scholar].

Özer, Y. Y. (2014). *Migration, Asylum and Refugees in Turkey: Studies in Control of Population at the Southeastern Borders of The European Union*. New York: Edwin Mellen Press. [Google Scholar].

Stahl, G. K., Chua, C. H., Caligiuri, P., Cerdin, J. L., & Taniguchi, M. (2009). Predictors of turnover intentions in learning-driven and demand-driven international assignments: The role of repatriation concerns, satisfaction with company support, and perceived career advancement opportunities. *Human Resource Management*, *48*(1), 89–109. doi: 10.1002/hrm.20268, [Web of Science ®], [Google Scholar].

United Nations. (2017). *The Rohingya Refugee Crisis*. Geneva: Office for the Coordination of Humanitarian Affairs. [Google Scholar].

Vassilieva, J. (2016). *Narrative Psychology: Identity, Transformation and Ethics*. London: Macmillan. doi: 10.1057/978-1-137-49195-4, [Google Scholar].

The effect of a career development programme based on the Hope-Action Theory: Hope to Work for refugees in British Columbia

Hyung Joon Yoon, Natasha Bailey, Norman Amundson and Spencer Niles

ABSTRACT

The purpose of this study was to assess the proximal and distal outcomes of a career development training programme for refugees that was developed based on the Hope-Action Theory (HAT). Adopting an experimental design, proximal outcomes such as self-efficacy, hope-action competencies, job search clarity, and career adaptability were assessed three times; and distal outcomes including employment status, job-seeking activities, career growth, hopeful career state, work engagement, and job satisfaction were assessed once at nine months. We used a two-way mixed effects analysis of covariance and a serial mediation analysis. The programme was effective in developing hope-action competencies, general self-efficacy, and job search clarity. The experimental group participants exhibited higher hopeful career state and work engagement. A serial mediation model of the HAT-based intervention predicting job satisfaction was found. Limitations and future directions are discussed.

Introduction

Refugees in Canada tend to exhibit higher unemployment rates than all other immigration classes (Wilkinson & Garcea, 2017). They are more likely to have precarious jobs, low job satisfaction and a higher degree of job status decline (Wilkinson, Chowdhury, Shen, Bucklaschuk, & Edkins, 2014). Muslim newcomers and refugees experience labour market penalties disproportionately to other religious groups and immigration classes (Fuller & Martin, 2012). The mean amount of time it takes for refugees to achieve employment and income parity with the Canadian-born population is 12–15 years (Affiliation of Multicultural Societies and Services Agencies of BC [AMSSA], 2017).

Unemployment is considered to put a refugee at risk of re-traumatization and deleterious mental health outcomes (Briggs, 2011). Moreover, trauma has been shown to result in dysfunctional career thoughts (Strauser, Lustig, Cogdal, & Uruk, 2006). These findings speak to the potential need to develop and test programmes that foster employment outcomes for refugees taking into account their unique experiences and the fact that their starting point for labour market integration is far behind that of other immigrant classes. UNHCR (Ott, 2013) supports this view suggesting that more could be known about refugee employment outcomes globally and the effectiveness of programmes through randomised controlled trials and research employing a quasi-experimental design. Ott (2013) also suggests that there is a theoretical gap in programming as it generally lacks an intervention logic or theory of change.

This study explores the outcome of a career development programme, called *Hope to Work* (H2W), for refugees in British Columbia. The programme is offered through MOSAIC, which is a charity serving immigrant communities in British Columbia, Canada. H2W is a 2-week long programme developed based on the Hope-Action Theory (HAT; previously known as the Hope-Centred Model of Career Development). Two types of outcomes are explored in this study: (a) proximal outcomes including hope-action competency, general self-efficacy, career adapt-ability, and job search clarity and (b) distal outcomes including job search activities, employment status, career growth, work engagement, hopeful career state, and job satisfaction.

Hope-Action Theory

The HAT is a positive approach to one's career development developed by Niles, Yoon, and Amundson (in Niles, Amundson, & Neault, 2011). The HAT integrated three theories: Bandura's (2001) human agency theory; Hall's (1996) career meta-competencies and Snyder's (2002) hope theory. It seeks to foster a set of competencies, called hope-action competencies, such as hope, self-reflection, self-clarity, visioning, goal setting, implementing, and adapting. Firmly situated within the positive psychology approach to human development, the model is strengths-based and incorporates innovative methods to foster these competencies, including kinaesthetic activities, storytelling, visualisation, and metaphor (Niles et al., 2011). Thus far, the model has been shown to have an impact on hope and related outcomes for internationally trained health professionals (Clarke, Amundson, Niles, & Yoon, in press), unemployed individuals (Amundson, Goddard, Yoon, & Niles, 2018), and post-secondary students (Yoon et al., 2015).

The HAT was chosen due to the salience of fostering hope as a mechanism for supporting refugee labour market integration. To date, almost no immigrant and refugee research has sought to explore the role of hope as a "state-like" attribute that is open to change and development as it relates to fostering newcomer employment outcomes. A notable exception is Clarke et al. (in press), where a hope-centred career development process with internationally trained health professionals resulted in significant improvements in levels of hope as well as progression towards licensure (as measured through a range of behavioural indicators). Clarke et al., however, applied only a pre- and post-design using a single group, suggesting the need to employing a more robust research approach combining time series and experimental designs, to which this study responded.

Hope and refugee employment

Hope is often mentioned in literature about immigrant and refugee employment. Elez (2014) scopes a central role for employment services in the restoration of career hope for newcomers. Employment offers social connections, status and identity, and income. Conversely, lack of access to the aforementioned pathways results in anxiety, depression, and isolation, all of which may involve feelings of hopelessness (Elez, 2014). According to Gilmore (2009), the type of employment that supports integration should be quality employment characterised by safety, financial and non-financial remuneration, not excessively long or short working hours, work–life balance, potential for social dialogue, skills development, and job satisfaction. He also notes that job stability or long-term employment is a quality employment criterion for newcomer labour market integration. However, these aforementioned criteria are generally not evident in refugee labour market attachment (Gilmore, 2009).

According to Snyder (2002), hope is defined with three elements: goals, the capacity to identify pathways to desired goals, and the capacity to motivate oneself to use those pathways. Moreover, the assertion is that high hope "allows for the rekindling of determination and willpower even when faced with blockages as additional alternative pathways have been proactively determined" (Youssef & Luthans, 2007, p. 779). In other words, people with high levels of hope are better at coming up with multiple, higher quality alternative routes when faced with barriers than those with low hope (Peterson & Byron, 2008). Given the significant employment barriers faced by refugees, developing or harnessing hope seems to be an important aspect of supporting their labour market integration.

Self-efficacy, career adaptability, and job search clarity

As proximal outcome measures for H2W, we chose self-efficacy, adaptability, and job search clarity in addition to the hope-action competencies. Hirschi (2014) shows that dispositional or learned hope is related to career self-efficacy as part of a model for self-directed career management, which incorporates career planning, career decision-making, career confidence and proactive career behaviours. Sulaiman-Hill and Thompson (2013) suggest that initiatives intending to foster general self-efficacy could have a positive effect on refugees' employment outcomes. They describe general self-efficacy as a "globalised confidence in one's coping ability to successfully manage a range of stressful situations" (p. 126).

General self-efficacy and career adaptability seem to play vital roles in predicting the quality of reemployment status. Zikic and Klehe (2006) explored the mediating roles of career environment and career adaptability in the relationship of social support and self-efficacy predicting reemployment quality with unemployed individuals in Canada. They measured reemployment quality with such indicators as job improvement, organisational identification, career growth, and turnover intentions. They conceptualised career adaptability with two subsets: career exploration and career planning. They found that social support at the instrumental level affects career exploration, and it, in turn, affects reemployment quality. In addition, they found that self-efficacy affects career planning, and it, in turn, affects reemployment quality.

Despite the positive role of career adaptability featured in Zikic and Klehe (2006), there is no consensus regarding its subsets. Koen, Klehe, Van Vianen, Zikic, and Nauta (2010) conceptualised career adaptability with decision-making, planning, exploration, and self-efficacy, using existing measures for each of the subsets. Maggiori, Rossier, and Savickas (2017), more recently, developed a career adapt-ability scale with four subscales including concern, control, curiosity, and confidence. Due to the differences in the conceptualisations of career adaptability, Johnston (2018) mapped different career adaptability variables into four dimensions: *adaptive readiness*, *adaptability resources*, *adapting response*, and *adaptive results*. Hope falls under adaptive readiness, Maggiori et al.'s (2017) conceptualisation falls under adaptability resources, and Koen et al.'s (2010) conceptualisation falls under adapting responses (Johnston, 2018).

An individual's job search clarity includes knowing the type of job they want, and when, where, how, and with whom to search for the job target (Zikic & Saks, 2009). Job search clarity shares some components of hope. If the clarity is about career goals, this satisfies the goals element of hope, and if the clarity is about how to achieve the career goal, it satisfies the pathway thinking element of hope. Similar to the relationship between hope and job satisfaction (Law & Guo, 2016), Hirschi (2014) found a positive relationship between job search clarity and job satisfaction. Guerrero and Rothstein (2012) found that immigrant job search clarity was positively related to job search intensity, which, in turn was positively related to the number of job offers. Since the HAT seeks to enhance an individual's ability to derive and pursue pathways, self-clarity, and goal setting; it seems reasonable to explore the impact of HAT-based interventions on job search clarity.

Hope, employee engagement, career growth, and job satisfaction

This study is interested in understanding the effect of the H2W on distal outcomes such as career growth, hopeful career state, work engagement, and job satisfaction, which do not tend to characterise refugee employment. Work engagement refers to a "positive, fulfilling, work-related state of mind characterized by vigour, dedication and absorption" (Schaufeli & Bakker, 2003, p. 4). Work engagement has been found to be related to job satisfaction and turnover intentions (Saks, 2006). Malinowski and Lim (2015) showed that hope is the only mediator among psychological capital variables such as self-efficacy, resiliency, and optimism in mindfulness predicting work engagement and general well-being. Peterson and Byron (2008) report that hope is predictive of job performance, and other researchers have found that work engagement is a key process or mechanism contributing to job performance (Alessandri, Borgogni, Schaufeli, Caprara, & Consiglio, 2015).

Career growth is "the individuals' subjective assessment of job loss as a positive growth opportunity, where new career goals are set and psychological success is experienced" (Waters, Briscoe, Hall, & Wang, 2014, p. 408). Zikic, Novicevic, Harvey, and Breland (2006) in their repatriate career exploration model posit that hope will affect career growth and success through career exploration as a mediator and personal, social, and organisational career support as moderators. Other than this hypothesis, no empirical study was found regarding the effect of hope on career growth.

In a study with correctional officers in Taiwanese prisons, hope was also found to be positively related to job satisfaction along with self-efficacy (Law & Guo, 2016). Research has consistently documented the positive impact of work engagement on job satisfaction (e.g. Karatepe, 2013; Wefald & Downey, 2009). Thus, this research explored if work engagement could potentially be a process by which hope results in job satisfaction. Since job satisfaction is positively related to turnover intention, it could be reasonably assumed that those participants with high job satisfaction would intend to stay in jobs for the long-term as long as satisfaction remains at reasonable levels.

Purpose of research and research questions

The purpose of this study was to assess the proximal and distal outcomes of a career development training programme for refugees that was developed based on the HAT. Proximal outcome measures were hope-action competencies, job search clarity, and career adaptability; and distal outcomes were employment status, job-seeking activities, career growth, hopeful career state, work engagement, and job satisfaction. To address the purpose, we developed the following research questions:

(1) *RQ1*. To what extent do the scores of the proximal outcome measures differ between the experimental group and the control group between T2 and T3, after controlling for T1 (pre-test) scores?
(2) *RQ2*. To what extent do the distal outcomes differ between the two groups at T4 (at 9 months)?
(3) *RQ3*. How does the participation to the H2W programme predict distal outcome variables?

Method

Participants

Participants were recruited through participating regional employment centres in British Columbia, internal marketing and promotion within an organisation that implemented the H2W programme, and word of mouth. The following criteria were employed to assess if someone was eligible for the project: had refugee status; were actively job-seeking; were legally able to work in British Columbia; had no barriers to participation; were fluent in Arabic; had at least 10 years of education (could be non-continuous) or 6 years of education plus at least 4 years of work experience and over the age of 18; had been in Canada for at least 6 months; could commit to participating in services, pre-, post-test and follow-ups; and were able to commit to full-time employment if they secured it.

Sixty-one refugees were recruited. Eighty percent were originally from Syria, while the remaining participants were from other Middle Eastern countries such as Afghanistan, Iraq, Iran, Jordan, and

Kuwait. One participant was from Sudan. The mean number of months in Canada at the time of the recruitment was 12 months ($SD = 15.34$). Of the participants, 31 were female and 30 were male. The mean age of participants was 38.51 years ($SD = 10.01$). Fifty-one percent had less than high school or no formal education. Their English levels ranged from Level 1 to Level 7 ($M = 2.85$, mode = 1) on the Canadian Language Benchmark (CLB), which has levels up to 12. After a pre-test (T1), which had demographic questions in addition to the same measures as T2 and T3 surveys, we randomly assigned them into two groups keeping similar proportions in terms of gender, age, country of origin, educational level, English level, and the Hope-Action Inventory (HAI) scores. Independent *t*-tests showed that there were no significant differences between the two groups in these categories. We randomly selected one group to be an experimental group ($n = 31$) and made the other group a control group ($n = 30$). The experimental group was further divided into 2 training cohorts of 15 and 16 participants, respectively.

Treatment

The experimental group members participated in a two-week-long career development training called *H2W*, which is based on the HAT; and the control group members started receiving typical employment services at local career centres. The experimental group members also had access to local career centres. The H2W programme (see Table 1) was offered in Arabic by a bilingual facilitator fluent in Arabic and English from 9:30am to 2:30pm each day for 10 days. The programme involved activities addressing each of the hope-action competencies along with employer workplace tours.

The experimental group participants engaged with five local employers to help them define their workplace attractors/values and envision the Canadian work environment. The last three days of the programme were dedicated to one-to-one meetings of the facilitator of the H2W programme with each participant to complete a detailed Enhanced Action Plan (EAP), which asks for answers addressing the hope-action competencies. Twenty-seven participants completed EAPs to support short and long-term goal attainment. The outline of the plan was as follows:

Table 1. H2W training programme.

Day	Corresponding hope-action competency	Training content
Day 1	Hope	• Introduction and icebreaker • Career flow metaphor • The role of hope and actions that enable hope
Day 2	Self-reflection Self-clarity	• Pursuing your interests and passions through paired interviews and assessments • Mapping your skills
Day 3	Self-reflection Self-clarity	• Personality style • Workplace attraction and values
Day 4	Visioning Goal setting and planning	• Ideal career flow through visualisation • Personal vision statement • Goal setting and action planning
Day 5–6	Visioning Goal setting and action planning	• Employer workplace tours • Reflection on the impact of the tours on the participants' personal vision statements and goals
Day 7	Adapting	• Realising dreams in challenging times utilising strengths • Selecting a motivational career metaphor/image
Day 8–10	All competencies	• Enhanced Action Planning through one-on-one coaching and independent work

(1) Goal setting and planning: Development of short-term and long-term employment goals.
(2) Self-reflection: Reflecting on the progress of goals and the relevance of their interests to their short and long-term goals.
(3) Self-clarity: Identifying transferable and personal skills and work values.
(4) Goal setting and planning: Identification of their career metaphor (Amundson, 1998) and its use for future action.
(5) Implementing: Taking steps to achieve short- and long-term goals.
(6) Adapting: Tactics to stay motivated and accountable for the goal implementation.
(7) Hope: Reflecting on career motivations and hopes for the future.

Measures and procedure

Along with outcome measures, demographics data was captured at T1 (pre-test) including gender, age, arrival date, country born, countries lived, first language, educational level, ethnicity, English level, and the nature of previous jobs. This demographics data was used, in part, for random assignment of the participants. All measures in this study were translated to Arabic due to the participants' limited English proficiency. In order to minimise errors in interpreting the meaning of the items, we listed both English and Arabic descriptions for each item.

Proximal outcome measures

The following instruments were used at T1, T2 (right after the intervention), and T3 (3 months after the intervention) to measure proximal outcomes.

- Hope-action competency. The HAI (Niles, Yoon, & Amundson, 2010) assesses the extent to which individuals demonstrate the following hope-action competencies: hope, self-reflection, self-clarity, visioning, goal setting and planning, implementing, and adapting. The scale consists of 28 items, each of which was rated on a 4-point scale (1 = Definitely false, 4 = Definitely true). In the current study, Cronbach's alpha for the composite scale ranged from 0.842 ($n = 60$) to 0.920 ($n = 52$).
- General self-efficacy. The General Self-Efficacy (GSE) scale (Schwarzer & Jerusalem, 1995) was chosen to assess a general sense of perceived self-efficacy. It has 10 items including "I can always manage to solve difficult problems if I try hard enough." A 4-point response scale was used (1 = Not at all true, 4 = Exactly true). In the current study, Cronbach's alpha for the scale ranged from 0.852 ($n = 61$) to 0.886 ($n = 60$).
- Career adapt-ability. The Career Adapt-Abilities Scale-Short Form (CAAS-SF; Maggiori et al., 2017) was used to measure career adaptability. There are 12 items in total with 4 subscales including concern, control, curiosity, and confidence. A 5-point response scale was used (1 = Not strong, 5 = Strongest). In the current study, Cronbach's alpha for the composite scale ranged from 0.908 ($n = 59$) to 0.921 ($n = 55$).
- Job search clarity. The Job Search Clarity (JSC) scale (Zikic & Saks, 2009) was adopted in order to assess the level of clarity in terms of career objectives and options and job search tactics. JSC has eight items with two reverse items. A sample item is "I have a clear idea of the type of job I want." A 5-point response scale was used in this study (1 = Strongly disagree, 5 = Strongly agree). In the current study, Cronbach's alpha for the scale ranged from 0.680 ($n = 58$) to 0.858 ($n = 59$).

Distal outcome measures

Nine months after the H2W intervention, we assessed distal outcomes by examining the frequency of 12 job-seeking activities, employment status, and measures listed below:

- Career growth. We used the Career Growth Scale (CGS; Waters et al., 2014) with four items – a combination of the two-item scale of Eby and Buch (1995) and the two-item scale of Bedeian, Kemery, and Pizzolatto (1991). The CGS assesses to what extent the current job provides opportunities for one's career growth and psychological success. A sample item is "My new job provides me new opportunities for psychological success." In the current study, Cronbach's alpha was .884.

- Work engagement. The nine-item Utrecht Work Engagement Scale-Short Form (UWES-SF; Schaufeli & Bakker, 2003) was used to measure the level of work engagement of the participants. It includes items such as: "At my work, I feel bursting with energy," "I am immersed in my work," and "My job inspires me." We used the overall composite scale in this study. The UWES is scored on a 7-point response scale indicating frequency, ranging from 0 (Never) to 6 (Every day). In the current study, Cronbach's alpha for the composite scale was 0.929 ($n = 28$).
- Hopeful career state. The Hopeful Career State (HCS) scale was developed to assess how hopeful individuals are at work considering their future career (Yoon, Niles, & Amundson, 2017). It has nine items including the following sample items: "What I am doing now is helping me to build skills and experiences for the future" and "I am hopeful that what I am doing now will help me in my career journey." A 4-point response scale was used (1 = Definitely false, 4 = Definitely true). In the current study, Cronbach's alpha was 0.958 ($n = 46$). Exploratory factor analysis employing principle axis factoring with promax rotation (Kappa = 4) revealed a one-factor structure explaining 75.9% of the variance (eigenvalue > 1).
- Job satisfaction. Job satisfaction was measured using the Job Satisfaction Subscale (JSS) of the Michigan Organizational Assessment Questionnaire (MOAQ) (Cammann, Fichman, Jenkins, & Klesh, 1979). JSS has three items, including, "All in all, I am satisfied with my job," "In general, I don't like my job," and "In general, I like working here." A 5-point scale was used for response options (1 = Strongly disagree, 5 = Strongly agree). In the current study, Cronbach's alpha was 0.905 ($n = 28$).

Data analysis

In order to answer RQ1, we adopted two-way mixed effects analyses of covariance (ANCOVA) because this study had two groups (between subjects) and a time series (within subject). While we made sure that the two groups were almost identical, we chose to control for pre-test results by using ANCOVA to capture the treatment effects more accurately. All analyses met the assumption of sphericity using Mauchly's test of sphericity. Therefore, we proceeded with analysing within-subjects effects and between-subjects effects. As for RQ2, independent samples *t*-test was used to compare the differences in the distal outcome measures at 9 Month (T4) between the two groups. SPSS 25 was used for both types of analyses.

Before analysing data for RQ3, correlation analyses were conducted to explore the bivariate relationships among the variables used in this study. Next, we conducted a serial mediation analysis (Hayes, 2013) in which we assessed the indirect effect of H2W participation on job satisfaction through hopeful career state and through work engagement. Utilising PROCESS v2.15 (Hayes, 2013), the bootstrapping technique (10,000 bootstrap resamples in this study) was used to generate an approximate sampling distribution of the indirect effect as well as confidence intervals for these effects. The indirect effect is considered significant if the confidence interval does not involve zero (Hayes, 2013). The serial mediation model allows researchers to test a specific theoretical sequence between variables. In the case of this study, we tested an alternative model by switching the positions of two serial mediators, hopeful career state and work engagement.

Results

Before analysing data to answer the research questions, correlation analysis was conducted to see whether there is any relationship between demographic variables – English level, educational level, gender, age, ethnicity, duration living in Canada – and outcome variables. No significant correlations were found.

Table 2. Difference between the two groups on proximal outcome measures at T2 and T3.

	T2		T3		Between-group effects		
Scale	Exp. group ($n = 29$)	Ctrl. group ($n = 26$)	Exp. group ($n = 29$)	Ctrl. group ($n = 26$)	F	p	η_p^2
HAI	3.629 (0.260)	3.470 (0.323)	3.583 (0.366)	3.489 (0.324)	6.114*	.017	0.105
GSE	3.667 (0.342)	3.492 (0.460)	3.364 (0.375)	3.565 (0.365)	4.128*	.047	0.074
CAAS	4.552 (0.602)	4.308 (0.410)	4.316 (0.546)	4.401 (0.515)	0.011	.917	0.000
JSC	4.116 (0.620)	3.655 (0.659)	3.953 (0.618)	3.723 (0.634)	6.720*	.012	0.114

Note: *$p < .05$. Standard Errors appear in parentheses below means.

Effects on proximal outcome measures across conditions (RQ1)

To answer RQ1, we used two-way mixed effects ANCOVA to examine the changes in the proximal outcome measures – hope-action competencies, general self-efficacy, career adaptability, and job search clarity – at three times (T1: pre-test, T2: post-test, and T3: post-test at 3 Month) between the experimental group and the control group. Time was the within-subject factor and group (i.e. experimental group or control group) was the between subject factor.

The HAI results were significantly different between the groups, $F(1, 52) = 6.114$, $p < .05$, $\eta_p^2 = 0.105$ (see Table 2). The experimental group had significantly higher mean scores of HAI than the control group. Examining within-subjects effects, i.e. differences according to time, there were neither statistically significant differences in the HAI mean scores between T2 and T3, $p = .296$, nor interaction effects between time and group, $p = .493$. The GSE results were significantly different between the two groups, $F(1, 52) = 4.128$, $p < .05$, $\eta_p^2 = 0.074$. The experimental group had significantly higher mean scores of GSE than the control group. Looking at within-subject effects, there was neither statistically significant difference in the GSE scores between T2 and T3, $p = .070$, nor interaction effects between time and group, $p = .185$. The CAAS results showed that there were no statistically significant differences between the groups, $p = .917$. There were neither within-subjects effects, $p = .281$, nor interaction effects between time and group, $p = .050$. The JSC results were significantly different between the groups, $F(1, 52) = 6.720$, $p < .05$, $\eta_p^2 = 0.114$ (see Table 2).

The same analyses were conducted with the HAI subscales – *hope, self-reflection, self-clarity, visioning, goal setting and planning, implementing,* and *adapting*. As for *hope*, there was a statistically significant difference between the groups, $F(1, 52) = 6.392$, $p < .05$, $\eta_p^2 = 0.109$, indicating that the experimental group had a higher level of *hope*. In addition, there was an interaction effect between time and group, $F(1, 52) = 9.928$, $p < .01$, $\eta_p^2 = 0.160$; in which the control group had higher hope at T3 than T2, and the experimental group had slightly lower hope at T3 than T2. There were significant differences between the two groups in three subscales: *self-clarity*, $F(1, 52) = 9.900$, $p < .01$, $\eta_p^2 = 0.160$; *goal setting and planning*, $F(1, 52) = 4.549$, $p < .05$, $\eta_p^2 = 0.080$; and *implementing*, $F(1, 52) = 4.052$, $p < .05$, $\eta_p^2 = 0.072$, which confirms that the experimental group had higher levels of these competencies than the control group. No significant differences were found in the cases of *self-reflection* ($p = .540$), *visioning* ($p = .265$), and *adapting* ($p = .067$). No significant differences were observed in terms of within-subjects effects – between T2 and T3 – for all of the subscales for both groups.

Effects on distal outcome measures (RQ2)

Job-seeking activities

We compared mean scores of all available outcome measures using independent *t*-tests. First, as for the frequency of job-seeking activities for their employment (see Table 3), there were no significant

Table 3. Independent samples *t*-test results on the frequency of job-seeking activities between the experimental and control groups.

Scale	Experimental group ($n = 25$)	Control group ($n = 21$)	t	df	p
Went to my local WorkBC Centre	3.52 (2.86)	5.33 (2.78)	−2.169*	44	.036
Used the Resource Room at my local WorkBC Centre	1.32 (2.98)	1.81 (2.52)	−0.594	44	.555
Saw or communicated by phone/email with my Case Manager at my WorkBC Centre	3.92 (3.48)	5.38 (3.09)	−1.493	44	.143
Searched for a job	5.88 (3.28)	5.90 (3.24)	−0.026	44	.980
Applied for a job	3.72 (2.85)	4.10 (3.84)	−0.380	44	.706
Went to a job interview	2.16 (2.21)	2.05 (2.20)	0.172	44	.864
Worked on my resume	2.76 (2.70)	2.48 (1.94)	0.402	44	.689
Attended an employment workshop at my local WorkBC Centre	0.92 (2.00)	1.67 (2.61)	−1.097	44	.278
Attended an Industry and Trades Authority Immigrants in Trades Programme	0.00 (0.00)	0.43 (1.165)	−1.686	44	.107
Attended English language training	3.72 (4.19)	4.86 (4.33)	−0.903	44	.371
Attended the A.C.A.P. – Pathways to Possibilities Programme	0.04 (0.200)	0.48 (1.57)	−1.265	44	.220
Attended a pre-employment training programme	0.36 (0.700)	1.24 (2.64)	−1.479	44	.153

Note: *$p < .05$. Standard Deviations appear in parentheses below means.

differences between the two groups except for going to local WorkBC Centres, which provide employment services.

Employment status

As for the employment status, out of 25 individuals within the experimental group who answered the 9 Month (T4) survey, 15 individuals (61%) were employed. Six were employed full-time (26%), eight were employed part-time (35%), and one was scheduled to start a part-time job soon (4%). In the control group, 13 out of 21 individuals (62%) were employed. Six were employed full-time (29%) and seven were employed part-time (33%). Independent samples *t*-test showed that there is no significant difference between the two groups in terms of employment status, $t(44) = -0.129$, $p = .898$. In terms of job type, taking both groups together, 67.9% were employed as entry-level employees (*assistant/support workers*). In the experimental group, 60% were employed as *assistant/support workers*, and 20% were employed as *technicians*. In the control group, 76.9% were employed as *assistant/support workers*, and 15.4% identified their roles as *other*. To see the difference between the two groups, independent samples *t*-test was conducted after making the variable dichotomous (*assistant/support worker* = 0, the rest = 1). There was no significant difference in job types between the two groups, $t(26) = -0.937$, $p = .074$.

Other distal outcome measures

In terms of the mean scores of the four scales used for distal outcomes, Table 4 indicates the differences between the two groups. The UWES scores turned out to be statistically different between the two groups, $t(26) = 2.514$, $p < .05$. This means that those who were working among the experimental group participants exhibited significantly higher levels of work engagement than those in the control group. Similarly, there was a significant difference in the HCS scores between the two groups, $t(26) =$

Table 4. Independent samples *t*-test results on career outcome measures between the experimental and control groups.

Scale	Experimental group ($n = 15$)	Control group ($n = 13$)	t	df	p
CGS	4.15 (0.83)	3.56 (0.64)	1.714	26	.104
UWES	6.22 (0.67)	4.97 (1.67)	2.514*	26	.023
HCS	3.68 (0.62)	3.16 (0.71)	2.072*	26	.048
JSS	4.20 (0.54)	3.54 (1.15)	0.402	26	.077

Note: $^*p < .05$. Standard Deviations appear in parentheses below means.

2.072, $p = .048$. While the scores of CGS and JSS of the experimental group were slightly higher than the control groups, there was no statistical difference in the scores between the two groups.

A mediation model (RQ3)

We identified a model that shows the effect of the H2W participation. Following Hayes (2013), we conducted a serial mediation analysis to see how employee engagement measured by the UWES will mediate the effect of the programme participation on job satisfaction (see Figure 1). The overall regression model was significant in predicting job satisfaction from H2W participation, hopeful career state, and work engagement, explaining 67.3% of the variance in job satisfaction, $R^2 = 0.673$, $F(3, 24) = 16.460$, $p < .001$. There was a significant indirect path from H2W participation to job satisfaction through hopeful career state and work engagement in a sequential order (indirect effect coefficient = 0.241, SE = 0.236, 95% CI = 0.001, 0.861). When substituting the order of the mediators so that work engagement preceded hopeful career state in the model, the indirect path was no longer significant (indirect effect coefficient = 0.028, SE = 0.067, 95% CI = −0.082, 0.183). Note that there was no significant direct path from H2W participation to either work engagement or job satisfaction, and there was also no indirect effect of H2W participation on job satisfaction through work engagement (95% CI = −0.151, 0.947).

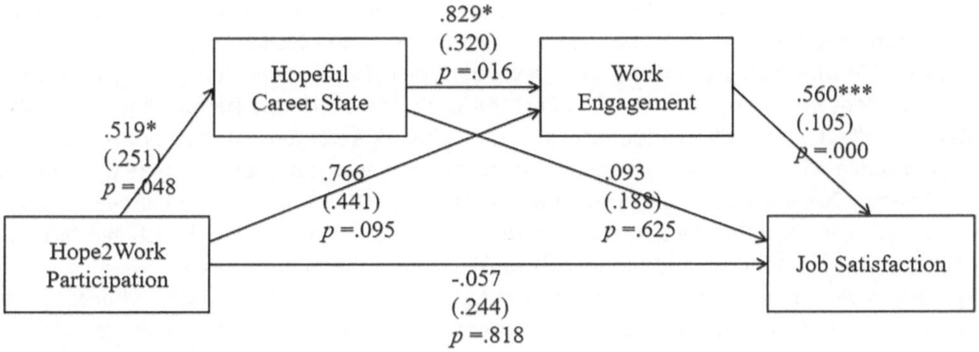

Figure 1. A mediation model between the H2W programme participation and job satisfaction.

Discussion

Considering data gathered from both groups at T2 and T3, it was confirmed that the H2W programme based on the HAT was effective in developing hope-action competencies (in particular, *hope, self-clarity, goal setting and planning,* and *implementing*), general self-efficacy, and job search clarity. Interestingly, however, there was no significant difference between the two groups in career adaptability. This is contrary to Zikic and Klehe's (2006) finding about the mediating role of adaptability between self-efficacy and reemployment quality. A potential cause of this non-significance is that this study did not use the career adaptability scale that Zikic and Klehe (2006) used, in an effort to try a newly developed and validated scale dedicated to measure career adaptability. While career adaptability is known to predict such results as a low turnover rate, positive job search behaviours, and reemployment quality (Johnston, 2018), a caution needs to be made when selecting an adaptability scale due to the conceptual differences.

In addition, the intensity of job-seeking activities over nine months (T1–T4) was not significantly different between the two groups, except for using a local employment centre. The experimental group participants utilised WorkBC Centres less compared to the control group. Although it needs to be confirmed, we hypothesise that they might have not felt the need to visit the Centres because they had gone through the 2-week programme that addressed a wide variety of topics already, which is far beyond what the Centres offer.

The employment status data also confirmed that there is no statistical difference between the two groups, with approximately a 60% employment rate in both groups. According to Minsky (2016), about 50% of adult Syrian refugees found work in Canada a year after their arrival. When considering British Columbia, 17% of refugee respondents of a survey conducted by the Immigrant Services Society of B.C. (2016) were employed approximately within one year after their arrival. Given these statistics, the H2W employment rate across the entire research group (experimental and control) seems to be high. While the control group achieved the same level of employment rate, one of the antecedents may be their repeated participation in assessing their hope-action competencies along with other measures. In qualitative feedback from the control group, some mentioned a perceived utility of completing the HAI in relation to their own employment hope.

The majority (67%) of the participants in both groups who obtained jobs were employed as *assistant/support workers*. Comparing this fact with their previous jobs in home countries, only 24.3% of the 61 participants reported that they were *assistant/support workers*. All others were technicians, managers, supervisors, and teachers, except for 8.2% who were either unemployed or did not answer. This reflects the challenging reality of them taking precarious and relatively lower level jobs (Wilkinson et al., 2014) and spending many years to secure jobs at the level of the Canadian-born population (AMSSA, 2017).

Considering their psychological status after gaining employment, the experimental group participants were more engaged at work and were in a more hopeful career state than the control group participants. This finding means that the H2W intervention contributed to forming a positive outlook on their current and future work as per the measures used in the research. This study expands on Yoon et al. (2015) where they examined the effects of hope on vocational identity and academic performance. Student engagement fully mediated the effect on academic performance and partially mediated the effect on vocational identity. In terms of work engagement, numerous studies have found its positive effect on task performance, retention, and job satisfaction (e.g. Giallonardo, Wong, & Iwasiw, 2010; Karatepe, 2013; Mendes & Stander, 2011; Saks, 2006; Salanova & Schaufeli, 2008). Thus, we can hypothesise that the experimental group participants will achieve higher task performance, longer retention, and higher job satisfaction at their current jobs.

This study is also significant as it used distal outcomes employing two groups whereas previous studies on the Hope-Action interventions used either pre-and post-tests with one group (Clarke et al., in press) or an experimental design with proximal outcomes (Amundson et al., 2018). The adoption of distal outcomes made it possible to explore and confirm a serial mediation model that depicts the path of the H2W programme participation affecting one's job satisfaction, which was achieved through hopeful career state, and in turn, work engagement.

Limitations, future research, and conclusions

The findings of this research are limited to the participant group – refugees in British Columbia – and no generalisation to other population, other places, or other times is possible. While HAT research along with this study has found positive outcomes with internationally trained health professionals (Clarke et al., in press) and unemployed individuals (Amundson et al., 2018) in Canada, the population and geographic location of future studies should be extended in order to confirm the utility of the HAT.

As for the serial mediation analysis, the findings are limited because the distal outcomes – the two serial mediators and the dependent variable – were captured at the same time, making it a semi-cross-sectional analysis. Future research, with a potential follow up on the current study participants, is needed to capture actual performance data, job satisfaction at a later time, and turnover.

A newly constructed measure, the HCS, was used for this study before validating its psychometric properties. While the EFA results and Cronbach alpha suggest that it has satisfactory psychometric properties, more validation studies need to follow to confirm its validity and utility. In addition, more research is needed using the hopeful career state variable as a potential mediator or a predictor for outcome measures such as job satisfaction, performance, and turnover, especially given the fact that it was one of the two serial mediators found in this study.

This study demonstrated the effectiveness of the H2W programme for refugees in British Columbia, Canada at both proximal and distal levels. In summary, the intervention based on HAT is confirmed to be effective in developing hope-action competencies, general self-efficacy, and job search clarity. While there was no difference between the two groups in terms of the employment rate or employment type, there was a significant difference in the quality of their job experiences measured by hopeful career state, work engagement, and job satisfaction. Nevertheless, this study cautions on the replication of the same programme for other refugee population or any other population. There could be other variables that may affect the success of the programme, and a customisation after assessing the need of the setting must precede offering a HAT-based career intervention.

Acknowledgements

The authors would like to acknowledge MOSAIC's role in leading project implementation and assisting the adaptation of the hope-action theory to the project target group, including delivery in participants' first language.

Disclosure statement

No potential conflict of interest was reported by the authors.

Funding

This research project was funded by the Ministry of Social Development and Poverty Reduction of British Columbia.

References

Affiliation of Multicultural Societies and Services Agencies of BC [AMSSA]. (2017, May). Integration outcomes of resettled refugees in Canada. *Migration Matters, 38*. Retrieved from http://www.amssa.org/wp-content/uploads/2017/06/Infosheet38_resettled_refugees.pdf

Alessandri, G., Borgogni, L., Schaufeli, W. B., Caprara, G. V., & Consiglio, C. (2015). From positive orientation to job performance: The role of work engagement and self-efficacy beliefs. *Journal of Happiness Studies, 16*(3), 767–788. doi:10.1007/s10902-014-9533-4

Amundson, N. E. (1998). *Active engagement: Enhancing the career counselling process*. Richmond: Ergon Communications.

Amundson, N. E., Goddard, T., Yoon, H. J., & Niles, S. G. (2018). Hope-centred interventions with unemployd clients. *The Canadian Journal of Career Development, 17*(2), 87–98. Retrieved from http://cjcdonline.ca/

Bandura, A. (2001). Social cognitive theory: An agentic perspective. *Annual Review of Psychology, 52*, 1–26. doi:10.1146/annurev.psych.52.1.1

Bedeian, A. G., Kemery, E. R., & Pizzolatto, A. B. (1991). Career commitment and expected utility of present job as predictors of turnover intentions and turnover behavior. *Journal of Vocational Behavior, 39*, 331–343. doi:10.1016/0001-8791(91)90042-K

Briggs, L. (2011). Demoralization and psychological distress in refugees: From research to practice. *Social Work in Mental Health, 9*(5), 336–345. doi:10.1080/15332985.2011.569444

Cammann, C., Fichman, M., Jenkins, D., & Klesh, J. (1979). *The Michigan organizational assessment questionnaire*. Unpublished manuscript, University of Michigan, Ann Arbor.

Clarke, A., Amundson, N., Niles, S., & Yoon, H. J. (in press). Action-oriented hope: An agent of change for internationally educated professionals. *Journal of Employment Counseling*.

Eby, L. T., & Buch, K. (1995). Job loss as career growth: Responses to involuntary career transitions. *Career Development Quarterly, 44*, 26–42. doi:10.1002/j.2161-0045.1995.tb00526.x

Elez, T. (2014). Restoring hope: Responding to career concerns of immigrant clients. *The Canadian Journal of Career Development/Revue Canadienne de Développement de Carrière, 13*(1), 32–45. Retrieved from http://cjcdonline.ca/

Fuller, S., & Martin, T. F. (2012). Predicting immigrant employment sequences in the first years of settlement. *International Migration Review, 46*(1), 138–190. doi:10.1111/j.1747-7379.2012.00883.x

Giallonardo, L. M., Wong, C. A., & Iwasiw, C. L. (2010). Authentic leadership of preceptors: Predictor of new graduate nurses' work engagement and job satisfaction. *Journal of Nursing Management, 18*(8), 993–1003. doi:10.1111/j.1365-2834.2010.01126.x

Gilmore, J. (2009). *The 2008 Canadian immigrant labour market: Analysis of quality of employment*. Ottawa: Statistics Canada, Labour Statistics Division.

Guerrero, L., & Rothstein, M. G. (2012). Antecedents of underemployment: Job search of skilled immigrants in Canada. *Applied Psychology, 61*, 323–346. doi:10.1111/j.1464-0597.2011.00470.x

Hall, D. T. (1996). Protean careers of the 21st century. *The Academy of Management Executive, 10*(4), 8–16. doi:10.5465/AME.1996.3145315

Hayes, A. F. (2013). *Introduction to mediation, moderation, and conditional process analysis: A regression-based approach*. New York: Guilford Press.

Hirschi, A. (2014). Hope as a resource for self-directed career management: Investigating mediating effects on proactive career behaviors and life and job satisfaction. *Journal of Happiness Studies, 15*(6), 1495–1512. doi:10.1007/s10902-013-9488-x

Immigrant Services Society of B.C. (2016). *Syrian refugee operation to British Columbia: One year in—A roadmap to integration and citizenship*. British Columbia, Canada: Immigrant Services Society of B.C. Retrieved from http://issbc.org/wp-content/uploads/2016/12/Syrian-Refugee-Operation-to-British-Columbia_final.pdf

Johnston, C. S. (2018). A systematic review of the career adaptability literature and future outlook. *Journal of Career Assessment, 26*(1), 3–30. doi:10.1177/1069072716679921

Karatepe, O. M. (2013). High-performance work practices and hotel employee performance: The mediation of work engagement. *International Journal of Hospitality Management, 32*, 132–140. doi:10.1016/j.ijhm.2012.05.003

Koen, J., Klehe, U.-C., Van Vianen, A. E. M., Zikic, J., & Nauta, A. (2010). Job-search strategies and reemployment quality: The impact of career adaptability. *Journal of Vocational Behavior, 77*(1), 126–139. doi:10.1016/j.jvb.2010.02.004

Law, F. M., & Guo, G. J. (2016). Correlation of hope and self-efficacy with job satisfaction, job stress, and organizational commitment for correctional officers in the Taiwan prison system. *International Journal of Offender Therapy and Comparative Criminology, 60*, 1257–1277. doi:10.1177/0306624X15574997

Maggiori, C., Rossier, J., & Savickas, M. L. (2017). Career adapt-abilities scale–short form (CAAS-SF) construction and validation. *Journal of Career Assessment, 25*, 312–325. doi:10.1177/1069072714565856

Malinowski, P., & Lim, H. J. (2015). Mindfulness at work: Positive affect, hope, and optimism mediate the relationship between dispositional mindfulness, work engagement, and well-being. *Mindfulness, 6*, 1250–1262. doi:10.1007/s12671-015-0388-5

Mendes, F., & Stander, M. W. (2011). Positive organisation: The role of leader behaviour in work engagement and retention. *SA Journal of Industrial Psychology, 37*(1), 1–13. doi:10.4102/sajip.v37i1.900

Minsky, A. (2016, December 11). Half of adult Syrian refugees unemployed 1 year later: Liberals. *Global News*. Retrieved from https://globalnews.ca/news/3119278/half-of-adult-syrian-refugees-unemployed-1-year-later-liberals/

Niles, S. G., Amundson, N. E., & Neault, R. (2011). *Career flow: A hope-centered approach to career development*. Boston, MA: Pearson.

Niles, S. G., Yoon, H. J., & Amundson, N. E. (2010). *Career flow index: Hope-centered career development competencies*. Unpublished manuscript, University Park, PA.

Ott, E. (2013). Conceptualising employment services for resettled Bhutanese refugees: A case study in Pittsburgh, Pennsylvania. *European Bulletin of Himalayan Research, 43*, 52–70. Retrieved from http://www.digitalhimalaya.com/collections/journals/ebhr/

Peterson, S. J., & Byron, K. (2008). Exploring the role of hope in job performance: Results from four studies. *Journal of Organizational Behavior, 29*(6), 785–803. doi:10.1002/job.492

Saks, A. M. (2006). Antecedents and consequences of employee engagement. *Journal of Managerial Psychology, 21*(7), 600–619. doi:10.1108/02683940610690169

Salanova, M., & Schaufeli, W. B. (2008). A cross-national study of work engagement as a mediator between job resources and proactive behaviour. *The International Journal of Human Resource Management, 19*(1), 116–131. doi:10.1080/09585190701763982

Schaufeli, W. B., & Bakker, A. B. (2003). *Utrecht work engagement scale: Preliminary manual*. Utrecht: Occupational Health Psychology Unit, Utrecht University.

Schwarzer, R., & Jerusalem, M. (1995). Generalized self-efficacy scale. In *Measures in health psychology: A user's portfolio. Causal and control beliefs* (pp. 35–37). Windsor: NFER-NELSON.

Snyder, C. R. (2002). Hope theory: Rainbows in the mind. *Psychological Inquiry, 13*, 249–275. doi:10.1207S15327965PLI1304_01

Strauser, D. R., Lustig, D. C., Cogdal, P. A., & Uruk, AÇ. (2006). Trauma symptoms: Relationship with career thoughts, vocational identity, and developmental work personality. *The Career Development Quarterly, 54*(4), 346–360. doi:10.1002/j.2161-0045.2006.tb00199.x

Sulaiman-Hill, C. M., & Thompson, S. C. (2013). Learning to fit in: An exploratory study of general perceived self efficacy in selected refugee groups. *Journal of Immigrant and Minority Health, 15*, 125–131. doi:10.1007/s10903-011-9547-5

Waters, L., Briscoe, J. P., Hall, D. T., & Wang, L. (2014). Protean career attitudes during unemployment and reemployment: A longitudinal perspective. *Journal of Vocational Behavior, 84*, 405–419. doi:10.1016/j.jvb.2014.03.003

Wefald, A. J., & Downey, R. G. (2009). Construct dimensionality of engagement and its relation with satisfaction. *The Journal of Psychology, 143*(1), 91–112. doi:10.3200/JRLP.143.1.91-112

Wilkinson, L., Chowdhury, I. A., Shen, Y., Bucklaschuk, J., & Edkins, T. (2014, September). *Labour market outcomes of refugees in Canada*. Presented at the Human Rights, Human Wrongs: Vulnerability in Comparative Perspective, Winnipeg, Manitoba. Retrieved from https://umanitoba.ca/faculties/arts/research/media/Labour_Market_Outcomes_of_Refugees.pdf

Wilkinson, L., & Garcea, J. (2017, April). *The economic integration of refugees in Canada: A mixed record?* Washington, DC: Migration Policy Institute. Retrieved from https://www.migrationpolicy.org/sites/default/files/publications/TCM-Asylum_Canada-FINAL.pdf

Yoon, H. J., In, H., Niles, S. G., Amundson, N. E., Smith, B. A., & Mills, L. (2015). The effects of hope on student engagement, academic performance, and vocational identity. *The Canadian Journal of Career Development/Revue Canadienne de Développement de Carrière, 14*(1), 34–45. Retrieved from http://cjcdonline.ca/

Yoon, H. J., Niles, S., & Amundson, N. (2017). *Hopeful employment scale*. Unpublished assessment.

Youssef, C. M., & Luthans, F. (2007). Positive organizational behavior in the workplace: The impact of hope, optimism, and resilience. *Journal of Management, 33*(5), 774–800. doi:10.1177/0149206307305562

Zikic, J., & Klehe, U.-C. (2006). Job loss as a blessing in disguise: The role of career exploration and career planning in predicting reemployment quality. *Journal of Vocational Behavior, 69*(3), 391–409. doi:10.1016/j.jvb.2006.05.007

Zikic, J., Novicevic, M. M., Harvey, M., & Breland, J. (2006). Repatriate career exploration: A path to career growth and success. *Career Development International, 11*, 633–649. doi:10.1108/13620430610713490

Zikic, J., & Saks, A. M. (2009). Job search and social cognitive theory: The role of career-relevant activities. *Journal of Vocational Behavior, 74*(1), 117–127. doi:10.1016/j.jvb.2008.11.001

The cultural preparedness model of aspiration and engagement: understanding the dynamics of integration

Gideon Arulmani

ABSTRACT

This paper uses the cultural preparedness approach to analyse the interface between the aspirations of immigrants and their engagement with systems of the host country. It draws upon interviews with 84 immigrants from 35 developing countries living in 9 high-income countries. Based upon Edmund Husserl's hermeneutical phenomenology, two studies are presented to understand the disturbance of equilibrium in cultural preparation status experienced by immigrants as they try to find their way in a host country. Aspiration-Engagement themes and responses to the challenges of integration are discussed. A model of aspiration and engagement based on the cultural preparedness approach is proposed as a framework that guidance and counselling workers could use to help immigrants optimise their engagement with the systems of the host country.

Introduction

The contemporary immigrant arrives in a location that is usually culturally occupied by others. While different push or pull factors influence migration (e.g. Van Hear, Oliver Bakewell, & Long, 2018), it is likely that nearly all immigrants aspire to a "better life" in the host country. From the side of the host, systems and supports are created and resources spent to help immigrants realise their aspirations. However, engagement with such services is not always optimal. In Sweden, for example, 10.5% of foreign-born students drop out of upper-secondary education compared with 5.4% native-born students, and 24.1% change educational choices compared to 12.6% of native-born (OECD, 2014). In Canada, recent immigrants are 2.5 times likelier than Canadian-born individuals to be working in low-skilled jobs and immigrants who have spent 15 years are still twice as likely as the Canadian-born to be working in low-skilled occupations (TIEDI, 2011). Similar trends are seen in other immigration destinations. Of concern is the fact that these disparities prevail despite substantial provisions made by "the system", where system is defined as the rules, mores, requirements, common practices and expectations that compose the social, educational, economic and cultural structure and organisation of the host country. An important mechanism available to the migrant to re-attain stability is through engagement with supports offered by the system. It is a moot point as to whether the system's offerings are consonant with the immigrant's cultural preparedness (described in greater detail below). Against this background, the relevance of this paper arises from growing concerns pertaining to the integration of immigrants (or lack thereof) into the cultural and economic fabric of host countries (e.g. OECD, 2014; TIEDI, 2011). This paper draws upon the constructs of aspiration, engagement and their interface to argue that identifying themes underlying engagement with systems of the host country and distinguishing responses to these themes could yield a frame of reference for deeper insights into the dynamics of immigrants' integration.

The paper begins with a discussion on the concepts of aspiration and engagement and juxtaposes these two constructs to show four theoretically interesting interactions referred to as the A–E matrix. The key constructs of the cultural preparedness approach are then described and used as a framework to understand the aspiration-engagement interaction. The philosophic moorings of the two studies reported here are Husserl's hermeneutic phenomenology and the nonlinear principles of Indian philosophy. Study 1 examines the author's interviews with immigrants conducted over a 17-year period and identifies themes reflecting the nature of immigrants' engagement with the systems of the host country. Study 2 examines data emerging from Study 1 to find descriptors for the four categories of the A–E matrix. These two studies suggest that the A–E matrix could provide clues that are useful for guidance and counselling workers to help immigrants re-establish their lives by discovering a new cultural preparedness equilibrium.

Aspiration and engagement: a matrix of interactions

Aspiration

In general terms, "to aspire" is defined as a longing, or aim; a goal or objective that is strongly desired (aspiration, n.d.). As a psychological construct, aspirations have been described to be expressions of personal agency involving intentionality, forethought, self-reactiveness and self-reflectiveness (Bandura, 2001). An interesting distinction that has emerged in the literature is between aspiration and expectation. For example, while Fouad and Byars-Winston (2005) in a meta-analysis (16 studies) found no significant difference between the career aspirations of ethnic minority and non-minority individuals, they did find that ethnic minorities expected fewer career opportunities and a larger number of career barriers than their nonminority peers. Therefore understanding congruence or discrepancy between an individual's career aspiration and expectation is important. The development of aspirations is not just an individual-specific matter. The prevailing opportunity structure (e.g. Schoon & Parsons, 2002), constraints of social circumstances along with systemic and structural barriers (e.g. Arulmani, Van Laar, & Easton, 2003), all affect the manner in which aspirations are formed and realised. Contemporary discourse pertaining to migration argues that the aspirations of immigrants are not linked merely to economic benefits and Meyer's (2018) conversations with immigrants, for example, found that aspirations were linked to their self-perceptions, their feelings about their home region and their concerns about their futures. Building upon such observations, Carling and Collins (2018) define aspiration as "... an intersection of personal, collective and normative dimensions" (p. 915). They point out that aspirations could be emulative, in that, immigrants find virtue in aligning with the aspirations of others like themselves in the host country. Also pertinent to the arguments that will be made in this paper is the introduction of the vocabulary of desire into the aspiration discourse which draws attention to the possibility that instigators of aspiration could refer to "... a wide range of conscious and sub-conscious influences ... combinations of strategic planning, opportunism and fancies that manifest in movements to take individuals into other worlds, to achieve or avoid (un)desirable futures" (Collins, 2018, p. 966). Viewed from this perspective, aspiration is not merely a cognition but implies a deep emotional investment on the part of the individual, the fulfilment of which is to be seen not only as future possibilities but also reflective of the immigrant's past experiences and present situation. Migration (whether by choice or coercion) may not be an end in itself but motivated rather by what the migrant aspires to achieve through immigration. This paper views immigrants' aspirations as indicators of the kind of transformation they desire. It is possible that the aspiration is for a better quality of life, greater opportunities, or for refuge, higher security and safety. It is also possible that the aspiration reflects the immigrant's desire for the above in conjunction with the freedom for continuance of an earlier way of life as dictated by the tenets of his/her home culture.

Engagement

In general terms, to "engage" is to bind (someone, such as oneself) to do something, to have contact and establish meaningful communication with someone or something (engage, n.d.). Prominent amongst attempts to operationalise engagement as a psychosocial construct are the person-environment models. Neufeld et al. (2006) define engagement as " … the quality of a person-environment relationship determined by the extent to which negotiation, participation, and evaluation processes occur during the interaction" (p. 251). Brown's (1987) research showed that locally specific working-class culture engenders cultural predispositions toward education that are seen as three forms of engagement: a positive, normative acceptance of schooling, a negative alienated rejection and between them, an alienated but instrumental orientation to schooling. Macdonald and Marsh (2004), nearly 20 years later, extend Brown's categorisations showing that the nature of engagement need not be fixed and stable. Pupils move from one form of engagement to another. Seen from another perspective is Schaufeli and colleagues' hypothesis that engagement is the opposite of burnout. They define engagement as " … a positive fulfilling, and work-related state of mind that is characterized by vigour, dedication, and absorption" (Schaufeli, Martínez, Pinto, Salanova, & Bakker, 2002, p. 465). The important point arising from these discussions is that engagement and disengagement ought to be viewed along a continuum and not as dichotomous, polar opposites (Macdonald & Marsh, 2004). Linked to the idea that the quality of engagement lies along a continuum is Neault and Pickerell's (2011) postulation that engagement is optimal when the challenges of job tasks match the individual's capabilities. Of particular relevance to this paper is Collins (2018) observation that although host countries invest considerable energy in developing modalities for engagement, rarely do immigrants " … act in the manner of rational calculating subjects, making decisions from available information, assessing risks and planning for determinate futures within the constraints of regulation" (Collins, 2018, p. 977). The quality of immigrants' engagement is instead strongly influenced by their willingness to acknowledge and accept the rules of the host country. In this paper, quality of engagement with the system is seen to reflect the depth of psychological connectedness between the individual and the system. This connectedness could be manifested as the ease, comfort, security and sense of belonging that the individual experiences in his/her interactions with the system.

Bringing aspiration and engagement together

It seems from the foregoing that aspiration and engagement taken severally and/or conjointly could throw light on immigrants' settlement into host locations. The juxtaposing of the constructs of aspiration and engagement (A–E) provides four theoretically interesting interactions between aspiration and engagement. Thus, interactions could show low aspiration-low engagement, high aspiration-low engagement, high aspiration-high engagement and low aspiration-high engagement. Each of these associations is a theoretical grouping and it is unlikely that any one individual would "fit" purely into any one category. Instead, the patterns presented are a theoretical starting point to explore the interplay between aspiration and engagement. These interactions are captured in Figure 1.

The cultural preparation process

This paper uses Arulmani's (2014, 2015, 2016) formulation of cultural preparedness as a theoretical framework to further understand the aspiration-engagement interaction. The cultural preparedness approach proposes that *global trends* form the backdrop against which human engagement with work and career play out. These are macro, external factors (social philosophies, economic trends, political changes, technological advances, natural phenomena) that affect the individual/group but over which they have little or no control. The process of *enculturation,* facilitated by the human

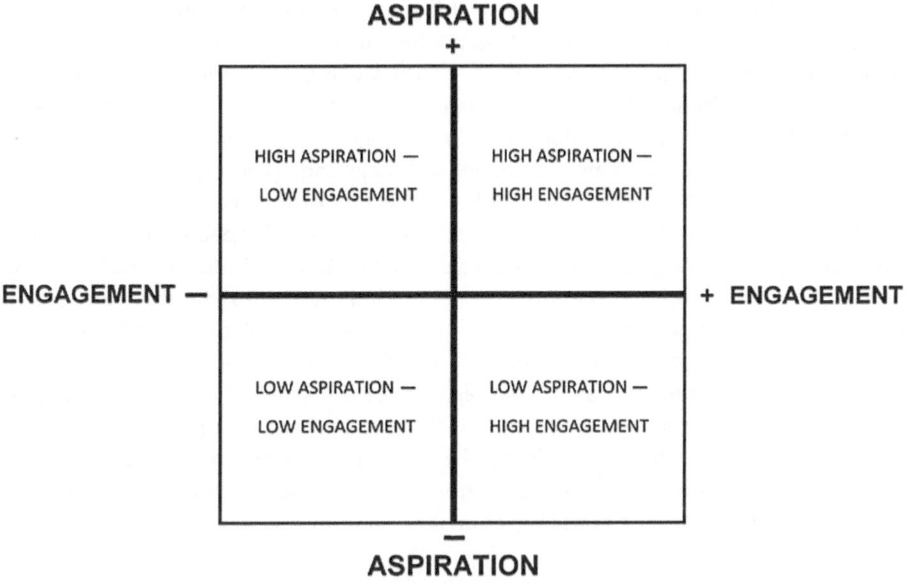

Figure 1. The cultural preparedness model of aspiration and engagement. Printed with permission from The Promise Foundation, 2010.

ability for *cultural learning,* leads the members of a group to absorb the ways of their culture. Enculturation is effected through three key factors: patterns of social organisation varying along the individualism-collectivism continuum, patterns of value attribution and processes of role allocation. Enculturation creates a unique state of balance and internal stability, reflected in the person's engagement with the world. This internal stability is described as the *cultural preparation status equilibrium*. This equilibrium is not permanent. The forces of *acculturation* can affect this state of equilibrium. Acculturative forces could be consonant or dissonant with the individual/group's cultural preparation status. Consonance would mean that the acculturative force supports, enhances, or further stabilises the existing equilibrium. Dissonance would mean that the existing equilibrium is disturbed. Underlying the hypothetical A–E categorisation shown in Figure 1, are propositions rooted within the processes of cultural preparedness. Accordingly, the immigrant is already in a state of cultural preparedness equilibrium when arriving in a new country. Immigration by its very nature results in the disturbance of this equilibrium. Immigrants' responses to this disturbance could range from establishing a new equilibrium by integrating with the host system to adopting a separatist position by rejecting the host and retaining the original cultural orientation. Understanding the variations seen in migrants' A–E responses to supports and services offered by the host country could throw light on the dynamics of integration and potentially inform policy and practice.

Philosophic moorings

This study is undergirded by philosophic constructs from Asian and Western thought with a strong emphasis on lived experience. Edmund Husserl's, hermeneutic phenomenology is of interest here (Husserl, 1913/1931). This style of enquiry seeks to create an intellectual ethos for the objective study of topics typically considered to be subjective such as judgements, perceptions, and emotions. Phenomenological data comprise conscious human experience rather than data emerging from experimentation. The fact remains however that perspective is ever present and cannot (perhaps need not) be neutralised. The notion of karmic dispassion from Asian philosophies is relevant here. The seeker of truth is exhorted to engage with life and its duties with vigour, but at the same time practice dispassion (Hiriyanna, 1993). This principle of distancing oneself from a task, yet engaging with it wholeheartedly could be relevant when applying the phenomenological approach.

Husserl and his colleagues (Heidegger, 1927/1996) draw upon the principles of hermeneutics to describe a hermeneutic phenomenology that strives to reflect upon basic experience before it has been coloured by theory, translated or elucidated in any way. One key tenet of hermeneutic phenomenology is phenomenological reduction (epoché) or bracketing. This requires the identification of personal assumptions about the external world and the bracketing of these assumptions in order to focus on the analysis of the original experience without bias. A repeated and consistent return to and a re-viewing of the original material is said to provide new insights which can inform the modification of earlier impressions creating a process of iterative reflexivity that continues throughout the examination of the data. Husserl's hermeneutic phenomenology guided this study. Reflections of this approach are seen in the nonlinear karmic principles of Asian thought. Cause and effect are not seen as polarities but as integral aspects of the same phenomenon. Enquiry is portrayed as an ever expanding spiral (Arulmani, 2014). Development occurs upon previous development, whereby one constantly learns from the past and looks to the future accepting all experience as integral to knowing. Applied to hermeneutic phenomenology one could conceive karmic engagement with data as a spirular (spiral-like) evolution of ideas.

Study 1

The objectives of Study 1 were twofold: identifying themes reflecting engagement with the systems of the host country and discovering responses to these themes. Study 1 draws upon interviews conducted by the author between the years 2000 and 2017 with 84 immigrants from 35 developing countries living at the time of the interview in 9 high-income countries (24 cities). Research indicates that the strongest impact of acculturation is felt by first-generation immigrants with subsequent generations assimilating the host culture with greater ease (e.g. OECD, 2014). The cultural preparedness approach suggests that the greater the cultural and economic difference between the home and host country (e.g. collectivist-individualistic social organisation, post-industrial work environment), the greater are the challenges faced by the immigrant (Arulmani, 2014). Hence Study 1 focused exclusively on first-generation immigrants. These interviews are a part of what is essentially the author's travelogue, compiled in the course of his travels on assignments. They are hence limited to immigrants one would encounter during international travel (e.g. in airports, hotels, restaurants). The collection of case material followed a serendipitous approach, "... making fortunate discoveries unexpectedly, by accident or coincidence" (Nutefall & Ryder, 2010. p. 3). The interviews were conducted in English with the duration ranging from 45 to 120 minutes ($M_{\text{interview time}} = 60$) depending on the availability of the interviewee. An invitation to a formal interview was made only after the person spontaneously began a conversation with the author over and above the transaction at hand. For example, some taxi drivers would remain silent throughout the drive while others would ask the author where he was from, why he was in the country, what he thought about the country and so on. This spontaneity was taken as an initial indication of the person's openness to engage in a broader conversation. The author then would introduce himself, explain his interest in understanding how immigrants settled into their new home and ask if this person would consent to have a more formal interview about these matters. All were informed that their narratives would be used to develop a deeper understanding of how immigrants engaged with the systems of the host countries and that these stories would finally be published (after anonymisation) for a public readership. About 40% of those whom the author approached declined participation. On the other hand, about 25% of those interviewed also brought their friends/relatives to meet the author. All interviews were conducted with verbal informed consent based on the assurance of confidentiality. The identity of participants was anonymised by transforming identifying data (e.g. name, place of employment) into alphanumeric codes, the expansion of which was known only to the author. No incentives were offered. Recordings were handwritten in the form of jottings which were transcribed into complete narratives. Participants could not be invited to verify the final version. When the author decided to analyse the interviews, ethics clearance for the study was obtained from the author's parent organisation, [identifying information removed for blind review], which researches and develops interventions related to mental health.

Interview protocol

The overarching objective of this study was to gain insights pertaining to the interaction between aspiration and engagement based on immigrants' *lived experience*. Interviewees were encouraged to look back to their earlier lives, compare and contrast it with their present situation and articulate plans for the future. After collection of preliminary background information, all interviews began with the question, "Tell me how your life has played out over the last few years". Other questions included, "Tell me about failures/successes/barriers you have experienced here", "How did you deal with any barriers you faced", "How has this move affected your family life/values/identity". Mother tongue expressions were encouraged and the author used prompts, encouragement and reflective statements to obtain as full a narrative as possible. All interviews were conducted by the author. An overview of the sample is presented in Table 1.

The research group

As described above, these interviews were conducted over many years, in multiple locations, within varying political, economic and cultural environments. Since the case material is multicultural in nature, it was important that the research team was itself varied and comprised individuals who were not only experienced and knowledgeable about the phenomenon being studied, but who were from different cultures. The author turned to colleagues with whom he had worked before. The project, as well as its philosophic orientation, was explained. All those the author approached, accepted to join the panel. The research group comprised three men and three women in the age

Table 1. Overview of sample.

Host country (city)	Number of interviews	Males	Females	Age range
Austria (Feldkirk, Vienna, Innsbruck, Salzburg)	8	4	4	18–47
Australia (Perth, Sydney, Melbourne)	9	5	4	28–55
Canada (Montreal, Quebec City, Toronto)	5	2	3	28–34
Liechtenstein	3	0	3	24–32
New Zealand (Wellington, Auckland)	8	6	2	22–45
Sweden (Stockholm, Gothenburg)	14	8	6	21–48
Switzerland (Zurich, Berne, Freiburg)	14	9	5	30–46
France (Paris, Nice, Roissy)	13	7	6	24–54
Italy (Rome, Bergamo, Turin)	10	6	4	28–54
Total	**84**	**47**	**37**	

Mean age: 36 years (range = 20–55 years).

Mean years of residence in host country: 6 years (range = 1–12 years).

Countries of origin: Afghanistan, Albania, Algeria, Andorra, Angola, Argentina, Bangladesh, Bulgaria, Cambodia, Cameroon, Caribbean, Congo, Côte d'Ivoire, Croatia, Eritrea, Ghana, India, Iraq (Kurdish), Kosovo, Lebanon, Morocco, Philippines, Poland, Serbia, Somalia, South Africa, Sri Lanka, Sudan, Syria, Thailand, Tunisia, Turkey, Turkey (Kurdish), Ukraine, Vietnam.

Occupation in home country: accountant, auto mechanic, bank teller, bus driver, businessman, carpenter, clerk, computer teacher, doctor, electrician, factory worker, farmer, fish canning industry, food technologist, graphic designer, head of school, history teacher, housewife, journalist, lab technician, lawyer, lecturer, miner, nongovernmental organisation worker, nun, nurse, nursery school teacher, physiotherapist, policeman, preschool teacher, psychologist, rug maker, scientist, senior teacher, shop attendant, shop keeper, shop owner, social worker, software programmer, soldier, student, teacher, tour guide, unoccupied, waitress.

Occupation at the time of interview: accountant, accounts clerk, auto mechanic, bar tender, box office clerk, bus driver, career counsellor, clerk, electrician, farmhand, front desk (hotel), housekeeping (hotel), housewife, janitor, junior accounts clerk, luggage handler, machine operator, maid, nun, nurse assistant, relief teacher, shop assistant, shop owner, software programmer, street vendor, student, supermarket clerk, taxi driver, tour guide, unoccupied, waiter/waitress.

Reason for shift: better prospects, loss of livelihood and property, marriage, political unrest, war.

range of 28–55 years. Three were from India. The others were from Sweden, Vietnam and Sri Lanka. Two held doctoral degrees in clinical psychology and one in human development. One was in the final year of a 4-year doctoral programme in career psychology, one held a Master's degree in social work and one a bachelor's degree in sociology. All members of the team were professionally engaged in counselling and guidance and had practical experience ranging from 10 to 25 years. Five had direct experience with immigrants. They were all closely acquainted with the author's work on cultural preparedness.

Procedure and data analysis

All team members were oriented to the concepts under study and the undergirding phenomenological principles. This was led by the author through discussions (group and individual) and written briefs. The following criteria for inclusion of a theme were set: the theme characterised at least 75% of the cases and concurrence between all members was 100%. The technique of memoing (Glaser, 1978) was used throughout the study.

Before the analysis, bracketing required all team members to describe their assumptions with particular reference to immigrants' aspirations and processes of engagement, cultural preparedness, as well as their expectations of the study. The objective was to achieve, as far as possible, a suspension of assumptions through the articulation of these assumptions, sharpening personal and mutual sensitivities to personal orientations and thereby mitigating the influence of bias. Over the next three months, each member of the group followed a two-step examination of each interview.

Step 1: Identifying key themes reflecting immigrants' aspirations and their engagement with the host country's systems and provisions, with primary reference to education and career. Thematic extractions were conducted to identify core phenomena (broad themes) specifically linked to finding one's way in the host country (e.g. learning the host country's language). This analysis of the case material was conducted in 6 rounds, over a period of 8 weeks, with each member examining 14 cases per round. Open coding (Strauss & Corbin, 1990) was used to identify distinct, independent concepts and categories in the case material. On completion of open coding, the study drew upon hermeneutic phenomenology to re-examine the first round of analysis. Each team member shared with the rest of the group, a written document listing identified themes with illustrative quotations from the case material. Each member was then required to perform two functions: firstly, indicate consensus with the themes in other members' lists and secondly, based on readings of others' lists, edit to include or delete themes they had originally listed. After one such round of editing, themes that found complete consensus were marked as selected. Members debated the inclusion/non-inclusion of remaining items on the theme list. This reflexive-hermeneutic iteration allowed the team to learn from each other, re-examine their own reflections and engage in an expanding spirular evolution of ideas. Three such rounds were held iteratively after which it was decided that the analysis was saturated and further analysis would not make substantial additions. Items that had not found consensus by this stage were dropped. The core phenomena listed were referred to as Aspiration-Engagement *themes* (A–E themes).

Step 2: Identifying responses to the A–E themes. Axial coding (Strauss & Corbin, 1990) was used to list the various ways in which interviewees engaged with the A–E themes. The same method of case allocation used in Step 1 was followed. Each A–E theme was examined across the cases to identify how the interviewee responded to the challenge, task or requirement presented by that theme (e.g. responding to failure to learn the language of the host country by *trying again*). The process of reflexive iteration was repeated. The objective this time was to find consensus about the best fit between the responses emerging from axial coding and the A–E theme to which each response best belonged (e.g. response of *failure* to learn the language best fits under the *failure experience* theme). Items that did not find consensus about fit with an A–E theme were dropped after the third iteration and the final list of responses referred to as Aspiration-Engagement *responses* (A–E responses) took shape.

Results

Open coding identified seven A–E themes and axial coding drew out four to ten A–E responses to each theme, together composing seven A–E *sets*. For example, Perception of the System is an A–E *theme* and corresponding responses of engagement such as acceptance, criticality or trust toward the system are the A–E *responses*. Together they compose the Perception of the System set. The following section presents illustrative vignette-pairs. Background information is given in parenthesis in the following order: gender, country of origin, age, present occupation, previous occupation, year of interview, location of interview, duration of stay in host country, reason for immigration. The superscripts AE and AER are used to mark phrases that open coding and axial coding identified as an A–E theme and A–E response respectively. A given vignette intends to illustrate one A–E set. All vignettes are verbatim extracts from the interviews.

Perception of the system

This A–E set reflecting attitudes toward and judgements of the host environment characterised every interview.

> *Vignette 1 (male, Sri Lanka, 45, front desk clerk in hotel, scientist, 2001, Zurich, 6 years, civil war).* Yeah … life is alright. The Swiss system is good[AE]. But just imagine what I was and what I am now. In Lanka I was a junior scientist in the ministry. But because of the war I could not proceed further. I thought I would be able to continue in the Swiss system. Initially I enrolled in a science programme. But for me this was not to be[AE]. With job duties and shift timings, how can I maintain a study schedule? So I guess I have given up[AER]. The money is there. Comforts are there. Children are in good school system. So I guess I just go on[AER]. My dreams are left behind[AER].

> *Vignette 2 (male, Serbia, 46, supermarket clerk, business, 2004, Zurich, 7, loss of livelihood and property).* I lost everything. But here I think I can gain back[AE]. Not what I lost, but something else. New start[AER]. Here they allow you to work[AE]. No thinking which people is which and no making differences[AE]. In this system all are equal[AE]. I had a bakery in Belgrade. But all gone. Bombed out! But here now I am studying also[AER]. Maybe I don't get all back. But sure my children will. We are happy[AER]. We are working for better future[AER].

The *Perception of the System* A–E set provides insights into how experiences of the system shape perception of the system. Vignette 1 shows a depletion in motivation for engagement characterised by indifference and a feeling of having tried and lost. Vignette 2 shows trust and hope leading to an alignment with the system.

Failure experiences

Experiences related to failure were common.

> *Vignette 3 (male, Somali, 35, unoccupied (engaged in gambling), farmer, 2015, Stockholm, 3, civil war).* The first thing to do – learn Swedish. Without that, no chance. I joined the classes. But it was too hard[AE]. The language is too hard[AE]. I did not pass[AE]. How can I pass? I am a farmer. I felt shame[AER]. Shame is very bad in my country. I am angry[AER]. How can I pass? Easy way is this … take money from foolish tourists with this number game[AER].

> *Vignette 4 (male, Turkey (Kurdish), 32, taxi driver, rug maker, 2015, Stockholm, 4, civil war).* I tried to continue my rug business. I thought I can bring from my country. But no chance. To export from my country, too much corruptions. To bring into Sweden, too much rules. So my idea of doing my business in Sweden, it failed[AE]. But in Sweden, at least I can drive taxi. So I am taking you to airport! So I am taxi driver. Fine! So is my destiny, so let it be[AER]. But please know, all my children they go to school. My work is for them[AER]. To make them success[AER].

The *Failure Experience* A–E set shows that while failure may be system induced, recovery requires concerted personal mediation. Vignette 3 shows anger and frustration along with the tendency to break rules. Vignette 4 is characterised by the acceptance of personal failure along with a shift from aspiring to personal success to the success of the children.

Motivation to engage with the system

Motivation is reflected by the enthusiasm and willingness to form and sustain a connection with a system.

> *Vignette 5 (female, Philippines, 34, maid, unoccupied, 2000, Rome, 6, better prospects).* Because my father died when I was young, I could only study till high school. Jobs were difficult to get in my country and low paid. Then through my church, I got the chance to come to Rome. Now I am still only a maid. But I have good hope for the future[AE]. I have learned Italian and I know English also[AER]. I am enrolled for a part time course in nursing[AER]. I am in my 2nd year. It is slow because of my work. Sometimes I get very stressed wondering how to keep studying successfully for 3 years more[AER]. I cannot sleep then! But okay. To make it I must keep on working and following the syllabus[AE].

> *Vignette 6 (female, India, 32, relief teacher, accountant, 2007, Perth, 6, better prospects).* I worked as a mid-level accountant for Ernst and Young in my country. I moved here after marriage. Look at me now. Just a relief teacher. I wait every day to be called. A daily wage worker! All my education, my experience, my status, all gone. I have no more desire left to make it here[AE]. The careers office told me I have to re-qualify. But no energy for all that[AE]. I would quit even what I have[AER]. But I need the money. I'm on tablets for depression[AER]. I can't take this[AER]. Sometimes I feel I should just end it all[AER].

Both these vignettes show the reality of the relative inflexibility of the system. The *Motivation to Engage with the System* A–E set shows that responsibility rests upon the individual to remain motivated and persistent despite expectations not being met. Vignette 5 is imbued with a positive orientation and high energy to maintain the engagement. At the same time, this person also seems to be anxious and experiencing stress not merely because she has to succeed at a set of tasks but because she has to continue to remain successful. Vignette 6 is a contrast. This person shows low motivation and desire. Her energy to persist is depleted and she seems to be dangerously depressed.

Integration and adjustment

This A–E set draws attention to the value placed on integration.

> ***Vignette 7*** *(female, Vietnam, 32, janitor, accountant, 2014, Toronto, 4, better prospects).* I was an accountant and I'm actually quite well qualified. But I've realised that won't work here[AE]. But still, I like it here[AE]. I think their system is good and everything is well organised and rational. I want to fit in[AE]. See this job I'm doing now is a very low job in my country. But here, it's okay. So I don't feel bad or anything[AER]. I think it would be easier if I just started again[AER]. Anyway I always wanted to change my career and become a chef! So here's my chance.

> ***Vignette 8*** *(female, India, 34, waitress, psychologist, 2014, Toronto, 2, better prospects).* I was head of a counselling service for 15,000 youth, pan India. I have a master's degree in counselling. I attended 14 interviews here. All said my qualifications are not relevant. This system is wacky[AE]. They want integration. Why should I?[AER] They won't do a thing to integrate[AE]. I got one job in a refugee centre. Didn't last a week. Then they asked me to leave citing no funds. Didn't they know that when they appointed me?[AE] You know what my boss said when she asked me to leave, that I won't have problems finding another job because of the colour of my skin! Racism in a refugee centre! I'm going back home [AER].

While integration may be desired by the system, the *Integration and Adjustment* A–E set points to variations in the value immigrants place on integration. Vignette 7 shows a strong desire to integrate, despite original desires not being fulfilled. Although the present job is low in status, there is a clear plan for optimally using the provisions made by the system. Vignette 8 shows anger, frustration and discontent. This person feels unrecognised and unaccepted. There is a strong feeling of alienation.

Opportunity awareness and planning

Almost all host systems make provisions and create opportunities for immigrants to make a new life. However, awareness of these opportunities and systematic planning are crucial if the benefit is to be gained.

Vignette 9 (female, Cameroon, 32, tour guide, non-governmental organisation worker, 2000, Paris, 7, better prospects). When I came I was lost and confused for two years. But the counsellor in the employment office helped me know more about what is suitable for me[AE]. Then I found my way. Now even though I am not doing what I used to do, I am still okay with this job[AER]. It is all about my talent to talk to people and guide them. I did not have to study a lot for it. Now I am going to study and develop in this area[AER]. It will take about 4 years and I have the plan[AER]. I know what to do and how.

Vignette 10 (male, Ghana, 33, street vendor, factory worker, 2016, Turin, 6, better prospects). I don't know what to do or where to go[AE]. Which office?[AE] I read in the posters, some information[AE]. But I don't understand[AER]. Once I found out some courses[AER]. But what is the use of that?[AER] So I am selling these items on the road side. You can call me a small business man. But I don't want to do this for always. Sometimes I feel like lost[AER]. I don't know how to move forward[AER].

The *Opportunity Awareness and Planning* A–E set shows variations in capitalising on opportunities. Vignette 9 shows a seeking attitude, and a concerted effort to plan and organise oneself. Vignette 10 shows a low level of awareness, poor quality planning and difficulties in linking opportunities with personal development.

Qualifications, credentials and recognition of past experience

Non-recognition of credentials and prior work and educational experience by the host country emerged as a theme across almost all interviews.

Vignette 11 (female, India, 28, unoccupied, food technologist, 2009, Melbourne, 6, better prospects). I have a master's degree in food technology[AE]. I worked in a large food processing firm in India[AE]. But here, these people don't recognise my degree or value my experience[AE]. They want me to do it all over again[AE]. WTF! I gave them the finger[AER]. I am making stuff[AER]. Pickles, jams, juices. My products are totally natural, homemade. Best you can have! I am selling to a growing circle of buyers[AER]. All off the record! No qualifications, no license. Let's see what they'll do[AER].

Vignette 12 (female, Poland, 40, shop assistant, nurse, 2000, Salzburg, 8, better prospects). I think what they say is true. The first generation of an immigrant family must sacrifice for the children[AE]. In the beginning I tried to study again and be a nurse here[AER]. But I could not[AER]. I am too old for that! So I could not qualify as a nurse[AE]. I felt bad that I could not get a job like in my country[AER]. But now I have accepted[AER]. I do this just to bring some income home. But I am mainly trying to be a good mother and wife[AER]. Forget a career for me[AER].

The *Qualifications, Credentials and Recognition of Past Experience* A–E set shows that host countries have their own regulations pertaining to certification which are usually more stringent than developing countries. Vignette 11 shows quite an aggressive and angry response to these pre-established standards. While it is true that this person is attempting to make her way forward, this effort may not be sustainable since it falls outside established regulatory frameworks. Vignette 12 shows a different response. There is a touch of sadness and disappointment about not qualifying to continue professionally. But at the same time there is acceptance and along with acceptance, a shift in perspectives from self to family.

View of the future

Personal development is intrinsically connected with the person's orientation to the future.

Vignette 13 (male, Syria, 48, bar tender, business, 2015, Gothenburg, 9, civil war). When I lost everything (even some loved ones) because of the war, I lost hope. I had a black view of the future[AE]. But somehow I managed to arrive here. I will never be a prosperous business man again[AER]. But now my future is not so black[AE]. I have a good job. It gives me what I need. I am also involved with the labour unions[AER]. That gives some meaning for what can happen in the future[AE]. I teach my children that nothing comes when we want it. We have to work for it, and plan for it and wait for the fruits to ripen[AER]. But, no plans no fruits!

Vignette 14 (male, Ukraine, 51, taxi driver, unoccupied, 2016, Bergamo, 8, political unrest). Before I came I lost my job and was unemployed in my country. Here I thought I will make it[AE]. But after many years, I am still only a taxi driver. I don't think there is anything more in the future for me[AE]. My children do not listen to me. They have grown up in this country and they think like these people. Our culture is lost but they will be alright. And me, I think I will just be a taxi driver. I can't go back. It is too late and I am too poor[AER]. So, I just carry on with this, day to day[AER]. I don't think so much now about the future[AER].

The *View of the Future* A–E set shows that the person's orientation to the future can have an impact on the quality of his/her preparation for the future. Vignette 13 begins with a bleak view but with the passage of time, much more positivity is seen. The importance of having a positive, planful view is highlighted. Vignette 14 shows a resigned acceptance. There seems to be a sense of giving up and focusing on immediate survival needs.

The A–E sets listed above comprising A–E themes and A–E responses were crystallised at the end of this study. Feedback received from presentations at multiple fora (e.g. international conferences, workshops, workshops) indicated that the information was useful in and of itself. However, such an A–E set still remained merely a list of responses tagged to a set of themes. The relevance of these themes and responses to the practice of guidance and counselling needed clarification. This was the objective of Study 2.

Study 2

This study considered how the A–E sets identified in Study 1 would relate to the aspiration-engagement *matrix* (A–E matrix) described in Figure 1. The objective was to use the A–E set to find descriptors for the four categories emerging from the A–E matrix. Since the objective now focused on application and practice, inputs from practitioners became imperative.

Practitioner group

The Practitioner Group comprised 120 Swedish counsellors in the age range of 24 to 61 years. All had gone through a three year, bachelor of arts programme in guidance and counselling. Their experience ranged between 2 and 21 years. They were all directly involved in interventions for immigrants to Sweden from Afghanistan, Bangladesh, Eritrea, Ghana, India, Iran, Iraq, Iraq, Kosovo, Lebanon, Morocco, Poland, Serbia, Somalia, Sri Lanka, Sudan, Syria and Turkey. About 15% of the participating counsellors were immigrants themselves. The author had no control over the selection of this group since they were a part of a mandatory municipality-wide cultural sensitivity workshop. All participants and the director of the government organisation that employed the participants were informed at the beginning of the workshop that the outputs of their discussions would be material for a larger research project. Informed verbal consent was obtained.

Procedure and data analysis

All members of the Practitioner Group went through a 4-day workshop on cultural preparedness aimed at improving sensitivity to the issues that surround immigrants' wellbeing. The practitioners were met over a period of two years (2015–2017) in six batches ranging in size from 15 to 20 persons. The data for this study is drawn from the culminating exercise of this training course. This was a day-long exercise that required participants to draw upon their experience as counsellors and map the A–E sets onto the A–E matrix. Each batch was further divided into groups comprising 3–4 counsellors and given one of the A–E sets. Written instructions were given to create an A–E map and each small group engaged in a 90 minute focus group discussion to complete the exercise. The author circulated amongst the groups providing explanations along with examples. Each group then presented their mapping exercise in a plenary session. The rest of the batch then added their comments and views. The A–E map created by each group was collected and retained as data.

Results

The frequency with which each response under each A–E theme was attributed by the Practitioner Group to one of the four types of A–E interactions was computed. Responses with the highest frequency for each type of A–E interaction were allocated to that type. Thereby the four A–E categories were populated with a set of descriptors drawn from the A–E sets of Study 1. Table 2 presents the final outcome of the mapping exercise. Drawing upon these findings the salient characteristics of the A–E groups could be described as follows.

The low-aspiration-low-engagement group

The low-aspiration-low-engagement group (LALE) situation is tinged with disappointment. There is an acceptance of the host system but as Neufeld et al. (2006) point out, these individuals could experience a sense of being neglected, overlooked or disregarded by their environment. This could be the result of being overwhelmed by circumstances. Original dreams and wishes are likely to have been discarded. Low contentment and an almost wistful sense of accepting one's lot could characterise their engagement.

The high-aspiration-low-engagement group

The high-aspiration-low-engagement group (HALE) situation depicts an overriding sense of anger and frustration. Criticality and a tendency to blame the system is common. Aspirations are high but could be unrealistic. It must be noted however that this group has not given up personal advancement. However, while the vigour described by Schaufeli et al. (2002) is present, the dedication required to overcome barriers described by these authors may not be persistent enough.

The high-aspiration-high-engagement group

The high-aspiration-high engagement group (HAHE) appears to be the "ideal group. Their aspirations are realistic and their engagement is sound. Rather than being a reason to complain, failure is a spur to try again. Information seeking and linking opportunities for personal advancement is common. This said, it is also important to note that the bidirectional process of evaluation occurring between the person and the environment (Neufeld et al., 2006), is tilted such that anxiety results from the need to maintain what has been achieved and to continue to move ahead.

The low-aspiration-high-engagement group

The low-aspiration-high engagement group (LAHE) is an interesting group. Engagement and contentment do seem to be high, while aspiration for personal success is low. Motivation seems to stem from working for the welfare of others. Interestingly, the frequency of responses of acceptance of the host culture is low with this group. This could point to an instrumental form of engagement (Brown, 1987). Thus, although engagement is present, there could be an underlying sense of disaffection where engagement is exercised only in so far as it is required for progress.

With this, Study 2 drew to a close and the central objective of creating the cultural preparedness model of aspiration and engagement was completed. It must be reiterated that the purpose of this exercise is not to box people into categories! It is unlikely that any individual would fall purely into any one A–E category. In fact, not all responses could be exclusively allocated to a single A–E type. Trust, for example, is a response that occurred in almost equal frequency both with the HAHE and LAHE groups. Anxiety in different shades characterised all the groups. It is important therefore that a given response is holistically interpreted along with the client's other responses.

Table 2. Mapping the aspiration-engagement set to the aspiration-engagement matrix.

A–E theme	LALE	HALE	HAHE	LAHE
Perception of the System: attitudes toward and judgements of the host environment based personal experiences of the host system	accepts the system but has grown indifferent and sceptical; feels let down by the system; feels requirements are overwhelming	critical of the system; does not align with the requirements of the system; does not trust the system	trusts the system; has learned how to align with and benefit from the system	trusts the system; is willing to contribute as a member
Failure experiences: the lack of success in obtaining what one desires despite effort	attributes failure to personal failings; given up	anger; frustration; unable to understand reasons for failure; attributes failure to flaws in the system; takes shortcuts to beat the system and circumvent failure (rule breaking)	learns from failure; tries again; anxious not to fail again; experiences stress and strain related to maintaining what has been achieved	acceptance; shifted priorities from self to others
Motivation to engage with the system: the quality of desire and energy to engage with activities and tasks set by the system and the interest and energy directed toward attaining goals using the provisions made by the system	low and indifferent; disappointed after trying hard; low motivation because of poor health/ trauma	high but unrealistic expectations; easily bored; dissatisfied with present level of success	high but realistic expectations; moving toward further development; but also experiencing stress because of the need to achieve	positively involved with family, community and social events
Integration and adjustment: experiencing a state of satisfaction and is at ease with one's situation having effectively combined aspects of the host culture with aspects of the own culture	low contentment; feels: I don't think I will ever make it	feels unrecognised and blocked; high sense of alienation from the system	feels content because of successes; satisfaction with the freedom to follow one's culture; accepts the host system	high contentment as a result of personal contribution to others' achievements
Opportunity Awareness and Planning: knowledge of chances available for advancement and preparing oneself in accordance with the system to benefit from these opportunities	is aware but shows low energy to engage with opportunities; not systematic when planning; poor preparation; has a long term view but low interest affects persistence	struggles to link opportunities to personal development; interested in opportunities for which personal suitability is low; plans but gives up easily; has a short term view; poor preparation	high awareness and able to plan appropriately; can identify sources of opportunities; plans effectively; makes long term plans; seeks information; shows persistence	high awareness of sources of opportunities and able to plan appropriately on behalf of others
Qualifications, Credentials and Recognition of Past Experience: evaluation and recognition of immigrants' qualifications, credentials and prior experience by regulatory bodies in the host country	feeling that solutions are too complicated/ expensive/take too long to actualise; unable to go through the process of re-certification; unable to allocate time for re-qualifying given the need to earn	feels earlier accomplishments not valued; unwilling for recertification; frustrated by educational requirements	willing to start afresh; has engaged in re-qualifying; able to make adaptations	may not possess the necessary credentials but has adjusted

(*Continued*)

Table 2. Continued.

A–E theme	LALE	HALE	HAHE	LAHE
View of the Future: thoughts and ideas about what is likely to happen in the future	bleak view of future; feels it's too late; working just for livelihood/survival needs of the present	unrealistic view of future; has a short-term view and wants quick results	has clarity about the future; is invested in long-term plans	has a positive long-term view of the future in relation to others

Note: LALE: low aspiration-low engagement; HALE: high aspiration-low engagement; HAHE: high aspiration-high engagement; LAHE: low aspiration-high engagement.

Discussion

This work has developed a cultural preparedness model of aspiration and engagement through a phenomenological analysis of a wide variety of case material. A limitation of this work could be its lack of reference to how individual differences emanating from personality features, gender and socioeconomic status influence the manner in which the A–E process plays out. This is worthy of further exploration through other studies Further, with the objective of grounding this work on lived experience, hermeneutic interpretation has been used as the primary tool of analysis. The word hermeneutic comes from Hermes, the inventor of language and speech, an interpreter of the gods. Hermes also is the archetype of the trickster and is often portrayed as a liar and a thief (Graves, 1955)! While this is stated here in lighter vein, it also flags for our attention the limitations one must be aware of when working with text and verbal material. These limitations are clearly articulated in Eastern epistemologies. Mimamsa (Sanskrit for reflection and critical investigation) rests upon a hermeneutics that describes the reliability of various modalities of knowing (Hiriyanna, 1993). The work reported in this paper rests on the mimamsa modality of *upamana*: vicarious learning about a phenomenon through someone else's description of their experience of the phenomenon. Upamana is categorised by mimamsa as the least reliable modality since it requires a high capacity for attention on the listener's side and true memories on the side of the speaker. Also, interpretation of words and text could be strongly mediated by cultural filters. It is essential that the limitations of drawing conclusions from a re-processing of the original experience are kept in mind.

Having acknowledged these limitations attention is drawn to the strong possibility that the equilibrium in cultural preparation status created through enculturation is disturbed by acculturative demands resulting from immigration. This disturbance could be further augmented by the higher likelihood of immigrants' aspirations being politicised (for better or for worse) than those of natives. The paper proposes the A–E model as a starting point from which to understand this disturbance. The A–E interaction is a dynamic one. Circumstances, experiences, opportunity structures and personal characteristics could cause a person to move from one A–E position to another. Vignette 1 (Study 1) for example shows that this person was initially at the HAHE position but succumbed to the stress and strain that characterises this group and slipped to the LALE position. By contrast, Vignette 9 (Study 1) shows a movement from the LALE status to the HAHE position because of the support received from the system. Central to this argument, therefore, is the notion of movement towards an equilibrium. The enculturated equilibrium with which the immigrant arrived perhaps can never be regained. The cultural preparedness model of aspiration and engagement could perhaps provide clues that guidance and counselling workers could use to help immigrants re-establish their lives by discovering a new equilibrium.

Disclosure statement

No potential conflict of interest was reported by the author.

References

Arulmani, G. (2014). The cultural preparation process model and career development. In G. Arulmani, A. J. Bakshi, F. T. L. Leong, & A. G. Watts (Eds.), *Handbook of career development: International perspectives* (pp. 81–104). New York, NY: Springer International.

Arulmani, G. (2015). The question is the answer: The cultural preparedness approach to assessment for career guidance. In M. McMahon, & M. Watson (Eds.), *Career assessment: Qualitative approaches* (pp. 207–218). Melbourne: Sense Publishers.

Arulmani, G. (2016). Contexts and circumstances: The cultural preparation process approach to career development. In M. McMahon (Ed.), *Career counselling: Constructivist approaches (2nd ed.)* (pp. 79–90). Abingdon: Routledge.

Arulmani, G., Van Laar, D., & Easton, S. (2003). The influence of career beliefs and socioeconomic status on the career decision-making of high school students in India. *International Journal for Educational and Vocational Guidance, 3*, 193–204.

Aspiration. (n.d.). *In Merriam-Webster's online dictionary* (11th ed). Retrieved from http://www.merriam-webster.com/dictionary/aspiration.

Bandura, A. (2001). Social cognitive theory: An agentic perspective. *Annual Review of Psychology, 52*(52), 1–26.

Brown, P. (1987). *Schooling ordinary kids*. London: Tavistock.

Carling, J., & Collins, F. (2018). Aspiration, desire and drivers of migration. *Journal of Ethnic and Migration Studies, 44*(6), 909–926.

Collins, F. L. (2018). Desire as a theory for migration studies: Temporality, assemblage and becoming in the narratives of migrants. *Journal of Ethnic and Migration Studies, 44*(6), 964–980.

Engage. (n.d.). *In Merriam-Webster's online dictionary (11th ed*). Retrieved from http://www.merriam-webster.com/dictionary/engage.

Fouad, N. A., & Byars-Winston, A. M. (2005). Cultural context of career choice: Meta-analysis of race/ethnicity differences. *Career Development Quarterly, 53*, 223–233.

Glaser, B. G. (1978). *Theoretical sensitivity: Advances in the methodology of grounded theory*. Mill Valley, CA: The Sociology Press.

Graves, R. (1955). *The Greek Myths*. London: Penguin.

Heidegger, M. (1927/1996). *Being and time* (J. Stambaugh, Trans.). Albany: University of New York Press. (Original work published in 1927).

Hiriyanna, M. (1993). *Outlines of Indian philosophy*. New Delhi: Motilal Banarsidass.

Husserl, E. (1913/1931). *Ideas: General introduction to pure phenomenology*. New York, NY: Humanities Press. (Original work published 1913).

Macdonald, R., & Marsh, J. (2004). Missing school: Educational engagement, youth transitions, and social exclusion. *Youth & Society, 36*(2), 143–162.

Meyer, F. (2018). Navigating aspirations and expectations: Adolescents' considerations of outmigration from rural eastern Germany. *Journal of Ethnic and Migration Studies, 44*(6), 1032–1049.

Neault, R. A., & Pickerell, D. A. (2011). Career engagement: Bridging career counseling and employee engagement. *Journal of Employment Counseling*, (48), 185–188.

Neufeld, J. E., Rasmussen, H. N., Lopez, S. J., Ryder, J. A., Magyar-Moe, J. L., Ford, A. I., et al. (2006). The engagement model of person-environment interaction. *The Counseling Psychologist, 34*(2), 245–259.

Nutefall, J. E., & Ryder, P. M. (2010). The serendipitous research process. *Journal of Academic Librarianship, 36*(3), 228–234.

OECD. (2014). *Finding the way: A discussion of the Swedish migrant integration system*. Paris: OECD Publishing.

The Promise Foundation. (2010). *Interventions for youth development and potential realisation: An overview*. Bangalore: The Promise Foundation.

Schaufeli, W. B., Martínez, I. M., Pinto, A. M., Salanova, M., & Bakker, A. B. (2002). Burnout and engagement in university students. *Journal of Cross-Cultural Psychology, 33*(5), 464–481.

Schoon, I., & Parsons, S. (2002). Teenage aspirations for future careers and occupational outcomes. *Journal of Vocational Behavior, 60*, 262–288.

Strauss, A., & Corbin, J. (1990). *Basics of qualitative research: Grounded theory procedures and techniques*. Newbury Park, CA: Sage.

TIEDI. (2011). *Continuity of employment for immigrants during the first four years in Canada (TIEDI Analytical Report 24)*. Toronto: Toronto Immigrant Employment Data Initiative.

Van Hear, N., Oliver Bakewell, O., & Long, K. (2018). Push-pull plus: Reconsidering the drivers of migration. *Journal of Ethnic and Migration Studies, 44*(6), 927–944.

'Where are you from?' Identity as a key to parenting by 1.5 generation Korean-New Zealand migrants and implications for counselling

Hyeeun Kim and Margaret Nelson Agee

ABSTRACT

In a qualitative study of the experiences of 1.5 generation Korean New Zealanders as parents, a notable finding was the significant part the participants' identity-related experiences as migrants played in shaping their parenting practices. Interviews were conducted with 18 Korean "Kiwis" (New Zealanders), colloquially referred to as "Kowis," who had arrived in New Zealand before 2002 as children or adolescents with their parents and were now married with children. Reflecting on the challenges of their migration and identity journeys enabled them to recognise their vulnerabilities and their advantages, and the multiple ways in which identity-related cultural conflicts and confusion influenced their parenting of their children. The implications are identified for further research and for counselling practice.

This article is based on findings from a qualitative study of the parenting experiences of 1.5 generation Korean New Zealanders (colloquially known as "Kowis") who had arrived in New Zealand themselves prior to 2002 as the children of migrant parents (Kim, 2014). The phrase "the 1.5 generation" refers to migrants' children who arrived in their host country before reaching adulthood, generally between the ages of 5 and 17 years (Bartley & Spoonley, 2008; Danico, 2004; Janes, 2004; Park, 1999; Zhou, 1997). The term "Kowi" (Korean-Kiwi) has been casually used by Korean New Zealanders since the 1990s until officially claimed and defined by the Kowiana Association of New Zealand in 2008 (Kowiana Association, 2008). Rather than a derogatory term, it represents their dual cultural heritage from both countries.

In the existing literature about migration and parenting, the focus is primarily on stressors, intergenerational dynamics, child development and parenting practices within the families of first generation migrants. Many factors influence the challenging task of parenting, and the cultural encounters and processes of change associated with migration and acculturation for families and individuals complicate parents' lives and roles in multiple ways (Berry, 2007; Fleck & Fleck, 2013; Tyyska, 2007). These processes have yet to be fully explored and understood from the perspectives of those experiencing these transitions.

Prior to undertaking this research, the first author worked with many 1.5 generation Kowis and their family members in over two decades of counselling practice and community work. A first-generation migrant herself, she kept hearing two contradictory statements that piqued her curiosity: "I can neither be a full Korean nor a full New Zealander," and "It is my strength that I have a dual cultural heritage from both Korea and New Zealand and speak both languages." She wondered where the sense of existential inadequacy and/or pride in their strengths had come from; whether their self-concept was influenced by the fact that their parents were first-generation migrants; how the speakers, as migrants, felt about bringing up their own second-generation children now; and how adequate they felt as parents. This seemed to be an aspect of Kowis' lives in which they were likely to experience cultural tension and "in-betweenness" (Bartley & Spoonley, 2008).

A sense of in-betweenness and of having to learn how to "walk in two worlds" seems commonly reported across various populations including not only migrants but also, e.g. "third culture kids" (TCKs) (Pollock & Van Reken, 2009), indigenous people with a history of colonisation and those with multi-ethnic heritages (e.g. Culbertson & Agee, 2007; Webber, 2008). However, a myriad of contextual factors – historical, political, social, ethnic and circumstantial – can render the nature of a particular group or individual's experiences unique. From a research perspective, little was known about Kowis' parenting experiences: the challenges they faced, the resources, hopes and aspirations they brought to their parenting, or their parenting practices. The current study was therefore undertaken to address this gap.

Unexpectedly, among other information, the findings of this original investigation (Kim, 2014) revealed multiple ways in which the participants' own identity journeys as 1.5 Kowis contributed to shaping their parenting practices. Although the matter of the identity development of migrant adolescents has been the focus of previous research (e.g. Berry, Phinney, Sam, & Vedder, 2006b; Phinney & Ong, 2007), there has been little research into Kowis' identity-related experiences as migrants, and no known studies that have associated such experiences with parenting. This article therefore focuses particularly on data from the first author's study that specifically illuminate the influence of the identity-related experiences of the 1.5 generation participants on their parenting perspectives and practices.

Korean migrants in New Zealand

At the time of the 2013 census, the total population of New Zealand was 4.24 million (Statistics New Zealand, 2013); in 2016 it was estimated to be 4.69 million (Statistics New Zealand, 2016). Seventy four percent identified with at least one European ethnicity, 14.9% of the population identified as Māori, the indigenous people of New Zealand, and 11.8% of the population identified as Asian, with Pacific peoples constituting 7.4% and Middle Eastern/Latin American/African 1.2%. Korean migrants are the fourth-largest Asian group in New Zealand, according to the 2013 census (Statistics New Zealand, 2014). In recent years the Korean population has grown from 920 in 1991, to 30,171 in 2013, hence the majority of Korean New Zealanders are relatively new settlers, and Koreans tend to live in the major urban centres.

In New Zealand, although members of the 1.5 generation are technically first-generation migrants, their socio-cultural experiences are different from those of the first and second generation. In addition, their self-perceptions are affected by the lenses through which others see and interact with them. The 1.5 generation often face ambiguity and confusion as they are usually perceived by the first generation as second generation, they are seen as first generation by the second generation, and they are identified as just Koreans by non-Koreans and locals (Danico, 2004).

Research into transnational childhoods (Orellana, Thorne, Chee, & Lam, 2001) and Asian migrants in New Zealand (Bartley & Spoonley, 2008) has revealed that 1.5 generation young people have struggled with disruption of normal roles, routines and power structures within their families, because changes to the dynamics between parents and children as they grow up overlap with the challenges of family migration. Such experiences are likely to have influenced the perspectives of Kowis on family dynamics including parenting, parent–child relationships, and their relationships with their own children, as well as their ways of coming to terms with different parenting styles in between two different cultures. It has also been found that the 1.5 generation display the development of some advanced life skills at a young age while coping with their settlement process

(Bartley & Spoonley, 2008; Kim, 2014), raising questions about whether these skills have any effect on their practices as parents themselves.

Most research into 1.5 generation migrants in general has been undertaken in the United States, primarily focusing on the identity formation and acculturation of young people (Berry, 2005; Berry, Phinney, Sam, & Vedder, 2006a; Danico, 2004; Kiang & Fuligni, 2008; Park, 1999; Phinney, Horenczyk, Liebkind, & Vedder, 2001; Yu, Huang, Shwalberg, Overpeck, & Kogan, 2003). New Zealand researchers have investigated the identities of 1.5 generation young people from other cultural groups such as Pacific Islanders (e.g. Anae, 1998; Cowley-Malcolm, 2013; Cowley-Malcolm, Fairbairn-Dunlop, Paterson, Gao, & Williams, 2009; Guo, 2013) whose circumstances, cultures and patterns of migration have been different from those of Koreans. In terms of parenting, however, both international and New Zealand-based studies have focused on first generation parents.

Cultural influences on parenting: challenges and change

Migrants inevitably face two fundamental challenges in acculturation: maintenance of their own inherited culture and their adoption of the new host culture (Berry, 2006). Of the many diverse influences that shape parenting, culture plays a major, overarching role (Bornstein & Cheah, 2006; Harkness & Super, 2002), given the different cultural values and forces in the new environment, and cultural influences are also integral to processes of identity development. Challenges and changes in parenting were exemplified in a study of first generation Korean American migrants encountering a culturally different kind of parenting (E. Kim & Hong, 2007) in the United States. Migration from a collectivistic society like Korea to a more individualistic society like Britain, the United States or New Zealand exposes migrants to continuous and direct contact between conflicting cultures. It is well-established that differences in cultural beliefs and values between parents and children create conflicts in the dynamics within migrant families between individuals and across generations (Berry et al., 2006a, 2006b; E. Kim & Cain, 2008; E. Kim & Hong, 2007; Phinney, Ong, & Madden, 2000). Compounding these stressors for Asian families are the disruption or loss of family and social support networks, and isolation in the process of integration into New Zealand society (Chang, Morris, & Vokes, 2006; Ho, Au, Bedford, & Cooper, 2003; Tan, 2010).

Parenting experiences during childhood

Parenting experiences during childhood have been documented in the international parenting literature as being especially influential in the way people parent (e.g. Barry, Bernard, & Beitel, 2009; Smith, 2013). As the parents of the Kowis were brought up in Korea, their parenting style will naturally have been shaped by Korean cultural parenting based on Confucian values such as Hyo (filial piety) (H. O. Kim & Hoppe-Graff, 2001; K. W. Kim, 2006), Samgang (three bonds)[1] and Oryun (five principal relationships)[2] (Won, 2002), shame[3] and Chemyon[4] (Oak & Martin, 2000), which form a hierarchal, authoritarian and patriarchal family system. These Korean values may conflict with the dominant New Zealand style of European parenting.

Migrant parents may have struggled with language and culture in New Zealand, even though the majority have held tertiary qualifications and have been highly skilled, wealthy entrepreneurs (J. Y. Lee, Kearns, & Friesen, 2009; Pio, 2010). They are unlikely to have had sufficient understanding and ability to integrate New Zealand ways of parenting, especially when there has been limited assistance with integrated parenting and parenting skills available to those migrants in need of this support (Ho & Bedford, 2008). Yet it has been found that mothers' confidence about integrating the positive aspects of discipline strategies from both cultures is beneficial for their 1.5 generation adolescent children's wellbeing (E. Kim, Cain, & McCubbin, 2006). Conversely, parental adaptation difficulties, particularly among fathers, tend to adversely influence their physical and psychological presence in their children's lives in migrant families (Qin, 2009). Overall, the degree of parents' cultural adaptation is likely to influence the wellbeing of their children, enhancing children's self-esteem and social involvement as well as the quality of the intergenerational relationships (Ying & Han, 2008).

In addition, research with young Korean American adults has revealed that compatible parent–child cultural value orientations and positive parent–child relationships are associated with the development of more positive attitudes toward their own ethnic origins (D. Kim, Sarason, & Sarason, 2006). These in turn have been found to engender a positive sense of identity and to create opportunities for children to engage in support networks from both host and ethnic communities (Zhou, 1997).

Parents' sense of adequacy about their role has been found to affect their confidence and, consequently, the quality of their parenting: the more skilled and effective they feel about parenting, the more satisfying it is likely to be (Coleman & Karraker, 2000), and the more their practices foster positive developmental outcomes for their children (Jones & Prinz, 2005). Childhood experiences of parenting they perceived as unhelpful or detrimental are therefore likely to have an adverse effect on their parenting of their own children, as the Kowis are likely to have limited skills, to lack confidence in their parenting role, and/or to lack positive role models (Zubrick, Smith, Nicholson, Sanson, & Jackiewicz, 2011).

In addition to the ways in which they were parented, forces within New Zealand culture such as individualism and gender equality are likely to influence Kowis' personal development. As well as observing how non-Korean families function, they are likely to acquire information about New Zealand and European cultural norms and parenting from the media, from local institutions, health professionals, and their own social networks. These and other social and psychological influences contribute to shaping their own identity development, a fluid process in the contemporary world which, in Franklin's (2003) words, touches into "the outer and inner limits of self/group awareness of having – or choosing – an 'identity' that enables rather than hinders" (p. 470).

Speaking of the close relationship between ethnicity and identity in the context of families, McGoldrick and Giordano (1996) noted the contextual influences such as family attitudes and community acceptance, as well as discrimination and rejection, that may affect parents, while identifying as "basic psychological needs" a sense of belonging and of historical continuity (p. 1). Despite the significance of identity in human lives and contemporary social science and the extensive literature in the field (Westin, 2010), La Barbera (2015) has commented that "little attention has been devoted to the influence of migration on identity formation and transformation" (p. 1). The influence of identity-related experiences on parenting that emerged in the results of the current study are therefore noteworthy.

Method

The current grounded theory study explored the perspectives of 1.5 generation Kowi on their experiences of parenting their own children, having grown up themselves as the children of migrants in New Zealand. In particular, the research aimed to investigate the influences on Kowis' parenting and the ways in which they perceive these influences as affecting their child–parent relationships and children's development, as well as the challenges the participants had confronted and the personal resources they utilised in bringing up their children at the interface between Korean and Kiwi cultures. The study aimed to access participants' perceptions of their world as parents, and their interpretations of their parenting experiences (Rubin & Rubin, 2012) through their own lenses, in order to amplify their voices and gather richer data than measuring their parenting practices would have done.

Grounded theory emphasises the construction of theory, rather than the analysis of others' experiences through the lens of a researcher's preconceived concepts and theories (Strauss & Corbin, 1994). In the current research, aspects of the constructivist approach to grounded theory methods were adopted because special attention was paid to the position of the researcher as an "insider" in bringing a strong sense of the participants' presence throughout, enriching the meaning and interpretation of the data (Charmaz, 2000, 2005; Mills, Bonner, & Francis, 2006, 2008). As Charmaz (2006) has acknowledged:

> … we are part of the world we study and the data we collect. We **construct** [emphasis in original] our grounded theories through our past and present involvements and interactions with people, perspectives, and research practices. (p. 10)

Reflexivity was a critical component in the research process, as the first author was aware of the strengths and limitations of one's own understanding. Hence, practicing reflexivity (Brannick & Coghlan, 2007; Cunliffe & Karunanyake, 2013; Finlay, 2002) throughout a robust process of data collection and analysis ensured that this study was informed and ethical. Permission to conduct the research was granted by the University of Auckland Human Participants Ethics Committee.

Participants

The participants included eighteen 1.5 generation Kowi adults – twelve women and six men, aged between 29 and 47 years – who in 2012 were married with their own children. They had migrated to New Zealand with their parents prior to 2002 when they were between the ages of five and 17 years. The participants had resided in New Zealand from 14.7 to 35 years, and had children aged between three months and 18 years.

Participants were recruited from four major New Zealand cities by distributing information about the study through professional networks, and through Korean community organisations, media and networks, as well as by snowballing. Inquirers who contacted the first author by telephone or email were screened for eligibility and were sent further information about the study and a consent form via email prior to arranging their interview.

Data gathering

Individual interviews were conducted with the participants in order to gain an in-depth understanding of each person's experiences as a 1.5 generation Kowi parent, and the meaning those held for them. In addition to being the approach "most consistent with people's ability to make meaning through language" (Seidman, 2006, p. 13), individual interviews allowed participants the privacy to share sensitive or emotionally distressing information or reflections on their experiences, while enabling them to describe their experiences and express their views in their own words.

A semi-structured interview guide consisting of open-ended questions was developed to facilitate the broad exploration of participants' parenting experiences, and to help keep the interviews focused on the aims of the current study while enabling unanticipated stories to emerge. Interviews were conducted for up to two hours in participants' preferred language – Korean and/or English – with 15 choosing Korean and three requesting English.

Most interviews were conducted in participants' homes, while several took place in mutually agreed-upon venues. Because of the relatively small size of the Korean community in New Zealand, efforts to protect participants' privacy included using pseudonyms of their own choosing and disguising potentially identifiable information in when reporting the research results.

Data analysis

Throughout the following series of steps and the use of NVivo software, data analysis incorporated the constant comparative method, memo writing and presentations (Holton, 2007), as well as concurrent collection and analysis of the data and refinement of the research questions.

(1) Initial coding – transcripts were coded by hand then imported into NVivo (qualitative data analysis computer software).
(2) Incorporation of post-data collection field notes.
(3) Focused coding in NVivo, and continued writing of theoretical memos.

(4) Development of categories from the focused codes. Elevating these categories to concepts and highlighting major emergent themes in order to build the framework to generate a grounded theory.
(5) Development of theory and theoretical model (Kowi Parenting Model) (see Kim, 2014).
(6) Writing and re-engaging with the data to strengthen validity of the Kowi Parenting Model.

Results

At an early stage in the interviews, it was noticeable how often the participants' responses to questions about their parenting became accounts of identity-related experiences. When reflecting on their life journeys, they recognised their strengths and weaknesses as well the challenges they had struggled with over the years. Their reflections encompassed their confidence, hopes and dreams, meaning and direction in life, and understanding their place in the world when they were faced with the task of parenting. Identity became one of the keys to explaining the ways in which the participants parented their children. Only when they had thoroughly reflected on their journey of migration and settlement, however, were they able to see the effect of these identity-related experiences on their parenting, and we have presented these results accordingly.

From childhood to adulthood: "Two countries in one"

As children, participants found it difficult to adjust to the unfamiliar environment – described by some as "a shock", "traumatic" and "overwhelming" – and to living in two distinct cultures: adhering to Korean cultural rules at home, while being forced to adapt to New Zealand cultural norms outside. As one put it, there were "two countries in one" in New Zealand:

> At home, you live as a Korean. Everything is Korean. Money matters, allowance from parents, Korean language, discipline styles, and what you eat. Everything is Korean. You watch Korean TV. But when you walk out of home, when you go to school, you now have to live the Kiwi way. That really didn't fit. (Jane)

The metaphor "two countries in one" came to describe Kowis' feelings about the cultural conflicts and challenges they faced in the process of adaptation and this umbrella concept explained the core of their identity crisis. Because the two cultures were significantly different, Kowis had to find or develop two very different internal systems by which to cope after migration: Korean at home and New Zealand elsewhere.

Identity confusion confronted Kowis with the task of redefining their identities in the host country. The developmental timing compounded the difficulties for adolescents in particular. One who had been well-settled with good friends in her school, loved her life in Korea, and did not want to emigrate, found the transition traumatic:

> We came and it was a real culture shock as a teenager because then you were starting to form a sense of identity of who you are as an individual, your nationality, all those and your social networks with friends. (Jean)

Another (Hana) who "hated" everything, including the language and the country, felt "forced to let go" of Koreanness when she first came to New Zealand, and described having to define who she was, "reform" her identity a number of times on her journey through migration, "and be comfortable with the mix, the unique mix of cultures that I was" as a 1.5 generation Kowi. Such experiences left their mark on Kowis' sense of self and later triggered anxiety in their parenting.

'Where are you from?' A question of belonging

For some participants, the experience of being "placed in the middle" of two cultures as a 1.5 generation migrant evoked a profoundly difficult struggle. One, for example, described 1.5 generation as "people without a citizenship or nationality ... neither Koreans nor New Zealanders." He returned to Korea with a plan for a long-term stay as a young adult, but struggled to adjust to Korean culture because he lacked a sense of a Korean identity, and ended up coming back to New Zealand feeling alienated from the culture:

> It was really hard. I was neither Korean nor New Zealander in my identity. When you visit Korea, you are treated like a foreigner, and when you come back New Zealand, Kiwis, they all ask you, "Where are you from?" I was in anguish when I was asked "Where are you from?" It was hard to answer it, whether I should say Korean or Kiwi. … You were from Korea but lived more than half of your life here. I wrestled with it for an answer, and often just replied "from Korea." (John)

> 'Where are you from?' was one of the most uncomfortable questions participants had to live with, that constantly brought up a question of their ethnic identity.

> We go to our work place, and people always ask "Where are you from?" They [third generation Chinese colleagues] have got Kiwi accents and they are Kiwi. You cannot be any more Kiwi than that. And yet because of their kind of outlook of appearance, they are always asked. (Peter)

Others' perceptions of her caused one participant to feel alienated from both Korean and Kiwi societies.

> When I go and socialise with Koreans, the Koreans will say "but you've been here so long … You are Kiwi" and then if I go and socialise with Kiwis, they go "you've been here a long time but you're still Korean, Asian." So I don't fit here and I don't fit there. (Bella)

Her brother also struggled with identity confusion.

> He wants to think he is all Western … Because he … he doesn't speak Korean as much as I do. And he's got only Kiwi friends. And … for a while, he almost just denied the fact that he was Korean … He was not very open … it took him a *long* [emphasis added] time to come around. (Bella)

In contrast, some participants chose to be Korean and stayed within the Korean community, removing themselves from the local culture and society. For one of the men, his declaration of a complete lack of interest in New Zealand politics spoke of his detachment. One of the women, who identified as a full Korean and had always resided in the Korean community, explained:

> I stayed with Korean friends at school and attended the Korean church at the weekend. Then I went back to school and hung around with Korean friends there during the break. I still believe I am a Korean and don't have two cultures mixed in me. I am a Korean living in special circumstances, the Western culture. I can accept and understand the Western culture but I've never struggled between the two cultures. (Abby)

Language barriers, cultural differences, and experiences of bullying and discrimination at school influenced another participant's choice of only Korean friends. However, when interviewed, she described feeling suffocated in a small, crowded Korean community while having difficulties integrating with the local society as an adult because she found it hard to meet Kiwis. This struggle was about a lost sense of belonging and her related dilemma.

> It is most difficult that you cannot belong to the Kiwi society, and feel uncomfortable belonging to the Korean society at the same time. (Hana)

The above experiences often influenced participants' identity development, and consequently their perceptions and decision-making as parents. Anxiety was transferred from the past into the present in terms of: concerns for their children's appearance and identity, for their sense of belonging at school and in New Zealand society in general, and for the development of their children's dual cultural heritages and languages.

Rating cultural identities

Some participants rated their cultural identities in the interview. A notable finding was that not everyone felt exactly in the middle as a 1.5 generation Kowi between the first generation and second generation. Some felt more Korean, were closer to the first generation, and rated 1.2 or 1.3, while others felt more Kiwi, closer to the second generation, and rated themselves 1.7 or 1.8. See the range below.

The stage of the Kowis' identity formation paralleled their migration and adaptation processes as they went through all or at least part of their adolescence in New Zealand. The migration process was significantly challenging for the Kowis, and their strengths and resilience varied depending on their experiences of migration and their adaptation processes including identity formation. In turn, they perceived these experiences as influencing their parenting positively or negatively.

Critical questions

Some critical questions resonated through Kowis' reflections on their identities: How do I manage being a Kowi? Do I hold on to Korean-ness or do I become just a New Zealander? But I can never be just a New Zealander. I look different. I am Korean, but I live in New Zealand. Do I have to be one or the other? Can't I be in-between? Will my children go through this agonising process too? How can I help when they ask who they are? These questions needed to be addressed and answered while they established their role as parents of second generation Kowis.

Identity and parenting: living with tensions

Wrestling with their identities formed an integral part of Kowis' cultural transition that involved maintaining their own cultural heritage while adapting to the new host culture. Tensions they lived with between conflicting cultural experiences and expectations undermined their self-confidence about the skills, knowledge and experience they needed to support their children. However, when Kowis were surer about their identities they demonstrated more confidence and resourcefulness in their parenting. Language fluency and cultural competency were important components that helped Kowis to rate their identities, and factors that affected their level of confidence in either culture. It became evident that when Kowi parents attained a coherent sense of identity, they could be instrumental in supporting their children's developmental journeys. They showed determination in their efforts to overcome significant challenges.

Limited frames of reference

Kowi parents who were isolated at home, had limited access to New Zealand public resources, or who stayed in a small circle of Koreans, remained Korean in their parenting. However, once their children started preschool, they were forced into a transition: they recognised that, for the sake of their children's well-being, this required them to "take what is right for our family" and negotiate their way between cultures and approaches to parenting, to find the best ways of supporting their children in this new stage of development. They experienced heightened anxiety because of their limited experience and cultural frame of reference, and lack of information and assistance in identifying what would work in their unique individual circumstances: they felt the lack of "Kiwi" experiences to guide their children into becoming well-integrated into the wider society.

Raised in Korean homes, they had few opportunities to observe the parenting of New Zealanders or to interact within the wider New Zealand society. They identified the need to make an effort and go beyond the limits of their experience in order to open up opportunities for their children to do things they had never done.

> When my son grows up, his friends will tell him what they do with their fathers. I will try to do what I can. But there will be some things that I haven't experienced before, but that Kiwis normally do. Like DIY [do it yourself]? (laugh) I think it will be challenging for me. (Scott)

> I actually have to make an effort. I can't teach them. I have to make sure they have a chance to go and learn somewhere else. I find quite a bit of lost opportunity for me. I feel like I wish I was able to experience what it is like and to grow up, studying or being at a primary school or having an experience in intermediate school. I know I've never experienced going out to yacht clubs or whatever, I've never experienced this. It is something I have to find out about and am trying to give them a chance to do. I kind of feel like, otherwise, we will end up teaching them to live like the 1.5 generation or even first generation, whereas they are not. (Peter)

Some were also concerned that they lacked understanding about Korean as well as Kiwi experiences to parent their children. For example:

> Both not 100 percent! I cannot show how Kiwis live. I cannot show how Koreans live either. I have only just very superficial knowledge. I can't really teach anything clearly. I find that frustrating. When you want to introduce something, you must know it really well (laugh). It is a weakness, weakness. (Ginny)

Participants emphasised the importance of teaching two languages and cultural heritages for the same reason: for children's well-being, sense of belonging and a secure identity.

> It [teaching Korean] is about the Korean identity. A language is not just a language. Culture comes with it. If you learn Korean as a second language, it is no different from learning English as a second language. I think along that line, and want to help my children to learn Korean well. (Suzan)

> I don't want her to go to school and not speak a word of English. And ... people say "You were born here. Why don't you speak English?" That I don't ... I want to prevent that happening (Bella)

As the Kowis spent their first formative five years or more in Korea and had very little knowledge about the first five years of child development in the culture of New Zealand, many indicated concerns about not knowing enough about the developmental process of pre-schoolers and what they needed to learn, such as rhymes and songs in English. Some also expressed concerns about their lack of confidence and skills to participate in their children's school, and to interact with other parents. They were anxious about taking the role of a parent who was expected to actively participate in the New Zealand system of education.

Kowis realised they needed to meet these challenges to be able to facilitate their children's integration into the community.

Language proficiency

Concerns about language proficiency were interwoven through Kowis' accounts of the challenges they faced as parents, regardless of their fluency in both languages.

> My English is limited. (laugh) My Korean is also limited. (Amy)

Despite speaking multiple languages, anxiety about their cultural competence led to reticence about participating in social conversations, as well as fear of difficulties in their communication with their children.

> I am most afraid of communication blockage with the children. I would really like them to speak Korean well. However, I don't want to pressure them to be Korean. But it is a bit of fear that I have [that I won't be able to communicate with my children]. (John)

Some participants expressed concern about the future transgenerational relationships with their second generation Kowi children. Over time, language barriers could contribute to alienation within the family once the children became more fluent in English.

> It is important to my husband [for our child to speak Korean]. His Korean is better than his English. He hardly uses English. My husband can still communicate with our child at this stage. When he grows up and goes to high school and university, I guess he may feel more comfortable to talk to his father, the male? However, I am worried what if they will be disconnected because his father doesn't speak English, and my child doesn't speak Korean well. (Erica)

It seemed that English proficiency was linked to success in schooling, socialising with friends, and belonging to New Zealand society. Korean proficiency was linked to knowing their cultural heritage, and their identity and confidence as a Korean–Kiwi, as well as to children's relationships with their Kowi parents and grandparents. Supporting the development of a healthy and integrated identity was therefore of major interest to Kowis because of their memories of their own challenging experiences in childhood.

'There is "between": it doesn't have to be black or white, yes or no'

The question, "Where are you from?" encapsulated these challenges of belonging and identity that Kowis had experienced since childhood, evoking confusion as well as anxiety about the well-being their own children belonging to neither one culture nor the other. It seemed that the longer they lived in New Zealand, however, the more developed and secure their own sense of identity was likely to be, and therefore the more able they were to accept and embrace their own dual heritages and their ability to be "both." When they recognised this they felt liberated. Once they developed a more integrated identity, what had once been a source of stress became a source of strength as they developed the ability to "take the best of both worlds", a strategy that was linked to a childhood coping skill of "dealing with things on their own" and "negotiating" at the interface between cultures (Kim, 2013). They named the advantages of being "in-between" and "in the middle" of the two cultures.

> Because I don't simply accept the Korean culture as it is, I can recognise weakness in the culture well. (Sarah).

Cultural competency provided a strong sense of belonging and identity. When John heard the term "between" used as a concept of integration, while talking with a Korean-American 1.5 generation person in Korea, he found this illuminating, and it enabled him to embrace his dual identities.

> There is "between," it doesn't have to be black or white, yes or no. (John)

Appreciating this reality, Kowis began speaking of themselves as "global citizens" and "part of this world" as their horizon had broadened. They were constantly exploring, redefining, changing, and creating a new culture and identity of their own.

Despite their eagerness to teach their children both cultural heritages and languages, they would give their children permission and give them the freedom to be themselves, rather than pressuring them to learn both languages and identify with both identities. At the same time, they could facilitate their children's development as second generation Kowis with awareness and insight, to the children's advantage. Interestingly, all wanted to do so, even though some were still engaged with their own identity-related struggles and lacked confidence. Mindful of these, they could see their children's potential, the advantages offered them, and what they would need for their future development, and hoped they could support their youngsters to excel.

Deeper, "broadened insights" followed, as the participants because aware of their "journey of self-discovery" and a process of "re-forming" in terms of identity formation and the migration process. They recognised this as a life-long journey, talked of becoming more open to "moulding" and "learning," and expressed excitement about navigating their way through as unique individuals, not required to fit into any predetermined mould any more. They enjoyed "moments of self-discovery" on this journey.

Discussion

In the context of exploring the parenting experiences of 1.5 generation Korean New Zealanders, the research participants reflected deeply on the question of their belonging and identities as the children of migrants and who had grown up in New Zealand. Understanding their identity-related challenges in childhood and adolescence proved essential to understanding a key influence on their parenting. This underlines the critical importance of maintaining open expectations about data that may emerge from interviews that can provide unexpected insights, and listening to the directions in which the participants lead. Similarly, holding open expectations and not foreclosing on the focus of the work is vital in a therapeutic context.

While aspects of these results correspond with the experiences of other migrants of diverse ethnicities, the findings reported here contribute to the international as well as the New Zealand-based body of knowledge about immigration and parenting. Just as traditional customs and values can differ significantly among cultures, so also are various kinds of cultural conflicts encountered, and diverse ways of coping are adaptive in different environments. It cannot be assumed that the experiences of members of any one group in a particular context will necessarily correspond with those of others. In addition, research that is most meaningful to particular communities is research in which community members recognise themselves – through which they can hear their own authentic voices and/ or identify with the experiences of the participants – and which can most effectively inform the work of professionals with their communities (Charmaz, 2006). This includes ensuring cultural safety and competence, and the creation of much-needed resources, in this instance to meet Kowis' needs in navigating the identity-related challenges they encounter in parenting their children in multigenerational migrant families between two cultures.

When counselling 1.5 generation migrants, exploring their childhood experiences of parenting, as well as their wider life experiences, seems important, particularly if the focus is the parenting of their own children. Parenting programmes also need to be developed for 1.5 generation migrants that are led with sensitivity, and validate flexibility and inclusiveness. It is also helpful when working with any individual 1.5 generation client to remind oneself that there is an invisible, multi-generational family also in the room: e.g. to hold the awareness that the client's values and beliefs are grounded in their family's culture-of-origin, influencing their position on matters and decision-making processes regarding their 2nd generation children who are very much part of the host society.

Given the painful struggles Kowis in the current study have experienced, it seems that suitably tailored resources are needed to assist families, school staff and peers, as well as other community organisations, to provide counselling and psychoeducational support to 1.5 generation young people and their parents. These would enable their unique needs, the distinction between the first generation and the 1.5 generation, and the diversity among the 1.5 generation (as evidenced in Figure 1) to be more widely and clearly understood.

This exploratory study paves the way for a range of further studies with migrant families into how they adjust, maintain healthy relationships and support 1.5 and 2nd generation members in their identity development. Research that gathers the voices of multiple generations about their identity journeys and explores in greater depth those of the 1.5 generation would provide valuable insights to inform professional practice and the wider community. Comparing the identity journeys of 1.5 parents with those of their 2nd generation children would also contribute further understandings.

Insights from an investigation of transitions in the parenting of migrants seems to offer useful points of comparison with the experiences of the Kowis in the current study (de Haan, 2011). Conducting the study in a multi-ethnic school in the Netherlands, de Haan used the term "cultural translation" (p. 396) as a conceptual grounding for the analysis of what happens when two different systems and parenting practices collide. While acknowledging uneven encounters and the power differential between the dominant and dominated culture, she demonstrated that through confrontation with the conflicting cultures, both frames of reference would be transformed and boundaries

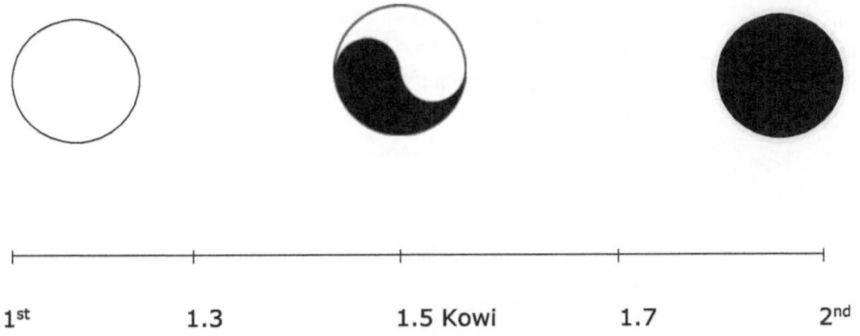

Figure 1. Self-rated identities of 1.5 generation Kowis.

stretched to accommodate new understandings. The confrontation between old and new practices led to a tension which resulted in the reconsideration of both.

The effectiveness of this reconsideration could arise from not losing touch with the immigrant parents' important moral grounding, but the simultaneous presence of two cultures and the constant tension between them that would provide "a potential energy to create new solutions" which de Haan called the "in-between position" (p. 395). In this position, migrants' traditional parenting practices from their homeland are not supported any more by the new environment, and new parenting practices must be defined by the directions that are newly experienced because of different needs and problems arising.

Conclusion

Since childhood, Kowis' identities and their parenting practices can also be seen – as participants acknowledged – in the "in-between position" (Bartley & Spoonley, 2008, p. 68). It will be intriguing to see, through further research, if such experiences have generated the energy to create new solutions and new understandings for the Kowis in their parenting while they are navigating and negotiating in their in-between position and negotiating different and conflicting cultures. As they developed a more integrated and confident sense of identity, participants expressed a greater appreciation of the positive nature and potential of the "in-between" space, and of the strengths they could draw on in their parenting. These results suggest that indeed these Kowis are generating creative energy and finding new solutions as they discover new understandings of themselves and their journeys.

Notes

1. *Samgang* expresses the hierarchal order between lord and subject, parent and child, and husband and wife. The latter in each relationship is seen as subordinate to the former.
2. *Oryun* expresses the ethical relationship between ruler and subjects (righteousness), parents and children (intimacy), husband and wife (distinction), elder and young (order), and betweenfriends (trust).
3. *Shame* is imposed on an individual when any of the five relationships (*Oryun*) is violated which may result in the family losing face in their relationships with others in the community.
4. *Chemyon* is one's prestige, pride, dignity, honour and reputation related to one's position.

Disclosure statement

No potential conflict of interest was reported by the authors.

ORCID

Hyeeun Kim http://orcid.org/0000-0003-3512-9739
Margaret Nelson Agee http://orcid.org/0000-0002-3124-8450

References

Anae, M. (1998). *Fofoa-i-vao-'ese: The identity journeys of NZ-born Samoans. (Doctoral dissertation)*. Retrieved from https://researchspace.auckland.ac.nz/handle/2292/66

Barry, D. T., Bernard, M. J., & Beitel, M. (2009). East Asian child-rearing attitudes: An exploration of cultural, demographic and self-disclosure factors among US immigrants. *International Journal of Psychology, 44*(5), 342–350.

Bartley, A., & Spoonley, P. (2008). Intergenerational transnationalism: 1.5 generation Asian migrants in New Zealand. *International Migration, 46*(4), 63–84.

Berry, J. W. (2005). Acculturation: Living successfully in two cultures. *International Journal of Intercultural Relations, 29*(6), 697–712.

Berry, J. W. (2006). Acculturation: A conceptual overview. In M. H. Bornstein, & L. R. Cote (Eds.), *Acculturation and parent-child relationships: Measurement and development* (Vol. 2, pp. 13–30). Mahwah, NJ: Lawrence Erlbaum Associates.

Berry, J. W. (2007). Acculturation strategies and adaptation. In J. E. Lansford, K. Deater-Deckard, & M. H. Bornstein (Eds.), *Immigrant families in contemporary society* (pp. 69–82). New York, NY: The Guilford Press.

Berry, J. W., Phinney, J. S., Sam, D. L., & Vedder, P. (2006a). Immigrant youth: Acculturation, identity, and adaptation. *Applied Psychology, 55*(3), 303–332.

Berry, J. W., Phinney, J. S., Sam, D. L., & Vedder, P. (Eds.). (2006b). *Immigrant youth in cultural transition: Acculturation, identity, and adaptation across national contexts*. Mahwah, NJ: Lawrence Erlbaum.

Bornstein, M. H., & Cheah, C. S. L. (2006). The place of "culture and parenting" in the ecological contextual perspective on developmental science. In K. H. Rubin, & O. B. Chung (Eds.), *Parenting beliefs, behaviors, and parent-child relations: A cross-cultural perspective* (pp. 3–33). New York, NY: Psychology Press.

Brannick, T., & Coghlan, D. (2007). In defense of being "native": The case for insider academic research. *Organizational Research Methods, 10*(1), 59–74.

Chang, S., Morris, C., & Vokes, R. (2006). *Korean migrant families in Christchurch: Expectations and experiences*. Wellington: The Families Commission.

Charmaz, K. (2000). Grounded theory: Objectivist and constructivist methods. In N. K. Denzin, & Y. S. Lincoln (Eds.), *Handbook of qualitative research* (pp. 509–535). Thousand Oaks, CA: Sage.

Charmaz, K. (2005). Grounded theory in the 21st century: Applications for advancing social justice studies. In N. K. Denzin, & Y. S. Lincoln (Eds.), *The SAGE Handbook of qualitative research* (3rd ed., pp. 507–535). Thousand Oaks, CA: Sage.

Charmaz, K. (2006). *Constructing grounded theory; A practical guide through qualitative analysis*. Los Angeles, CA: Sage.

Coleman, P. K., & Karraker, K. H. (2000). Parenting self-efficacy among mothers of school-age children: Conceptualization, measurement, and correlates. *Family Relations, 49*(1), 13–24.

Cowley-Malcolm, E. (2013). *Perceptions of Samoan parents from a small town in New Zealand on parenting, childhood aggression, and the CD-ROM Play Nicely* (Unpublished PhD thesis). The Victoria University of Wellington, Wellington.

Cowley-Malcolm, E. T., Fairbairn-Dunlop, T. P., Paterson, J., Gao, W., & Williams, M. (2009). Child discipline and nurturing practices among a cohort of Pacific mothers living in New Zealand. *Pacific Health Dialogue, 15*(1), 36–45.

Culbertson, P., & Agee, M. (2007). 'What's so "identity" about that word?': Pasifika men's experience of being 'afakasi'. *New Zealand Journal of Counselling, 27*(2), 77–95.

Cunliffe, A. L., & Karunanyake, G. (2013). Working within hyphen-space in ethnographic research; implication for research identities and practice. *Organizational Research Methods, 16*(3), 364–392.

Danico, M. Y. (2004). *The 1.5 generation: Becoming Korean American in Hawaii*. Honolulu, HI: University of Hawaii Press.

de Haan, M. (2011). The reconstruction of parenting after migration: A perspective from cultural translation. *Human Development, 54*, 376–399.

Finlay, L. (2002). "Outing" the researcher: The provenance, process, and practice of reflexivity. *Qualitative Health Research, 12*(4), 531–545.

Fleck, J. R., & Fleck, D. T. (2013). Immigrant family: Parent-child dilemmas and therapy considerations. *International Journal of Contemporary Research, 3*(8), 13–17.

Franklin, M. (2003). I define my own identity: Pacific articulations of "race" and "culture" on the internet. *Ethnicities, 3*(4), 465–490. doi:10.1177/1468796803003004002

Guo, S. P. (2013). *"娩" 与 "通"; Migrant ethnic Chinese mothers' intercultural communication experiences with their maternity-care and health providers in New Zealand (Unpublished PhD thesis)*. Waikato University, Hamilton.

Harkness, S., & Super, C. M. (2002). Culture and parenting: Biology and ecology of parenting. In M. H. Bornstein (Ed.), *Handbook of parenting* (2nd ed., Vol. 2, pp. 253–280). Mahwah, NJ: Lawrence Erlbaum Associates.

Ho, E., Au, S., Bedford, C., & Cooper, J. (2003). *Mental health issues for Asians in New Zealand: A literature review*. Wellington: Mental Health Commission.

Ho, E., & Bedford, R. (2008). Asian transnational families in New Zealand: Dynamics and challenges. *International Migration, 46*(4), 41–62.

Holton, J. A. (2007). The coding process and its challenges. In A. Bryant, & K. Charmaz (Eds.), *The SAGE handbook of grounded theory* (pp. 265–289). Thousand Oaks, CA: Sage.

Janes, A. (2004, July 17). The 1.5 generation. *New Zealand Listener*, pp. 17–23.

Jones, T. L., & Prinz, R. J. (2005). Potential roles of parental self-efficacy in parent and child adjustment: A review. *Clinical Psychology Review, 25*, 341–363.

Kiang, L., & Fuligni, A. J. (2008). Ethnic identity and family processes among adolescents from Latin American, Asian, and European backgrounds. *Journal of Youth and Adolescence, 38*(2), 228–241. doi:10.1007/s10964-008-9353-0

Kim, D.-Y., Sarason, B. R., & Sarason, I. G. (2006). Implicit social cognition and culture: Explicit and implicit psychological acculturation, and distress of Korean-American young adults. *Journal of Social and Clinical Psychology, 25*(1), 1–32.

Kim, E., & Cain, K. C. (2008). Korean American adolescent depression and parenting. *Journal of Child and Adolescent Psychiatric Nursing, 21*(2), 105–115.

Kim, E., Cain, K., & McCubbin, M. (2006). Maternal and paternal parenting, acculturation, and young adolescents' psychological adjustment in Korean American families. *Journal of Child and Adolescent Psychiatric Nursing, 19*(3), 112–129.

Kim, E., & Hong, S. (2007). First-generation Korean-American parents' perceptions of discipline. *Journal of Professional Nursing, 23*(1), 60–68.

Kim, H. (2013). Parenting patterns of "1.5 generation Kowis" in New Zealand: Take best of both worlds to raise the next generation. *New Zealand Journal of Asian Studies, 15*(2), 78–93.

Kim, H. (2014). *Parenting experiences of 1.5 generation Kowi parents*. Auckland: University of Auckland. Retrieved from https://researchspace.auckland.ac.nz/handle/2292/24659.

Kim, H. O., & Hoppe-Graff, S. (2001). Mothers' roles in traditional and modern Korean families:The consequences for parental practices and adolescent socialization. *Asia Pacific Education Review, 2*(1), 85–93.

Kim, K. W. (2006). Hyo and parenting in Korea. In K. Rubin, & O. K. Chung (Eds.), *Parenting beliefs, behaviors, and parent-child relationships: A cross-cultural perspective* (pp. 207–224). New York, NY: Psychology Press.

Kowiana Association. (2008). *Kimchi and Marmite Conference: Finding Kowi. What does it mean to be Kiwi-Korean?* Retrieved from http://www.kowiana.org.nz/conference/2008/27-kimchi-a-marmite-2008.

La Barbera, M. C. (2015). Identity and migration: An introduction. In M. C. La Barbera (Ed.), *Identity and migration in Europe: Multidisciplinary perspectives* (pp. 1–13). Cham: Springer.

Lee, J. Y., Kearns, R. A., & Friesen, W. (2009). Seeking affective health care: Korean immigrants' use of homeland medical services. *Health & Place, 16*(1), 108–115.

McGoldrick, M., & Giordano, J. (1996). Overview: Ethnicity and family therapy. In M. McGoldrick, J. Giordano, & J. K. Pearce (Eds.), *Ethnicity and family therapy* (2nd ed., pp. 1–27). New York, NY: The Guilford Press.

Mills, J., Bonner, A., & Francis, K. (2006). Adopting a constructivist approach to grounded theory: Implications for research design. *International Journal of Nursing Practice, 12*(1), 8–13.

Mills, J., Bonner, A., & Francis, K. (2008). The development of constructivist grounded theory. *International Journal of Qualitative Methods, 5*(1), 25–35.

Oak, S., & Martin, V. (2000). *American/ Korean contrasts: Patterns and expectations in the US and Korea*. Elizabeth, NJ: Hollym International.

Orellana, M. F., Thorne, B., Chee, A., & Lam, W. S. E. (2001). Transnational childhoods: The participation of children in the process of family migration. *Social Problems, 48*(4), 572–591.

Park, K. (1999). "I really do feel I'm 1.5!": The construction of self and community. *Amerasia Journal, 25*(1), 139–163.

Phinney, J. S., Horenczyk, G., Liebkind, K., & Vedder, P. (2001). Ethnic identity, immigration and well-being: An interactional perspective. *Journal of Social Issues, 57*(3), 493–510.

Phinney, J. S., & Ong, A. D. (2007). Ethnic identity development in migrant families. In J. E. Lansford, K. Deater-Deckard, & M. H. Bornstein (Eds.), *Immigrant families in contemporary society* (pp. 51–68). New York, NY: The Guilford Press.

Phinney, J. S., Ong, A., & Madden, T. (2000). Cultural values and intergenerational value discrepancies in immigrant and non-immigrant families. *Child Development, 71*(2), 528–539.

Pio, E. (2010). *Longing and belonging*. Wellington: Dunmore Press.

Pollock, D. C., & Van Reken, R. E. (2009). *Third culture kids: Growing up among two worlds* (3rd ed.). Boston, MA: Nicholas Brearley Publishing.

Qin, D. B. (2009). Gendered processes of adaptation: Understanding parent–child relations in Chinese immigrant families. *Sex Roles, 60*(7), 467–481.

Rubin, H. J., & Rubin, I. S. (Eds.). (2012). *Qualitative interviewing: The art of hearing data* (3rd ed.). Thousand Oaks, CA: Sage.

Seidman, I. (Eds.). (2006). *Interviewing as qualitative research: A guide for researchers in education*. New York, NY: Teachers College Press.

Smith, A. B. (2013). *Understanding children and childhood* (5th ed.). Wellington: Bridget Williams Books.

Statistics New Zealand. (2013). *2013 Census usually resident population counts*. Retrieved from http://www.stats.govt.nz/browse_for_stats/population/census_counts/2013CensusUsuallyResidentPopulationCounts_HOTP2013Census.aspx.

Statistics New Zealand. (2014). *Ethnic group (total responses) by age group and sex, for the census usually resident population count, 2001, 2006, and 2013 Censuses* Retrieved from http://nzdotstat.stats.govt.nz/wbos/Index.aspx?DataSetCode = TABLECODE8021#.

Statistics New Zealand. (2016). *National populaton estimates: At 30th June 2016*. http://www.stats.govt.nz/browse_for_stats/population/estimates_and_projections/NationalPopulationEstimates_HOTPAt30Jun16.aspx.

Strauss, A. L., & Corbin, J. M. (1994). Gounded theory methodology: An overview. In N. K. Denzin, & Y. S. Lincoln (Eds.), *Handbook of qualitative research* (pp. 273–285). Thousand Oaks, CA: Sage.

Tan, L. (2010, August 9). Religion gives salvation for migrants. *New Zealand Herald*. Retrieved from http://msn.nzherald.co.nz/nz/news/090909090909090909090909090909090909/nz/news/article.cfm?c_id = 1&objectid = 10664624&pnum = 0.

Tyyska, V. (2007). Immigrant families in sociology. In J. E. Lansford, K. Deater-Deckard, & M. H. Bornstein (Eds.), *Immigrant families in contemporary society* (pp. 83–99). New York, NY: The Guilford Press.

Webber, M. (2008). *Walking the space between: Identity and Māori/ Pākehā*. Wellington: NZCER Press.

Westin, C. (2010). Identity and inter-ethnic relations. In C. Westin, J. Bastos, J. Dahinden, & P. Gois (Eds.), *Identity processes and dynamics in multi-ethnic Europe* (pp. 9–51). Amsterdam: Amsterdam University Press.

Won, P. (2002). *Traditional Korean thought*. Incheon: Inha University Press.

Ying, Y.-W., & Han, M. (2008). Parental acculturation, parental involvement, intergenerational relationship and adolescent outcomes in immigrant Filipino American families. *Journal of Immigrant & Refugee Studies*, *6*(1), 112–131.

Yu, S. M., Huang, Z. J., Shwalberg, R. H., Overpeck, M., & Kogan, M. D. (2003). Acculturation and the health and well-being of U.S. Immigrant adolescents. *Journal of Adolescent Health*, *33*, 479–488.

Zhou, M. (1997). Growing up American: The challenge confronting immigrant children and children of immigrants. *Annual Review of Sociology*, *23*, 63–95.

Zubrick, S. R., Smith, G. J., Nicholson, J. M., Sanson, A. V., & Jackiewicz, T. A. (2011). *Parenting and families in Australia: SSRN working paper series No.34*. Canberra: Australian Government Department of Families, Housing, Community Services and Indigenous Affairs.

Considering boundaries when doing therapeutic work with people who are seeking asylum: a reflective case study

Megan Cowles and Mary Griggs

ABSTRACT

People who are seeking asylum often have lived experience of their personal boundaries and human rights being violated. For this reason, it is especially important that we consider the impact of boundaries in therapeutic work with this population. This paper explores work with a woman with a severe trauma history who was seeking asylum in England. Examples of perceived boundary crossings in the therapeutic relationship are examined. Considerations for other clinicians working with asylum seekers are discussed. These include: addressing socio-political factors; being sensitive to cultural differences; the importance of supervision and reflective practice; the personal impact of such work; and using critical thinking and warmth to manage boundaries rather than rigidly following rules.

Introduction

Asylum seekers often have lived experience of their personal boundaries and human rights being violated. For this reason, it is especially important that we consider the impact of boundaries in therapeutic work with this population. This paper will briefly discuss the role of boundaries in therapeutic work generally, and more specifically with people who are seeking asylum. A reflective case-study approach will be used to explore some of these issues in the context of trauma-focused work with a woman who was seeking asylum.

The importance of boundaries in therapeutic work

Therapeutic relationships have an inherent power imbalance and intimacy that, without careful attention, could become fertile ground for inflicting harm. A potentially vulnerable person seeking help is expected to share intimate information with an expert professional whose opinions can influence their future care. In order to prevent abuses of power and keep the service-user's best interest at heart, professional bodies provide guidelines around what is considered ethical practice. This is often brought to life with the metaphor of "boundaries", a demarcation of what is included and what is excluded from the therapeutic relationship. By clarifying what can be expected in a therapeutic relationship, boundaries can help to build trust, allow appropriate levels of vulnerability, and ensure ethical practice, increasing the likelihood that both the service-user and the therapist have a sense of safeness in the relationship.

However, a boundary suggests a clear cut-off of what is right and wrong, but things are rarely black or white when it comes to human interaction. Most clinicians agree that boundaries should not be hard and fast rules, although they differ to what extent they feel that boundaries can be flexible. How a therapist decides what boundaries are appropriate depends on a variety of factors, including the therapeutic model, the needs of the client, the training of the therapist, the nature of the therapeutic relationship, and the treatment setting. It has been suggested that using the metaphor of territory, rather than boundaries, may be more appropriate for promoting important reflective questions to help with decision-making about the therapeutic relationship:

> Is this territory familiar, unfamiliar, or dangerous? Accordingly, of what do I need to be wary? Have I been here before? What was it like? What do I have to look out for? How can I determine if I have gone too far? Should I bring someone with me? What brings my client to this shared space? What can I do to increase the safety of both? When I come back from this territory, will I feel comfortable telling others where I have been? If not, why might this be so? (Austin, Bergum, Nuttgens, & Peternelj-Taylor, 2010, pp. 90–91)

Gutheil and Brodsky (2011) offer some helpful terminology from which to consider behaviour that does not neatly fit within our usual boundaries. They use the term "boundary crossing" to refer to behaviours that go beyond what we would normally expect in therapy but that do not have adverse consequences, and in fact may be beneficial for therapy. They use the term "boundary violation" to refer to therapist behaviours that breach an ethical standard and can put the service-user at risk of harm. For example, sexual conduct of any kind with a service-user would always be considered a boundary violation. As a good rule of thumb you should be able to document the boundary crossing, discuss it in supervision and address it in the next session with the service-user if necessary; inability to document and discuss a boundary crossing could be a sign that a boundary violation has occurred and presents a real problem.

Lazarus (1994) offers examples where a number of boundary crossings in his professional work have felt appropriate, improved the therapeutic alliance, and helped the service-user make further progress. Such examples include giving and receiving gifts, engaging in activities outside of the clinic room, self-disclosure, having a hug, and sharing lifts in the car. He argues that certain boundaries can actually diminish, rather than promote, the therapeutic relationship. His paper has provoked a number of reactions both for and against his flexible stance to boundaries. Hermansson (2007) offers a review of some of these reactions and goes on to argue that tightening boundaries, despite good intentions, can be controlling and stifle the very essence of what is therapeutic for service-users. He explores empathy as a key therapeutic element that he argues requires boundary crossing to be genuine; he promotes training, reflective-practise, and supervision as important ways to monitor and make informed decisions about the fluid and dynamic process of boundary management. The British Psychological Society (2018) offers four pillars – respect, competence, responsibility and integrity – to guide ethical practice when working psychologically. The details of this guidance map well on to the issues raised by Lazarus and Hermansson, including: considering issues of power and environment; compassion; training and appropriate skills; being accountable and transparent; avoiding misconduct; and maintaining professionalism.

Essentially proponents appear to agree that having fluid boundaries that can be crossed, but never violated, involves using clinical judgement to make reasoned decisions. Lazarus and Zur (2002) argue that taking a humanistic, person-centred (rather than fear-based) approach, that is transparent and based on critical thinking, allows us to make informed decisions about how best to act with service-users to maximise the therapeutic potential; this may involve perceived boundary crossings. It is proposed that if we recognise the inherent power differential in therapeutic relationships and only cross boundaries when this is genuinely done from a place of warmth then "[b]oundary crossings are likely to increase familiarity, understanding and connection and hence increase the likelihood of success for the clinical work" (Zur & Lazarus, 2002, p. 6). Black (2017) offers a helpful summary of recent research into boundaries in psychological practice, outlining how flexible boundaries have not been found to lead down a "slippery slope" to boundary violations, as has been suggested elsewhere (e.g. Gutheil & Gabbard, 1993; Strasburger, Jorgenson, & Sutherland, 1992).

Boundaries in therapeutic work with people who are seeking asylum

There are complex issues around professional and personal boundaries that can arise when working with people who are seeking asylum or are refugees. This paper will focus particularly on people seeking asylum, although much of what is discussed will be applicable to people who are refugees.

Asylum seekers are usually facing insecure immigration status, attempting to navigate unfamiliar and complex systems whilst living in poverty, and dealing with the increased psychological stress that accompanies this (Chu, Keller, & Rasmussen, 2013; Laban, Gernaat, Komproe, Schreuders, & De Jong, 2004; Silove, Sinnerbrink, Field, Manicavasagar, & Steel, 1997; Silove, Steel, McGorry, & Mohan, 1998). Furthermore, protracted asylum claims and asylum claim rejections have been found to increase or maintain psychological distress, including that defined as depression, anxiety and post-traumatic stress disorder (PTSD). Li, Liddell, and Nickerson (2016) offer a review of the link between post-migration stress and psychological health in asylum seekers and refugees, concluding that psycho-social factors have a substantial deleterious impact that can complicate the picture for therapeutic intervention. This does not create the optimal foundation from which to carry out therapeutic work, yet despite this it has been shown that trauma-focused therapy has a large effect size on depression and PTSD symptomology in refugees and asylum seekers (Lambert & Alhassoon, 2015). Thus therapy can potentially place asylum seekers in a better position from which to manage the stressors that they are facing by reducing some of their distressing experiences.

It has been suggested by several research teams that interventions to support asylum seekers must include a psycho-social perspective that takes everyday stressors into account (e.g. Miller & Rasmussen, 2010; Murray, Davidson, & Schweitzer, 2010). For example, Chantler (2012) argues that interventions for psychological distress in asylum seekers should consider and seek to address the effects of insecure immigration status, poverty, gender, and societal & organisational influences. The American Psychological Association guidance on multicultural working states that psychologists should seek to address institutional barriers and inequalities in their work, and promote culturally adaptive interventions (APA, 2017: guidelines 5 and 6). Consideration of the research outlined above raises some important questions for therapeutic work and what the role of therapists, or other healthcare professionals, should be. Expanding therapeutic work to consider broader psycho-social factors may involve different working practices and boundaries than professionals are used to, or even prepared for. Indeed Century, Leavey, and Payne (2017) found that counsellors reported "an erosion of usual counselling boundaries" (p. 23) when working with asylum seekers and refugees.

Additionally, cultural factors are important to consider when thinking about working with asylum seekers and refugee populations. Zur (2005) argues that many non-Western cultures promote interdependence and familiarity between care-providers and service-users. Such approaches can arguably help us move away from the medical model and "helpless" patient approach towards a more equal and empowering relationship. It can be important to explore the cultural norms in an asylum seeker's home country about therapeutic relationships and how the boundaries may be similar or different in the host country, being open to the possibility of crossing boundaries if appropriate. Speight (2012) discusses how culturally competent practice necessitates a broader view of therapeutic boundaries, including understanding boundaries from the perspective of solidarity. As such, boundaries should communicate warmth, empathic understanding and a willingness to hear and respond to the individual's needs. This may involve moving beyond our normal therapeutic boundaries both in the room, for example by being willing to show our personal reaction to their stories and thus demonstrate our unity with them, and beyond the session, for example by being an advocate for the needs of the individual and their community.

Aims of this paper

This paper will use a case example to explore how work with people who are seeking asylum can involve both creating containment by having clear boundaries, and addressing psycho-social issues by crossing boundaries that one might otherwise have in place. Reflective-practise and supervision will be highlighted as two key ways to identify, test-out and evaluate therapeutic boundaries. In this case interactions that were different from what the therapist (MC) would normally do in her trauma work were considered as boundary crossings (Gutheil & Brodsky, 2011).

Case description

This paper describes the case of Mirella (pseudonym), a woman in her late 20s seeking asylum in the UK. Mirella had two sons aged 7 years old and 6 months old with whom she was living in a room provided by the city council. Mirella had been referred to a primary-care Traumatic Stress Service for asylum seekers and refugees following an assessment at her local Improving Access to Psychological Therapies (IAPT) service.

Mirella had been an asylum seeker in the UK for 18 months at the start of therapy. Her first claim for asylum was rejected and she was waiting to hear if there was enough evidence to open a fresh claim. Mirella had experienced chronic traumas across her lifespan, including extreme physical, sexual, psychological and emotional abuse, at the hands of her birth family and her husband's family. This included being forced into hard manual labour without breaks or water from a young age, being chained up, being repetitively and brutally raped, being locked in a dark shed with rats, being starved, not being provided with any food or clothes for her baby who she worried would die, being severely beaten, and much more than can be detailed here.

Mirella came from a rural part of Eastern Europe where traditional customs meant honour killings were not uncommon. Her escape to the UK with her eldest son had been experienced as traumatic and the possibility of being murdered should she be returned to her home country was a constant worry. The rejection of her first asylum claim had led to the possibility of Mirella losing her accommodation, the threat of deportation, and bills from the National Health Service (NHS), which were causing her a substantial amount of distress. Mirella reported that her uncertain asylum status left her feeling unsafe and increased her sense that her abusers were going to find her. Mirella's difficulties were having a significant impact on her, causing her to struggle to complete daily tasks due to the severity of her psychological distress. Despite this, Mirella demonstrated good care-giving skills for both of her children as witnessed by the therapist in session and reported by her eldest son's school.

A risk assessment indicated that Mirella had chronic suicidal thoughts but with no intention to act on them. However, Mirella disclosed that if she was deported she would kill herself rather than go back to be murdered in her home country; she believed her children would be allowed to stay in the UK if this happened. A risk management plan was put in place, including education about what would happen to her children if she died, providing a crisis line number and developing grounding strategies.

Mirella and the interpreter gave verbal and written consent for this case study to be written and submitted for publication.

Formulation

The initial assessment sessions had explored culturally informed perceptions of the presenting problems, what they meant, how Mirella had been coping with them and her worries about the service-user/therapist relationship, as suggested in the Cultural Formulation Interview, DSM-5 (APA, 2013). This revealed that Mirella believed she was crazy, weak and bad to be experiencing these things.

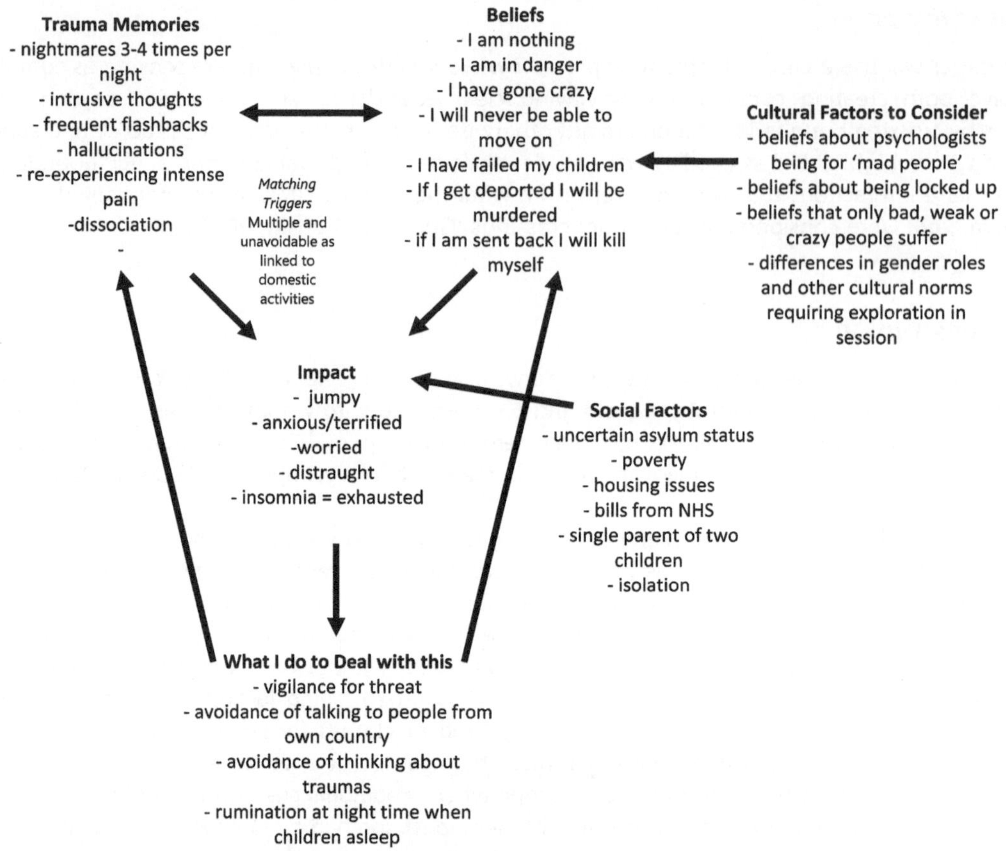

Figure 1. Diagram of formulation of Mirella's presenting problems.

She discussed hating being associated with her home country and wishing she could forget how to speak the language. She was worried that the therapist would lock her up in an institution.

A modified version of Ehlers and Clark's (2000) model for PTSD was used to conceptualise Mirella's experiences and inform the intervention (see Figure 1). This, alongside psycho-education about trauma, helped to gently explore some of the culturally informed beliefs Mirella held.

A virtuous flower formulation was also drawn out and added to throughout therapy to highlight Mirella's strengths, with the belief "I can have a life worth living" in the centre. The petals were each of the behaviours, feelings and thoughts that this belief inspired – including having the strength to escape with her children.

Measures showed that Mirella was having experiences that would meet the diagnostic criteria for severe depression, anxiety and PTSD (Table 1), as confirmed during assessment. Mirella had been using anti-depressant medication for 12 months prior to the start of therapy.

Table 1. Outcome measures for Mirella.

Measure	Score at session 1	Score at session 12	Score at final session
PHQ-9	25/27	22/27	19/27
GAD-7	21/21	19/21	16/21
PDS-5	77/80	N/A	59/80

Note: PHQ-9 = Patient Health Questionnaire (Kroenke, Spitzer, & Williams, 2001), a measure of depression; GAD-7 = Generalised Anxiety Disorder Questionnaire (Spitzer, Kroenke, Williams, & Lowe, 2006), a measure of general anxiety; PDS-5 = Post-traumatic Diagnostic Scale for DSM 5 (Foa et al., 2016), a measure of PTSD-related experiences.

Intervention

Culturally informed trauma-focused cognitive behavioural therapy (TF-CBT) was used based on Ehlers and Clark's (2000) model in line with findings that culturally sensitive TF-CBT and NET have the most evidence in this population (Lambert & Alhassoon, 2015). The therapist was a final year clinical psychology trainee who had worked at a specialist trauma centre specialising in TF-CBT for two years prior to commencing training. Recommended modifications to TF-CBT (e.g. Stallworthy, 2013) were implemented due to the extensive and severe nature of Mirella's trauma history. To accommodate some of these modifications to traditional TF-CBT, including extending the stabilisation phase, the number of sessions was extended to the maximum 25 sessions allowed within the service. All sessions were conducted with the same female interpreter, who received supervision before and after each session.

The therapist considered moving to a Narrative Exposure Therapy approach, based on TF-CBT, to structure the reliving sessions. However, as therapy progressed it became clear that the therapist was the only person that Mirella was willing to open up to and as such the focus was moved to "telling the story" using a timeline rather than the recommended *in-sensu* reliving. This was decided upon in order that a detailed report could be provided as supporting evidence for Mirella to have a new asylum case opened. Despite the lack of in depth re-living, Mirella was able to further process some of the trauma memories through telling her story, and much of the work focused on updating her trauma-related beliefs, modifying unhelpful coping strategies, and working towards "reclaiming her life" as recommended in TF-CBT (e.g. Ehlers & Clark, 2000).

Boundary crossings

Several elements of therapy went beyond the therapist's normal boundaries when working with people using TF-CBT. These are summarised below with an exploration of how reflection and supervision were used to make sense of these and how they were received by Mirella.

Helping to liaise with other organisations

Much time was spent in sessions liaising with other organisations including: the NHS debt line, the hospital, the dentist, the GP, the local refugee support centre, a local mentoring scheme, Mirella's eldest son's school, her solicitor and the home office.

The therapist was unclear whether the amount of time she was dedicating to addressing these social needs was appropriate as it could significantly reduce the time available in the session for more targeted therapeutic work. During supervision the therapist identified that these needs were being raised by Mirella when she was invited to contribute to the session agenda; the supervisor (MG) reflected that this demonstrated a truly collaborative approach, addressing those needs that the client identified as meaningful for her. Social and cultural issues relevant to asylum seekers were also discussed; the supervisor suggested that the uncertainty around Mirella's asylum status, the complexity of the organisations she was liaising with, the cultural and language differences she was having to navigate, the poverty she was living in, and the stress associated with these could all be potential barriers to Mirella being in the right space to make use of TF-CBT. Signposting Mirella to other sources of support where possible, or helping Mirella to address social difficulties during sessions, was felt to be a valuable use of time that could be seen as part of the stabilisation and preparation stage of therapy. This was supported in feedback from Mirella, "The tricks, or things we've learned, have helped me to cope better. Also everything you have done to help me with my letters and making phone calls. Thank you".

Addressing other needs

Mirella was carrying her baby in her arms as she no longer had access to a pram; this was exacerbating her trauma-related back pains and limiting her daily activities. A pram was sourced from a local charity and delivered by the therapist at the end of the working day. At this time Mirella was insistent that she wanted to show her thanks by offering the therapist a drink in her home. After attempting to refuse the invitation the therapist accepted a glass of water and engaged in a 10-minute conversation with Mirella about her children and her neighbours.

Whilst community visits are common for many CBT therapists, the visit to drop off the pram was not a pre-organised therapy session; although Mirella had been informed that the therapist and interpreter would be attempting to locate a pram, a time had not been agreed until one hour before and the interpreter was not present. For this reason, the therapist felt very uncomfortable accepting a drink and staying to talk, leaving after a 10-minute conversation when it was clear Mirella would like her to stay for longer. The language barrier meant it was difficult to explore the reasons for the therapist's hesitation at the time, which clearly left Mirella somewhat perplexed.

The supervisor noted that when working with asylum seekers who are in poverty it often makes sense for the professionals working with them to help them access resources, but that it is hard to draw a definitive line about what is appropriate and not; this will largely come down to reflective decision-making and critical thinking. When asked to reflect, the therapist felt that providing the pram, which she was very clear was not a gift from her but rather from a charity, was a helpful and appropriate gesture. It would have been preferable if this could have been delivered at the usual session time but this would have meant another week with Mirella carrying her baby; it felt uncomfortable for the therapist to deny this resource due to questions such as "is this my role?", it felt more appropriate to respond as a human being to someone in distress. Mirella later reflected on this as a key turning point in the therapeutic relationship where she began to trust that she could open up, "It felt so good that you were looking out for me and making an effort to show you cared. You understand my struggles". The key issue for the therapist was being in a hostess/visitor dynamic rather than a service-user/professional dynamic. This could have been avoided had roles and boundaries been discussed in more detail previously. The fact that the therapist had felt hesitant to bring this up in supervision had flagged for her that this was an issue. In supervision it was decided that the best way to address the situation was to have a conversation with Mirella about what happened and professional boundaries (see below).

Managing expectations

There had been an initial conversation exploring what therapists do at the first meeting with Mirella, but it was clear after the pram-delivery incident that this had not been explicit or detailed enough. On reflection, the therapist felt that further discussion about the limits of the relationship should have happened right at the beginning of the sessions to help form expectations. This was especially relevant given that the therapist and Mirella were similar in age and appearance, and Mirella was very isolated, making it potentially more likely that Mirella would see the therapist as a friend rather than as a professional providing support.

After the therapist had shown some discomfort at being asked to stay for a glass of water at Mirella's when dropping off the pram, Mirella asked in the next session if she had done something wrong. The therapist discussed cultural differences between Mirella's home country and England in terms of professional relationships. The interpreter was also invited to add to the conversation given her knowledge. Professionals in Mirella's home country were described as being local people who would know you and your family well and would often be friends. Mirella linked this to being akin to her health visitor in England, who she described would stay at her home for an hour having an informal chat whilst carrying out her duties. The therapist explained how the therapy relationship was different from other professional relationships and may be different from how therapists work in Mirella's home country. The boundaries around not being friends with your clients were explored, as were the differences between different types of professionals. The reasons for these boundaries, such as creating containment and helping to make the sessions about Mirella rather than about the therapist, were explored. Mirella reported finding this conversation helpful,

> At first it was a bit awkward as I used to have a support worker who would come for a drink and have a chat and I didn't understand why you didn't want to. It was upsetting me. Now we had that conversation the next week I understand that the work we do is different and needs different rules.

Endings were also discussed as something inevitable that is understandably upsetting but that can be prepared for in advance, "[in joking tone] I don't know, maybe I'll be calling you every day saying 'I miss you, come and have a coffee with me!' But really I don't know how it will feel to end. I know it will come and we will have to say goodbye".

In supervision, time was used to reflect on this situation. It was felt that the conversation was helpful to reduce Mirella's anxiety about what was expected of her and to set a strong and clear foundation from which the rest of the therapeutic work could continue. This conversation would be referred to in later sessions when it was felt to be useful to clarify an interaction; for example after receiving a gift for Christmas or giving a birthday cake (see below) these were discussed as examples of appreciation and a demonstration of respecting someone as a valued human rather than tokens of friendship. However, Mirella still perceived the relationship as a friendship of sorts,

> I do call what we have a friendship because I see the warmth in your eyes and that helps me feel reassured that you and I can talk about things here. I feel really pleased it was you and not someone else.

Giving and receiving a gift

At Christmas time Mirella gave the therapist a scarf and a bar of chocolate. The therapist felt very uncomfortable receiving a gift from Mirella, especially in light of her financial situation. It felt important not to refuse the gift or to explore whether it was appropriate, but rather to gratefully accept the gift whilst making it clear that this was not expected of Mirella. Using supervision to reflect on the incident it was agreed that this was an appropriate course of action, especially given Mirella's inter-personal history where none of her kind actions towards others had even been acknowledged or appreciated.

Mirella had shared some horrific stories about what happened to her after her birth and told us she had never celebrated a birthday. Mirella often raised existential questions when discussing her suicidal thoughts, including seeing no value or purpose in her existence. The day before Mirella's birthday the therapist brought a boxed birthday cake to the session and asked Mirella to enjoy it with her children on her birthday. The birthday cake was planned by the therapist and supervisor in advance as an important way to validate Mirella's existence. It felt important to give Mirella an experience of being valued as a human being, which her comments suggest was achieved, "I wasn't expecting a cake. It was such a nice thing to do. My son was so happy too. It was the first time in my life that I felt my birthday was a good thing". Both the therapist and supervisor felt this was a simple, appropriate and powerful gesture that complemented the TF-CBT.

Self-disclosure and emotional expression

On a handful of occasions Mirella would ask the therapist and interpreter for their honest answers to questions. These questions were either to clarify cultural norms in England, for example, "Do women here get killed if they are not virgins on their wedding night?" and, "Do you think women should be servants to men?"; or to ask what was thought of her actions, for example, "What would you have done in my situation?" and, "Do you think I should have killed myself?" These questions were infrequent and when they were asked the therapist would seek to answer them in a balanced way. The interpreter would also ask permission to give her own perspective, as a woman who knew Mirella's home culture well. On one occasion Mirella was very emotional and stated that she felt she should be dead and she was weak for not killing herself and her eldest son when he was born, to protect them both from enduring what they had. She then stated that perhaps the therapist and interpreter were only kind to her as they had to be and they also saw her as weak. The therapist stated that she was actually very moved by Mirella's story and was in awe of how strong she was for surviving what she had been through and emerging as such a great mother and woman. The therapist welled-up as she spoke and a single tear came down her cheek; Mirella looked shocked and leaned forward out of her chair to put her arms around the therapist's shoulders and give her a brief hug whilst saying, "Thank you". This was the only time the therapist had ever been so visibly emotional in a session and had ever received a comforting hug from a client. This was discussed with Mirella and the interpreter as a response to the therapist getting in touch with her personal feelings about what Mirella was saying, which was not something the therapist would normally explore in session but which had felt appropriate – or perhaps unavoidable – at that time. The rest of the session continued as normal.

Initially, the therapist felt incredibly embarrassed that she had allowed herself to show emotion like this and she wondered what the interpreter had thought of her. However, Mirella's response suggested that this display of emotion had been beneficial. The interpreter had also spoken to the therapist after the session and reflected that she felt the incident had "snapped [Mirella] out of her suicidal thinking and desperation". Had the therapist began to cry uncontrollably or leaned into the hug it would have felt like a loss of control or a signal that the contained space was no longer safe. However, the calm content of the therapist's speech and the ability to retain composure seemed to communicate a human recognition of Mirella's suffering without questioning the abilities of the therapist to keep professional boundaries that felt acceptable to all three of them in the room. Mirella's comments suggest that the incident had been empowering for her, "I saw you upset and it was hard for me to see that but at the same time it gave me strength. I saw that I had been through a lot, and that I am still here". The therapist used accounts of much more intense physical contact or emotional expression being used in a therapeutic way with trauma survivors (e.g. Heitzler, 2013) to help her think further about whether such interactions can be helpful or should always be avoided.

In supervision, the emotional and personal impact of hearing torture and trauma stories was explored. The supervisor reflected that when working with people within a human rights framework it is normal to have strong responses, and communicating these to our clients in a contained way can help to validate their experiences as unacceptable. For similar reasons, it was felt that responding to Mirella's questions was appropriate and helpful; this was seen as part of the cognitive restricting part of therapy, allowing Mirella to question and explore alternative ways of perceiving situations she had been through.

Endings

Mirella asked that the final session take place at her home as her son was ill. Due to service-limitations it was not possible to delay the ending session any further and the therapist and interpreter agreed to meet Mirella at her home. During this session Mirella served hot drinks and snacks and the conversation was kept quite "light", summarising the work that had been done and re-iterating what Mirella had found helpful and would be taking forwards. At the end of the session, both the therapist and the interpreter gave Mirella a hug.

The therapist had worried that the dynamics would be inappropriate given the previous interaction when the pram was delivered. However, the therapist had also held a session at Mirella's house since then to work on trigger discrimination, a part of TF-CBT, and conversations had been held around the boundaries of the relationship. On reflection, the therapist felt that such a coming together, in a different environment from the clinic room, was a pertinent symbol of Mirella moving forwards and a way to celebrate the relationship. This was confirmed by Mirella's final feedback, "It was so nice to be able to show you how much your support has meant to me. I'm so sad it has to end but I feel more positive about my future life now". In supervision it was agreed that sharing food and drinks was a culturally appropriate way to mark the ending and allow Mirella to feel empowered.

Evaluation

Patient's experience

Mirella reported finding therapy a rewarding process,

> At the beginning it was extremely difficult for me working with a psychologist. In my country it means you are going mad, you are crazy. You helped me understand why I am like this, that I am not crazy, that we can do something to try and make it better.

Although Mirella had been very anxious at the start of the sessions, overtime she had come to trust the therapist and see positive outcomes from the intervention, "I start to feel stronger and stronger as time goes by."

Mirella's goals besides reducing her trauma-related distress had included being able to talk more about what had happened to her. Initial attempts to talk about the traumas had been difficult for Mirella but with development of the therapeutic relationship she began to open up; "I feel stronger when I'm here and feel able to talk about almost everything with you. Things I have never spoken to anyone about." The interpreter reflected that when she had worked with Mirella two years ago Mirella had not been able to share any details with the solicitors about her traumas, likely part of the reason that her claim was rejected. She told Mirella how great it was to see her develop a voice to tell her story.

The parts of the session dedicated to dealing with liaising with other organisations had also helped Mirella to start thinking about her final goal of engaging more in the community. She had begun attending an English class with other mothers at her son's school and was enrolled in a mentorship scheme.

Outcome measures

Outcome measures demonstrated that ratings for depression, anxiety and PTSD had shown a reliable reduction (IAPT, 2014), although all were still rated well within clinical levels (see Table 1). Mirella had reduced the intensity of her conviction in several of the beliefs she had held and no longer believed the traumas were her fault; she had reduced unhelpful coping strategies and instead was using more of the helpful coping strategies she had developed in therapy as well as focussing on her strengths; Mirella reported having less re-experiencing symptoms now she had developed skills to ground herself in the here-and-now.

Given the extreme and prolonged nature of Mirella's traumas, plus the requirement for the therapist to gather a very detailed account in order to write a legal report, 25 sessions had not been long enough to complete all aspects of recommended TF-CBT. The therapist suggested that Mirella engages in some more trauma-focused work in the future through the same service (TF-CBT, NET or EMDR). Service guidelines required a 6-month gap between interventions, which was discussed as a good amount of time for Mirella to further digest some of the skills from therapy and have energy to focus on fighting for a new asylum case to be opened. In truth, the therapist felt it would have been more beneficial for Mirella to continue to be held in the therapeutic relationship she had developed and carry-on with the work. A frustrating reality of primary-care mental health services in the NHS is the limitation on how long therapy can continue for.

Perceived costs and benefits of boundary crossings

Incidents of boundary crossing (e.g. delivering the pram, expressing emotion and exchanging gifts) were highlighted by Mirella as key turning points in her perception of, and ability to trust in, the therapist. On the other hand, there were also concerns that the loss of Mirella's first meaningful relationship where she was treated with compassion could be incredibly painful for her, and that the boundary crossings may have increased the likelihood of this. However, having explicit conversations where the limits of the relationship and the reality of endings were discussed appeared to support Mirella to emotionally prepare herself for this. She was not particularly emotional at the end of the sessions and her comments suggested that she was prepared for moving on. The gains for Mirella in terms of having a mutually respectful relationship, having her experience witnessed and validated, having a new framework from which to understand her experiences, developing new skills to manage, and believing in her capacity to enjoy life were felt to outweigh any potential sadness she may feel at ending the relationship. Unfortunately it has not been possible to liaise with Mirella since the end of the sessions to seek any follow-up or to learn about her journey through the immigration system.

In supervision, the process was compared to the idea of crossing a border more metaphorically. The deviations from "normal" practice were seen as attempts to reach someone therapeutically but being in unfamiliar territory and leaning on a human right's framework to make sense of the experience. These crossings were not without their challenges but in this case appeared to facilitate greater connection. Whether this helped or hindered in terms of outcome measures is unclear, but there was a sense that such crossings enabled a human connection that instilled hope.

Discussion and reflections

This paper has described a case of culturally informed TF-CBT with a woman who was seeking asylum, in order to explore the role of boundaries when working therapeutically with this population. The paper has attempted to unpick how supervision and reflective-practise were used to consider boundaries, and the impact of perceived boundary crossings on the therapist, service-user and therapeutic relationship.

Clear expectations of what can be expected from a therapeutic relationship, often referred to as the boundaries of the relationship, are crucial to create a sense of safety for the service-user and therapist. The importance of explicitly defining and exploring boundaries, especially in cases where cultural differences may lead to diverging expectations, was highlighted in this case by the therapist needing to come back to further define and discuss the nature of the relationship once therapy was already underway. This helped to reduce confusion and clarify expectations, something that may be especially important when working with trauma survivors (e.g. Borys, 1994).

The value of broadening the usual remit of therapeutic work to include addressing social and cultural issues was demonstrated by Mirella, the service-user in this case study, raising these as important items for the weekly agenda that were then included in the formulation. This echoes recommendations that therapists seek to explore factors such as immigration status, poverty, gender and societal influences (e.g. Chantler, 2012). In this case, such work communicated to the service-user that her needs were important, and helped her to feel in a safer place from which to engage in trauma work. Supervision has also been found to offer space to develop cultural, political and legislative knowledge when working with asylum seekers (Apostolidou & Schweitzer, 2017).

The possibility of therapists expressing personal responses when working with this client group was raised by the therapist's examples of expressing emotion and opinion, as well as giving a birthday cake. Reflections from Mirella and the therapist suggest that such boundary crossings helped to build a stronger therapeutic alliance and helped to empower Mirella, allowing her to see herself more as an equal than a "helpless patient". This echoes Speight's (2012) and Zur's (2005) work arguing that boundaries that come from a place of warmth and empathy, and that are handled in a thoughtful way focusing on the service-user's wellbeing and needs, can be validating and give a strong message of solidarity.

This paper also explored how reflective-practise and supervision are crucial to critically examine perceived boundary crossings, as encouraged by Hermansson (2007). This was particularly relevant when the therapist delivered the pram to Mirella's house as she noticed on reflection that she did not feel comfortable telling her supervisor that she had accepted a glass of water and stayed to talk. Despite this, it *was* raised in supervision and the therapist was helped to realise that her discomfort was due to the differing dynamics involved in meeting outside of the usual session and without the interpreter to aid communication. The therapist had worried that the interaction could cause confusion for Mirella and impact negatively on therapeutic work. Thinking this through allowed the therapist to "repair" the boundary crossing in the next session. It may be that the therapist's level of expertise (she was a final year clinical psychology student) contributed to her anxiety about the interaction, supporting Hermansson's (2007) assertion that training is also important in developing a professional's skills in managing boundaries.

Listening to graphic details of extreme abuse and torture is challenging; reflecting on our personal responses, including how boundaries may have been challenged or crossed, is important not only to ensure best-practice for the service-user but also for ourselves as professionals and human beings. Understandably, it may be tempting in such cases to set up clear and rigid boundaries in order to prevent a personal attachment forming and thus limiting the emotional impact of such work. However, such rigid boundaries may not allow for the level of alliance that is required to support people whose human rights have been violated where rigid boundaries may be perceived as punitive. On the other hand, maintaining professional distance is important to prevent the therapist becoming overwhelmed or vicariously traumatised by what they are hearing. Supervision and reflection are key to maintaining the right balance for the therapist.

This paper touched on the personal and subjective nature of boundaries. For example, some clinicians have detailed far more contentious boundary crossings (e.g. Heitzler, 2013; Lazarus, 1994). It may be that the boundary crossings outlined in this paper are practise-as-normal for some clinicians whilst for others they go too far. The considerations raised in this paper posit that rather than attempting to categorise boundaries as good or bad, or to have fixed rules about boundaries, it is much more important for decisions in therapy to be based on critical reasoning about case-specific factors by trained, supervised and reflective practitioners (Lazarus & Zur, 2002). This allows for ethical practise to be maintained whilst making space for creativity that may enhance the therapeutic relationship and lead to greater gains for the service-user. This is particularly pertinent for work with people who are seeking asylum who are likely to be facing a number of challenges with a limited support network in a new culture. A person-centred, warm and collaborative therapeutic relationship can be invaluable in such circumstances, although of course having firm boundaries does not necessitate that these are lacking. It is of note that in this case a CBT approach was employed, which lends itself naturally to more flexible boundaries; such boundary crossings may not have been possible for therapists working within certain models. Helpful guidance around considering boundaries has been written by Pope and Keith-Spiegel (2008).

A final reflection comes around the term "boundary". A boundary brings to mind the idea of keeping something out, of a barrier, a clear demarcation of what's in and what's out. As argued in this paper and elsewhere, perhaps this is not the most helpful terminology to use when we are promoting empathic interactions based on flexible and critical thinking, rather than firm rules? Alternative metaphors, such as those suggested by Austin et al. (2010), may be preferrable and offer a helpful starting point from which this avenue of thinking may be further explored.

Implications

Therapists working with asylum seekers should consider including social needs and cultural factors in their formulations and interventions with service-users. This may involve using session time to help liaise with other organisations and to have discussions about the impact of social and cultural factors on the service-user, making use of the expertise of interpreters where appropriate. Where serious human rights violations have taken place it is important to work with sensitivity, warmth and an awareness of the personal impact of the work. Self-reflection, supervision, critical thinking and discussions with the service-user can help to guide appropriate boundary management. This may include therapists being open to showing more of their human and personal reactions than they might normally do, as well as advocating for the needs of the service-user and this client group in the community more widely. Of course these decisions will be made on a case-by-case basis with a variety of factors in the balance including the therapeutic model being used, characteristics of the service-user and therapist, and personal preferences. However, it feels important that these are thoughtful decisions rather than rigid rule following.

There were some interesting dynamics raised by involving the interpreter in a different capacity than would be usual at certain points, for example, to offer her opinion. It is beyond the scope of this paper to explore this in any detail although it appeared in this case that such interactions strengthened the alliance between all three people and facilitated cross-cultural working. The importance of regular supervision for interpreters, even just fifteen minutes after a session, should not be overlooked.

It would be interesting to think about how ideas around boundary crossings might apply to other populations. For example, working with older age adults in the community entails engaging with people from a potentially different era (depending on the therapist's age) that was culturally distinct in many ways. Many healthcare workers find themselves accepting tea and cake, and discussing their families, as part of the therapeutic work with older populations. Arguably it is these very real and human interactions that lay the foundations for meaningful work to take place. Further research may include a combination of qualitative methods, such as interviewing service-users about how they experienced interactions that therapists may have viewed as boundary crossings, and quantitative measures, such as including other outcome measures, for example looking at self-compassion, quality of life, resilience and daily functioning.

Limitations

As it is a case study, this paper does not tell us whether different approaches to boundaries would have led to different outcomes. It would be interesting to explore this further but difficult to operationalise given the various domains that the term "boundary" can cover and the subjective nature of what constitutes a flexible versus a rigid boundary. However, the improvement in functioning, the positive feedback of the service-user and the positive results of the used outcome measures suggested that having more flexible boundaries was unlikely to be detrimental to the therapy. As this case study is reflective in nature, the discussion is based largely on the authors' experience and may not be shared by other clinicians. It is hoped that in the very least the paper can provide some food for thought.

Disclosure statement

No potential conflict of interest was reported by the authors.

References

American Psychiatric Association. (2013). Cultural formulation. In *Diagnostic and statistical manual of mental disorders* (5th ed., pp. 749–759). Washington, DC: Author.

American Psychological Association. (2017). *Multicultural guidelines: An ecological approach to context, identity, and intersectionality*. Retrieved from http://www.apa.org/about/policy/multicultural-guidelines.pdf

Apostolidou, Z., & Schweitzer, R. (2017). Practitioners' perspectives on the use of clinical supervision in their therapeutic engagement with asylum seekers and refugee clients. *British Journal of Guidance and Counselling, 45*(1). doi:10.1080/03069885.2015.1125852

Austin, W., Bergum, V., Nuttgens, S., & Peternelj-Taylor, C. (2010). A re-visioning of boundaries in professional helping relationships: Exploring other metaphors. *Ethics & Behavior, 16*(2), 77–94. doi:10.1207/s15327019eb1602_1

Black, S. (2017). To cross or not to cross; ethical boundaries in psychological practice. *Journal of the Australian and New Zealand Student Services Association, 25*(1), 1–17.

Borys, D. S. (1994). Maintaining therapeutic boundaries: The motive is therapeutic effectiveness, not defensive practice. *Ethics & Behavior, 4*(3), 267–273. doi:10.1207/s15327019eb0403_12

British Psychological Society. (2018). *Code of ethics and conduct*. Retrieved from https://www.bps.org.uk/sites/bps.org.uk/files/Policy20-20Files/BPS20Code20of20Ethics20and20Conduct2028201829.pdf

Century, G., Leavey, G., & Payne, H. (2017). The experience of working with refugees: Counsellors in primary care. *British Journal of Guidance and Counselling, 1*. doi:10.1080/03069880601106765

Chantler, K. (2012). Gender, asylum seekers and mental distress: Challenges for mental health social work. *The British Journal of Social Work, 42*(2), 318–334. doi:10.1093/bjsw/bcr062

Chu, T., Keller, A. S., & Rasmussen, A. (2013). Effects of post-migration factors on PTSD outcomes among immigrant survivors of political violence. *Journal of Immigrant and Minority Health, 15*(5), 890–897. doi:10.1007/s10903-012-9696-1

Ehlers, A., & Clark, D. M. (2000). A cognitive model of posttraumatic stress disorder. *Behaviour Research and Therapy, 38*(4), 319–345.

Foa, E. B., McLean, C. P., Zang, Y., Zhong, J., Powers, M. B., Kauffman, B. Y., … Knowles, K. (2016). Psychometric properties of the posttraumatic diagnostic scale for DSM-5 (PDS-5). *Psychological Assessment, 28*(10), 1166–1171. doi:10.1037/pas0000258

Gutheil, T. G., & Brodsky, A. (2011). *Preventing boundary violations in clinical practice*. New York: The Guilford Press.

Gutheil, T. G., & Gabbard, G. O. (1993). The concept of boundaries in clinical practice: Theoretical and risk-management dimensions. *American Journal of Psychiatry, 150*(2), 188–196. doi:10.1176/ajp.150.2.188

Heitzler, M. (2013). Broken boundaries, invaded territories – the challenges of containment in trauma work. *International Body Psychotherapy Journal, 12*(1), 28–41. Retrieved from www.ibpj.org/issues/124008_EABP_Journal-Vol-12-No1.pdf

Hermansson, G. (2007). Boundaries and boundary management in counselling: The never-ending story. *British Journal of Guidance & Counselling, 25*(2), 133–146.

IAPT. (2014). *Measuring improvement and recovery adult services*. Retrieved from http://www.theguardian.com/lifeandstyle/2017/sep/24/why-lack-of-sleep-health-worst-enemy-matthew-walker-why-we-sleep

Kroenke, K., Spitzer, R. L., & Williams, J. B. (2001). The PHQ-9: Validity of a brief depression severity measure. *Journal of General Internal Medicine, 16*(9), 606–613.

Laban, C. J., Gernaat, H. B., Komproe, I. H., Schreuders, B. A., & De Jong, J. T. (2004). Impact of a long asylum procedure on the prevalence of psychiatric disorders in Iraqi asylum seekers in the Netherlands. *Journal of Nervous and Mental Disorders, 192*(12), 843–851.

Lambert, J. E., & Alhassoon, O. M. (2015). Trauma-focused therapy for refugees: Meta-analytic findings. *Journal of Counselling Psychology, 62*(1), 28–37. doi:10.1037/cou0000048

Lazarus, A. (1994). How certain boundaries and ethics diminish therapeutic effectiveness. *Ethics & Behavior, 4*(3), 255–261. doi:10.1207/s15327019eb0403_10

Lazarus, A., & Zur, O. (2002). *Dual relationships and psychotherapy*. New York: Springer.

Li, S. S., Liddell, B. J., & Nickerson, A. (2016). The relationship between post-migration stress and psychological disorders in refugees and asylum seekers. *Current Psychiatry Reports, 18*(9), 82. doi:10.1007/s11920-016-0723-0

Miller, K. E., & Rasmussen, A. (2010). War exposure, daily stressors, and mental health in conflict and post-conflict settings: Bridging the divide between trauma-focused and psychosocial frameworks. *Social Science and Medicine, 70*(1), 7–16. doi:10.1016/j.socscimed.2009.09.029

Murray, K. E., Davidson, G. R., & Schweitzer, R. D. (2010). Review of refugee mental health interventions following resettlement: Best practices and recommendations. *American Journal of Orthopsychiatry, 80*(4), 576–585. doi:10.1111/j.1939-0025.2010.01062.x

Pope, K. S., & Keith-Spiegel, P. (2008). A practical approach to boundaries in psychotherapy: Making decisions, bypassing blunders, and mending fences. *Journal of Clinical Psychology, 64*(5), 638–652. doi:10.1002/jclp.20477

Silove, D., Sinnerbrink, I., Field, A., Manicavasagar, V., & Steel, Z. (1997). Anxiety, depression and PTSD in asylum-seekers: Assocations with pre-migration trauma and post-migration stressors. *British Journal of Psychiatry, 170*, 351–357.

Silove, D., Steel, Z., McGorry, P., & Mohan, P. (1998). Trauma exposure, postmigration stressors, and symptoms of anxiety, depression and post-traumatic stress in Tamil asylum-seekers: Comparison with refugees and immigrants. *Acta Psychiatrica Scandinavia, 97*(3), 175–181.

Speight, S. L. (2012). An exploration of boundaries and solidarity in counseling relationships. *The Counseling Psychologist, 40*(1), 133–157. doi:10.1177_0011000011399783

Spitzer, R. L., Kroenke, K., Williams, J. B., & Lowe, B. (2006). A brief measure for assessing generalized anxiety disorder: The GAD-7. *Archives of Internal Medicine, 166*(10), 1092–1097. doi:10.1001/archinte.166.10.1092

Stallworthy, P. (2013). Cognitive therapy for people with post-traumatic stress disorder to multiple events: Working out where to start. In N. Grey (Ed.), *A casebook of cognitive therapy for traumatic stress reactions* (pp. 194–312). East Sussex: Routledge.

Strasburger, L. H., Jorgenson, L., & Sutherland, P. (1992). The prevention of psychotherapist sexual misconduct: Avoiding the slippery slope. *American Journal of Psychotherapy, 46*(4), 544–555.

Zur, O. (2005). The dumbing down of psychology: Faulty beliefs about boundary crossings and dual relationships. In R. H. Wright & N. A. Cummings (Eds.), *Destructive trends in mental health: The well intentioned path to harm* (pp. 253–282). New York: Routledge.

Zur, O., & Lazarus, A. (2002). Six arguments against dual relationships and their rebuttal. In A. Lazarus & O. Zur (Eds.), *Dual relationships and psychotherapy* (pp. 3–24). New York: Springer.

Ready or not – Here we come! Is Europe ready for career guidance in an intercultural society?

Daniel Hailemariam

ABSTRACT

In today's increasingly diverse and multicultural societies, the need for effective intercultural counselling is more significant than ever. This chapter explores the nuances of intercultural counselling within a multifaceted and dynamic cultural landscape. It delves into the challenges and opportunities presented by multiculturalism, emphasising the importance of culturally competent career guidance approaches. The discussion focuses on understanding the role of professional careers practitioners as bridges between different cultural contexts and the strategies and skills necessary for fostering meaningful cross-cultural relationships. Ethical considerations and potential pitfalls faced by intercultural practitioners are discussed. The findings underscore the significance of intercultural counselling in promoting integration in an increasingly interconnected and diverse world.

Is Europe ready?

Europe is a diverse continent with a history of being a haven for different cultures and ethnicities. The concept and idea of multiculturalism, which stands for the coexistence and integration of various cultural groups, has been present in Europe for decades (Dijkstra, Geuijen & de Ruijter, 2001). However, the level of readiness to embrace multiculturalism that promotes interaction, understanding, and respect between people of different cultural and ethnic backgrounds, can vary significantly across European countries. Cantle (2012) argues for a focus on interculturalism rather than multiculturalism. He suggests this can facilitate changing mindsets by creating new opportunities across cultures to support intercultural activity in communities. Interculturalism provides the opportunity to address five significant issues that it could be argued multiculturalism has largely ignored. As Cantle indicates these are crucial in the new context of globalisation and 'super diversity' namely, (1) identity as a dynamic concept; (2) from 'race' to recognition of all other forms of difference; (3) from national to global/international drivers of difference; (4) new power and political structures; and (5) an interdisciplinary approach.

Kastoryano (2018) highlights the management of diversity has led to the normative theories of multiculturalism, interculturalism, inspired by Canadian political theory and by Canadian reality. Transposed into European context, each approach has its own conception of national unity, equality and solidarity. Most analyses have been single-theory-oriented, leading to multiple, contested and controversial interpretations of integration and democratic public spaces.

Different countries excel in different aspects of integration, and success can be evaluated through various indicators such as employment rates, educational attainment, social cohesion, cultural acceptance, and political participation. Many European countries have embraced multiculturalism and worked to foster diversity and integration. They have implemented policies and initiatives to accommodate and respect the rights of different cultural groups, promote intercultural dialogue, and provide support for newcomers. Yet, integration is a complex issue with multiple perspectives to consider. There have been instances of cultural clashes, discrimination, social tensions, and social injustice due to differences in values, traditions, and beliefs. The arrival of hundreds of thousands of refugees to Europe in a short period around and after 2015 has put immense strain on the host country's resources and systems, including housing, healthcare, and education (Metcalfe-Hough, 2015; BBC, 2020). More recent waves of migration have resulted in countries experiencing more difficulties in managing integration and have certainly tested the willingness of societies to accept people from other countries. The irony is that global migration flows have created the movement of people from varied cultural, ethnic, linguistic, and religious backgrounds, but with an increase in inequality and tensions between individuals and groups.

This chapter argues from a practitioner's perspective that career guidance can play a major role in societies working beyond multiculturalism and striving for interculturalism. Training practitioners in intercultural counselling competencies and training them within the context of an intercultural society will help them provide targeted and more effective services to inform and support individuals from diverse cultural backgrounds. Intercultural career guidance serves as a compass, guiding the practitioner toward a deeper understanding of cultural identity and how it has a bearing on career choices.

Intercultural perspectives in an intercultural society could emerge as a beacon of hope, offering a profound and dynamic approach to address the unique challenges and complexities faced by practitioners. This topic should be a significant concern for policymakers and practitioners in their endeavour to make Europe ready for the new reality and address the unique needs of individuals from different cultural backgrounds. By incorporating intercultural perspectives into policies and practices, career guidance can better serve the needs of an increasingly diverse global population in Europe. This makes cultural competence no longer optional but essential.

Demographic changes and challenges

About 184 million people—2.3 percent of the world's population—live outside of their country of nationality, of these 20 percent are refugees. Almost half of them are in low- and middle-income countries (The World Bank, 2023). Changes over the years in the population structure have resulted in numerous demographic challenges. Some of the challenges inter alia include for example, low birth rates, low death rates (longevity), an ageing population, and high immigration. These changes can have significant social, economic, and political implications. One of the main demographic changes and challenges in Europe in recent years is immigration.

Increased globalisation and mass immigration have brought people from diverse backgrounds and cultures into closer proximity, leading to both enriching exchanges and potential challenges. The challenges include issues related to integration, cultural diversity, social cohesion, social integration, intercultural understanding, and managing multicultural communities. Addressing these and other demographic challenges requires proactive and thoughtful policies, effective integration programmes, language training, employment opportunities, and social support systems. And these challenges compel us to rethink how we deliver career guidance most effectively.

The challenges ahead are significant, but so too are the opportunities. With an unreserved commitment to lifelong learning, an openness to new ideas, and a willingness to embrace diversity and inclusion, we can contribute to making Europe ready for the 'new norm'. While the demographics shift and challenges surmount and propel societies forward, one thing that remains constant is the need for compassion and empathy. It is our humanity that will guide us to give the right services and make the right policies.

One of the prominent challenges of demographic change is the so-called 'brain wastage', also known as the 'credential recognition gap'. Both issues refer to situations where highly skilled individuals, who have obtained education, training, and professional experience in their home countries, face difficulties in being recognised and fully utilising their skills and qualifications in the new country to which they have migrated (Frykman, 2012). This leads to a situation wherein highly skilled immigrants may end up in jobs that are below their qualifications and professional expertise (Damelang, Ebensperger & Stumpf, 2020). Consequently, immigrants may experience lower wages and reduced job satisfaction. This can lead to frustration, loss of self-esteem, and a sense of unfulfilled potential as well as social isolation, and decreased motivation to integrate into the new society and contribute positively. At the same time, the host country may miss out on the full economic potential and contribution of these skilled individuals. A country's ability to recognise people's credentials gained in foreign countries remains central to making the most of a country's labour force. Addressing these dual issues requires a system for credential recognition and targeted support for immigrants to integrate into the local job market by fostering policies that promote diversity and inclusion in the workforce. By tapping into the full potential of highly skilled immigrants, countries can benefit from their expertise and contribute to a more inclusive and prosperous society.

Response to demographic challenges

The concept of career guidance (sometimes described as career counselling, career development, or vocational guidance), originated with the emergence of industrialisation as a response to the demographic changes in the early 1900s (Parsons, 1909). Since then, career support services have in a formalised and structured approach been implemented in societies to meet demographic shifts and help individuals explore and plan their career paths by providing them with decision-making tools, resources, and support.

Career guidance as a response to demographic changes can contribute the following:

- Assist migrants, refugees and asylum seekers in understanding local job markets, transferring skills, and navigating cultural differences.
- Support their integration into the workforce.
- Empower displaced women to break through traditional gender roles and enter fields traditionally dominated by men.
- Help individuals find careers that align with their values and priorities, promoting work-life balance in an evolving workforce.
- Introduce and explain the educational system with an emphasis on lifelong learning.

Overall, career guidance is essential in helping individuals adapt, thrive, and contribute positively to society amid demographic challenges. By addressing the unique needs and circumstances of individuals with immigrant backgrounds, career guidance can play a crucial role in shaping a more inclusive, resilient, and responsive workforce (Patton, & McMahon, 2014).

Understanding culture

Geert Hofstede, a Dutch social psychologist and anthropologist, is best known for his research on understanding culture and its impact. One of Hofstede's most influential academic contributions is the development of the 'Cultural Dimensions Theory' (CDT) (Hofstede, 1984, 2001).

Hofstede's CDT identifies six cultural dimensions that help explain cultural differences. The six dimensions are:

- Power Distance Index (PDI)
- Individualism versus Collectivism (IDV)
- Masculinity versus Femininity (MAS)
- Uncertainty Avoidance Index (UAI)
- Long-Term Orientation versus Short-Term Orientation (LTO)
- Indulgence versus Restraint (IND).

Each dimension represents a fundamental value orientation that influences how people in a culture perceive and interact with the world. By identifying these dimensions, Hofstede's work has provided a systematic way to compare cultural values, norms, and behaviours across different cultures. His cultural dimensions give insight into the impact of culture on areas like communication patterns and decision-making processes. The theory encourages us to develop cultural awareness and sensitivity, recognising that cultural differences can significantly influence perceptions, beliefs, and behaviours.

For years, assimilationism and multiculturalism have been the models of explanation for understanding and dealing with diversity. Assimilation emphasises equality at the expense of ignoring diversity, and multiculturalism emphasises cultural differences at the expense of unity. The aim of *interculturalism* is to realise equality and societal cohesion by building on diversity. CDT helps careers counsellors appreciate and strive for *interculturalism*, which seeks to embrace the richness of cultural diversity while recognising the shared humanity that binds us all. What all of humanity shares goes beyond individual differences and contributes to building bridges of understanding between different cultures. Understanding CDT helps us cultivate an inclusive society that celebrates the beauty of differences and upholds the principles of equality and social justice.

Group- and individual-oriented societies

Limited space in this chapter does not allow for discussion on all six dimensions, however, one dimension needs to be addressed, namely the Individualism versus Collectivism (IDV) dimension. Sociologists have studied how cultural orientations influence how people interact with each other and make decisions (Hofstede, 1984, 2001). Group-oriented and individual-oriented societies represent two distinct cultural orientations. These cultural orientations have a significant impact on various aspects of social behaviour, values, and norms. Here are the key differences between group- and individual-oriented societies:

It is important to note, however, that these are general cultural orientations, and real-world societies often exhibit a mix of both group-oriented and individual-oriented traits. Different societies may fall on a spectrum between these two cultural orientations, and individuals within a society may also express a combination of these values and behaviours. Understanding these cultural orientations and major differences, however, can help in promoting cross-cultural understanding and effective communication in career guidance settings.

Table 1. Key differences between collectivism and individualism

Factors	Collectivism (Group-oriented)	Individualism (Individual-Oriented)
Social identity and interpersonal relationships	Individuals primarily identify themselves with their social groups, such as family, community, or ethnic groups. The sense of belonging and loyalty to the group is strong, and people often prioritise collective interests over individual ones.	Individuals tend to emphasise personal identity and self-expression. They focus on their own needs, aspirations, and achievements, valuing individualism, and independence.
	Relationships are often characterised by interconnectedness and interdependence. People place importance on maintaining harmony and social cohesion within the group. Identity is connected to the group.	Relationships may be more individualistic and transactional. People may value personal space and privacy and emphasise personal choices and autonomy. Identity is based on self-image, competencies, and personal qualities.
	Conformity to social norms and group expectations is highly valued. Deviating from the group's norms may be seen as disruptive to social harmony.	There may be greater acceptance of nonconformity and individual expression. People may be encouraged to pursue their unique interests and ideas.
Decision-making	Decisions are often made collectively, considering the opinions and interests of the group one belongs to. Consensus and group harmony are important factors in decision-making.	Decisions are more likely to be based on individual preferences, goals, and aspirations. Autonomy and personal choice play a significant role in decision-making.
Values and norms	Collectivist values such as cooperation, loyalty, and duty to the group are highly regarded. Maintaining social harmony and avoiding being a shame for the group are valued virtues.	Individualistic values such as personal achievement, self-expression, and personal freedom are emphasised. Independence and self-reliance are often valued traits.
Social support	Social support and assistance are readily available within the close-knit community or extended family. People rely on their social networks for help and guidance.	People may rely more on themselves and formal support systems, such as government agencies or professional services, for assistance.

Sources: Hofstede, 1984, 2001; Launikari, & Puukari, 2005.

The role of culture and values in career choice

Values and culture impact career decisions, including the type of career pursued, the work environment preferred, and the career goals set (Brown, 2002). Some people prioritise family, personal time, or leisure activities over work, while others prioritise career advancement. Some may emphasise the importance of pursuing traditional and stable career options, while others may prefer more entrepreneurial or creative pursuits, still others seek to consider careers that are respected and valued within their cultural context. In some cultures, certain careers are considered more suitable for men or women that limits individuals' choices to societal gender expectations (Sue & Sue, 1990).

Individuals who choose careers that align with their core values are more likely to find fulfilment and contentment in their work. They feel a sense of purpose and meaning, which contributes to higher job satisfaction, and they tend to be more committed and dedicated to their roles, leading to improved performance and productivity. It is therefore essential for individuals and practitioners to reflect on values and consider them when exploring potential career paths and making career decisions. Understanding cultural differences and influences can help practitioners be constructive in their guidance of individuals in their career-related decisions.

Intercultural counselling

Western and Eastern countries vary in their approach to career guidance due to cultural, educational, economic, and societal differences. Career guidance, with the underlying idea of assisting individuals in making career choices and navigating career transitions, is closely associated with Western societies. In contrast, Eastern countries, particularly Asia may prioritise collectivism, valuing family and societal expectation in career decision-making. Also, formalised access to career guidance services is not available in all cultures.

At its core, intercultural counselling acknowledges that every person's worldview is an intricate mosaic woven from their cultural, ethnic, and societal backgrounds. It recognises that these cultural influences significantly shape beliefs, values, communication styles, and coping mechanisms. As practitioners embrace the principles of intercultural counselling, they 'step into the shoes' of their clients, creating a safe and non-judgmental space where cultural differences are neither ignored, discredited, or minimised, but embraced and respected. Moreover, intercultural counselling encourages empathy and open dialogue breaking down the barriers that divide us and cultivating a society that values inclusivity, equity, and social justice.

However, we need to recognise the differences that exist between Western and non-Western counselling regarding cultural perspectives and underlying assumptions about human behaviour (Tanaka-Matsumi, 2022).

Despite the differences, it is also essential to recognise that both Western and non-Western counselling approaches have their strengths and limitations. Culturally competent counsellors seek to bridge the gap between different cultural perspectives, acknowledging the importance of cultural context in understanding human behaviour and providing effective counselling interventions. Moreover, the best counselling practice is one that respects and adapts to the unique needs of the clients being served.

Table 2. Norms in different cultures

	The norm in Western cultures	The norm in non-Western cultures
Guidance and counselling	Guidance is based on Western ways of thinking rooted in Euro-American cultural values and individualistic orientations. It emphasises personal autonomy, self-expression, and individual achievement and is focused on exploring what the client wants to achieve. The support is indirect with the emphasis on the individual helping him/herself. The individual is expected to follow his/her wish.	Guidance is informal and is conducted through various social interactions influenced by cultural traditions and rooted in collectivistic values, and community-oriented perspectives. The focus is on advising the client. The support is direct with the emphasis on the expert providing advice to the individual. The individual is expected to do as it is expected of him/her more authoritarian.
Expert and client relationship	The client is regarded as the expert on what he or she wants to achieve and therefore is encouraged to explore what he or she wants. The counsellor focuses on asking questions and listening to the client. Direct advice is *not* appreciated.	The helper is regarded as the expert and therefore focuses on informing and answering questions from the client. The client is expected to listen to the helper. Direct advice is appreciated.

(*Continued*)

Table 2. Continued.

	The norm in Western cultures	The norm in non-Western cultures
Decision-making	Individualism is a central value and counselling focuses on promoting personal growth, self-awareness, and individual goals. Career decisions are therefore made by the individual based on what is best for him/her. The individual is first and foremost loyal to self with an emphasis on personal choices, development, and independence.	The well-being of the group or community is prioritised over individual desires. Therefore, in decision-making, the individual is loyal to the community he or she belongs to. Extended families and community structures hold more power and influence in decision-making.
Power structure	Places stronger emphasis on egalitarianism, advocating for equal rights and opportunities. Hierarchical power structures are often challenged and questioned with a focus on power balance and power proximity.	Hierarchical power structures exist and are often accepted. Social roles and relationships are often defined by clear hierarchies. Elders hold significant authority and are highly respected. Power structures play a significant role in decision-making.
Communication	Emphasises direct and explicit communication between counsellor and client, with a focus on verbal expression of thoughts and emotions – what is said is important. Direct communication is valued, and speaking up and challenging is encouraged.	Indirect communication might be preferred, especially when addressing authority figures or discussing sensitive matters. Who says it, why it is said, and the context it is said in matters the most. In certain cultures, being too direct can be perceived as impolite or confrontational. Indirect communication allows individuals to maintain a sense of politeness and avoid offending.
Gender roles	Have made progress in breaking down traditional gender divisions of labour, allowing individuals to pursue a wider range of careers and roles. Women and men have relatively equal access to public spaces and activities, and there is an acceptance of shared participation in all areas of life.	Have more defined divisions of labour, with certain jobs and responsibilities traditionally associated with specific genders. Public roles and spaces are more gender-segregated and are constrained by traditional norms. In many cases to the disadvantage of girls and women.
Body language	Personal space is valued, and people tend to maintain larger physical distances during interactions. Standing too close can be perceived as unpleasant. Direct eye contact is generally seen as a sign of attentiveness, honesty, and engagement. Facial expressions often convey emotions openly, and smiling is considered friendly and approachable. Touching can be seen as personal and intimate.	Personal space may be smaller, and physical contact and proximity during conversations are often more acceptable. Eye contact norms vary widely. In some cultures, prolonged direct eye contact might be considered impolite or confrontational, while averting one's gaze may be a sign of respect. Have more reserved facial expressions in public spaces, and smiling might not be as common. Physical touch can be more common and accepted – whether it is to express warmth or anger.

Interculturalism and counselling in a changing society

In a globalised era, individuals often find themselves caught between multiple cultural identities, grappling with questions of belonging, cultural clashes, and the delicate balance of integration or assimilation versus safeguarding their own. In such moments of cultural tension, intercultural counselling extends a compassionate and culturally sensitive hand. This can be done by providing a safe space where clients can explore their unique cultural contexts and make meaning of their career choices (Piller, 2017).

With the rising tide of migration and globalisation, individuals from diverse cultural backgrounds increasingly seek help in navigating the challenges of living in multicultural societies. With this realisation in mind, it is crucial to shift focus from what type of counselling to the *counselee* and the context he/she is living in. The shift should be from 'multicultural counselling' to '*counselling in a multicultural society*'. Counselling in a multicultural society requires a deep understanding of cultural diversity, effective communication skills, and a commitment to providing culturally sensitive and respectful support. The goal is to create a safe counselling environment where clients from different backgrounds can explore their concerns, navigate challenges, and work toward improved well-being that embraces interculturalism.

Interculturalism is a concept and approach that emphasises the interaction and exchange of cultures within a society while promoting dialogue, mutual understanding, and respect among different cultural groups. It is a response to the cultural diversity present in modern societies, aiming to create inclusive and cohesive communities where individuals from various cultural backgrounds can interact and learn from each other.

Interculturalism seeks to go beyond the mere coexistence of different cultures and aims to create a dynamic and interactive environment that benefits from the richness of cultural diversity. It values the distinctiveness of each culture and seeks to foster a sense of belonging and shared responsibility among all members of society. This encourages active and meaningful interactions between individuals from different cultural backgrounds, allowing for the sharing of experiences, traditions, and knowledge. It promotes communication and understanding between different cultural groups, allowing them to learn from each other and build bridges of mutual respect. Facilitating communication and dialogue among diverse cultural groups helps break down barriers and reduce stereotypes and prejudices. It also includes ensuring that all cultural groups have equal access to rights, opportunities, and resources. Interculturalism involves supporting newcomers to society, whether through language programmes, employment assistance, or cultural integration initiatives (Hurn & Tomalin, 2013). This helps newcomers feel welcome and facilitates their integration into the community.

Interculturalism celebrates and embraces diversity, recognising the value of different cultural backgrounds, languages, and traditions. It promotes inclusive policies and practices that ensure equal rights and opportunities for all individuals, regardless of their cultural heritage. Intercultural dialogue and exchange foster understanding and appreciation for each other's perspectives, customs, and values. This helps break down stereotypes and misconceptions and promotes empathy and mutual respect. At its best it also promotes social cohesion, creating a sense of belonging and unity among individuals from various cultural backgrounds. It encourages collaboration and cooperation, leading to stronger and more resilient communities. Intercultural societies benefit from the richness of cultural exchange, which can lead to creative innovation and the blending of different ideas and traditions. This cultural fusion contributes to a vibrant and dynamic society (Nasar & Tariq, 2011).

Mismanaged multiculturalism on the other hand creates situations where diverse cultural groups in society experience significant challenges, conflicts, or negative consequences due to their coexistence. Some characteristics of multiculturalism at its worst are segregation, discrimination, prejudice, social inequality, lack of social cohesion, cultural stereotyping, ethnocentrism, and xenophobia just to mention a few. These negative outcomes often arise due to a lack of effective policies, inadequate intercultural communication, and due to some structural factors, that have not been updated to fit the situation of immigrants.

Intercultural competencies and skills

Carrying out career guidance in a multicultural society is about helping individuals from diverse cultural backgrounds navigate their career development and make informed career decisions (Peavy & Li, 2003). To effectively provide career guidance to this target group, professionals need a unique set of competencies and skills that go beyond traditional career guidance techniques (Poehnell & Amundson, 2011). Intercultural competencies and skills refer to the ability to effectively communicate, interact, and work with people from diverse cultural backgrounds. In an increasingly interconnected and globalised world, these skills are essential to build positive and productive counselling relationships with people from different cultures.

These and other competencies enable counsellors to provide culturally responsive and effective counselling services, fostering a therapeutic environment that respects and celebrates the diverse identities and experiences of their clients. These competencies are essential for promoting positive client outcomes and creating an inclusive and affirming counselling experience for clients from different cultural backgrounds (Thomas & Inkson, 2004).

Table 3. Some key competencies and skills for intercultural career guidance

Competency/Skill	Explanation
Cultural competence	Understanding different cultures, including values, beliefs, norms, and communication styles. Recognising and addressing cultural factors that may influence a client's career choices.
	Understanding one's own cultural values, biases, and assumptions, and being aware of how they may influence the counselling process. This includes engaging in ongoing self-reflection and cultural humility to recognise personal biases and limitations and to continually improve cultural responsiveness in counselling practices.
Cross-cultural communication	Developing effective communication skills that are sensitive to cultural differences in verbal and non-verbal expressions. Utilising counselling techniques and interventions that are inclusive and appropriate for clients from diverse cultural backgrounds.
Empathy and respect	Empathising and understanding the experiences and emotions of clients from different cultural backgrounds. It also includes understanding how cultural factors may impact their career aspirations and challenges.
Identity development	Helping clients explore and understand their cultural identities and how these identities intersect with their career goals and professional growth.
Intersectionality awareness	Recognising the complex interplay of various social identities, such as race, gender, ethnicity, and religion, and understanding how these factors shape a client's career path and opportunities.
Advocacy and inclusivity	Advocating for inclusive practices and policies to ensure equal opportunities for clients from diverse cultural backgrounds and empowering them to overcome systemic barriers.
Collaboration, networking, and training	Building relationships with diverse cultural communities, various other professions, and organisations to enhance career opportunities and resources available to clients.
	Conducting workshops and training sessions to promote intercultural competence and career development among diverse groups.
Counselling methods	See norms of Western and non-Western counselling above

Overall, intercultural career guidance requires a commitment to understanding and appreciating diverse cultural perspectives, as well as a willingness to adapt counselling approaches to meet the unique needs of clients from different cultural backgrounds. Effective intercultural career counsellors play a crucial role in helping individuals from diverse cultures achieve their career aspirations and contribute to creating more inclusive and diverse workplaces. Intercultural competencies and skills are crucial not only to foster mutual understanding and cooperation but also to help prevent misunderstandings and conflicts that can arise due to cultural differences. Developing these competencies and skills is an ongoing process that requires self-awareness, learning, and practice.

Normality and norm-critical

Another area for practitioners to reflect upon is the question of what is *normal* and how to view *normality*. Normality can be seen as something *universal* and *local*. The concept of 'universal normality' refers to the idea that certain behaviours, activities, and needs are considered normal across all cultures and societies. It suggests that some universal standards or activities apply to all human beings, regardless of their cultural background. These include eating, dancing, crying, and greeting, just to mention a few. These are basic human behaviours and are practiced across borders – this is the '*what*'.

The expression or '*the how*' of these behaviours and the norms surrounding them, however, is contextual and local. For example, eating habits, clothing choices, gender roles, and social customs exist in all cultures but how they are carried out and expressed can vary widely across different cultures. In some cultures, it is customary to eat with hands, while in others, using cutlery is the norm. Similarly, what is considered appropriate behaviour for men and women may differ significantly from one culture to another. This means that no culture's norms can be objectively judged as superior or inferior – good or bad. The difference after all, is not in what we do, but in *how* we do things.

Therefore, embracing cultural relativism and acknowledging normality as universal and local is essential for promoting mutual understanding and respect between different societies. It helps prevent ethnocentrism, which is the tendency to judge other cultures based on one's cultural standards. Instead, recognising cultural differences allows for more open and empathetic cross-cultural interactions.

Career counsellors need to approach the concept of normality with caution, as it can be used to perpetuate harmful stereotypes, marginalise certain groups, or dismiss the diversity of human experiences. The notion of normality can be used to maintain power structures, exclude certain groups, and perpetuate discrimination.

Being norm-critical is an approach that aims to question and challenge societal norms and power structures that perpetuate inequalities and discrimination. Norm criticism seeks to analyse and deconstruct norms related to gender, race, sexuality, disability, and other social categories to create awareness of their impact on individuals and groups within a society. The goal of norm criticism is to promote social justice and equality by challenging oppressive norms and advocating for more inclusive and equitable societies. Norm criticism acknowledges the complexity of these interactions and the unique experiences that result from them. Norm criticism questions the taken-for-granted norms and expectations that govern behaviour and social roles. It seeks to reveal the power dynamics behind these norms and their consequences for marginalised groups.

Norm criticism also addresses the privilege that certain groups enjoy due to societal norms. It encourages individuals to reflect on their privileges and how these privileges can contribute to inequality. Norm criticism empowers individuals to question norms and resist societal pressures that limit their freedom and self-expression. By challenging harmful norms, norm criticism strives to create more inclusive spaces that value diversity and difference. Finally, norm criticism emphasises the importance of understanding norms within their historical, cultural, and social contexts to identify the roots of discrimination and inequality.

Conclusion

Is Europe ready? The readiness of Europe for career guidance services for immigrants can vary from one country to another and depends on a range of factors, including government policies, available resources, and the overall approach to immigration and integration. Each country has its own approach to immigration and integration. Some countries have well-established career guidance and support programmes for immigrants, while others may lag behind. Countries that allocate sufficient resources to immigrant integration programmes and provide practitioners with training are often better equipped to support transitions through career guidance services.

Europe, in general, has a strong education system, but challenges related to equipping and training career counsellors, the recognition of foreign qualifications, and avoiding 'Brain wastage' remain to be 'ready'. Career guidance programmes in Europe need to be culturally sensitive and tailored to the specific needs of immigrants from diverse backgrounds. Understanding the unique challenges and experiences of immigrants is essential for effective guidance. Career guidance can play a role in supporting not only economic integration but also the social inclusion of immigrants. The effectiveness of the activities leading to integration and inclusion depends on adaptability, cultural sensitivity, and the allocation of resources. There is still room for improvement in ensuring that immigrants receive the support they need to successfully integrate into the labour market and society. Collaboration between governments, practitioners, and employers is essential to enhance personalised career guidance services for immigrants.

As argued above, career counsellors play a unique and vital role in the integration of immigrants in Europe. Their role is multi-faceted and encompasses several key aspects that contribute to the successful integration of immigrants into the host society. As mentioned above career counsellors can fill in the gap by being cultural bridges helping immigrants understand the nuances of the job market and workplace culture in the host country. They can provide skill assessment and recognition schemes and help them navigate the process of having foreign qualifications recognised in the host country. They can assist immigrants in building professional networks and connecting with local employers, industry associations, and mentors who can provide guidance and job opportunities. In general career counsellors can provide tailored, culturally sensitive, and holistic guidance that addresses the specific needs and challenges immigrants face as they strive to become self-reliant, contributing members of their host societies.

> *"I have learned that people will forget what you said, people will forget what you did, but people will not forget how you made them feel".*
>
> *Maya Angelou*

This quote above by Maya Angelou highlights the profound impact that emotions and interpersonal interactions have on our memories and perceptions of others. While words and actions may fade from memory over time, the emotions experienced during an interaction tend to stay with people. Positive or negative feelings attached to a person's presence are often remembered far longer than the specifics of the conversation or action. The quote also underscores the significance of human connection. The way we engage with others on an emotional level has a far-reaching impact. It shapes our relationships, influences our interactions, and contributes to the overall quality of our interactions.

This perspective emphasises once again, the value of empathy and understanding. When we genuinely empathise with others and try to understand their feelings, it creates a deeper connection and leaves a lasting positive impression. Our ability to make people feel valued, respected, and cared for has a direct influence on the quality of our relationships. People are more likely to be drawn to those who consistently make them feel good about themselves. Authenticity in our interactions is crucial. People tend to remember how we genuinely made them feel, whether it was through sincere kindness, empathy, or genuine interest in their well-being.

As we move forward, the journey of intercultural career guidance remains ongoing and evolving. It prompts us to continually educate ourselves, challenge our biases, and adapt our approaches to ensure that careers support, including specialist guidance (and any other kind of support) is accessible, respectful, and effective for individuals from all walks of life. In embracing the principles of intercultural counselling, we take a crucial step toward a more compassionate and interconnected world, where the pursuit of a good life knows no cultural boundaries.

Ultimately, reflection in general encourages us to be mindful of the emotional resonance we create in our interactions. It reminds us that the way we treat others, the kindness we show, and the empathy we extend are powerful ways to make a positive and enduring impact on people's career choices and ultimately on people's lives. What a privilege to be in the business of career guidance and help one person at a time reestablish their lives in a new country and what a responsibility it is to be prepared for the new reality.

References

BBC News. (2020). Europe's migrant crisis: The year that changed a continent. British Broadcasting Corporation, 31st August 2020. Retrieved from: www.bbc.co.uk/news/world-europe-53925209

Brown, D. (2002). The Role of Work and Cultural Values in Occupational Choice, Satisfaction and Success: A Theoretical Statement. *Journal of Counselling and Development, 80* (1), 48–56. https://doi.org/10.1002/j.1556-6678.2002.tb00165.x

Cantle, T. (2012) *Interculturalism: For the Era of Cohesion and Diversity*. Basingstoke: Palgrave Macmillan.

Damelang, A., Ebensperger S., & Stumpf, F. (2020). Foreign Credential Recognition and Immigrants' Chances of Being Hired for Skilled Jobs—Evidence from a Survey Experiment Among Employers. *Social Forces*, 99 (2), 648–671. https://doi.org/10.1093/sf/soz154

Dijkstra, S., Geuijen, K., & de Ruijter, A. (2001). Multiculturalism and Social Integration in Europe. *International Political Science Review*, 22 (1), 55–84. https://doi.org/10.1177/0192512101221004

Frykman P. M. (2012*)*. Struggle for Recognition: Bosnian Refugees' Employment Experiences in Sweden. *Refugee Survey Quarterly*, 31 (1), 54–79.

Hofstede, G. (1984). *Culture's Consequences: International Differences in Work-related Values*. Newbury Park, CA: Sage.

Hofstede, G. (2001). *Culture's Consequences: Comparing Values, Behaviors, Institutions, and Organizations across Nations*. Thousand Oaks, CA: Sage Publications.

Hurn, B. J., & Tomalin, B. (2013). *Cross-Cultural Communication: Theory and Practice*. Palgrave Macmillan.

Kastoryano, R. (2018). Multiculturalism and Interculturalism: Redefining Nationhood and Solidarity. *Comparitive Migration Studies*, 6 (1):17. doi: 10.1186/s40878-018-0082-6. Epub 17th May 2018.

Launikari, M., & Puukari, S. (Eds.) (2005). *Multicultural Guidance and Counselling –Theoretical Foundations and Best Practices in Europe*. Jyväskylä.

Metcalfe-Hugh, V. (2015). The migration crisis? Facts, challenges and possible solutions, ODI, October 2015. Retrieved from: https://cdn.odi.org/media/documents/9913.pdf, 29th September 2023.

Nasar, M., & Tariq, M. (2011): How Does Interculturalism Contrast with Multiculturalism? *Journal of Intercultural Studies*, 33 (2), 175–196. doi: 10.1080/07256868.2011.618266

Parsons, F. (1909). *Choosing a Vocation*. Houghton, Mifflin and Company.

Patton, W., & McMahon, M. (2014). *Career Development and Systems Theory Connecting Theory and Practice*, 3rd edition. Sense Publishers.

Peavy, V., & Li, H. Z. (2003), Social and Cultural Context of Intercultural Counselling. *Canadian Journal of Counselling*, 37 (3), 186–196.

Piller, I. (2017). *Intercultural Communication: A Critical Introduction*. EUP.

Poehnell, G., & Amundson, N. E. (2011). *Hope-filled Engagement: Creating New Possibilities in Life/Career Counselling*. Ergon Communications.

Sue, D. W., & Sue, S. (1990). *Counselling the Culturally Different: Theory and Practice*, 2nd edition. Wiley.

Tanaka-Matsumi, J. (2022). Counselling Across Cultures: A Half-Century Assessment. *Journal of Cross-Cultural Psychology*, 53 (7–8), 957–975.

The World Bank (2023). World Development Report: *Migrants, Refugees and Societies*. A Flagship World Bank Development Group Report, 2023, p.43.

Thomas, D. C., & Inkson, K. C. (2004). *Cultural Intelligence: People Skills for Global Business*. Berrett-Koehler.

Factors that impact the sociocultural adjustment and well-being of Syrian refugees in Stuttgart, Germany

Samar Jean El Khoury

ABSTRACT
This study investigated the impact of age, gender, language and acculturation choice on the sociocultural adjustment and well-being of Syrian refugees in Stuttgart, Germany. A total of 214 Syrian refugees participated in this study by filling a demographics questionnaire, the Acculturation Attitudes Scale (AAS-16), the Revised Sociocultural Adjustment Scale (R-SCAS), and the Mental Health Inventory (MHI-18). The results showed that the level of German language acquisition significantly correlated with sociocultural adjustment. No significant correlation was found between age and depression level and no significant difference in depression scores were found as a function of gender. Integration significantly correlated with sociocultural adjustment and mental health. Assimilation correlated significantly with sociocultural adjustment, and separation correlated negatively with mental health.

Introduction

The Syrian War that started in 2011 has led to the displacement of 6.1 million Syrians inside Syria and 4.8 million outside Syria (UNHCR, 2017). Some fled to the neighbouring Middle-Eastern countries with great numbers residing in Jordan, Lebanon, and Turkey (Weaver, 2017), while others went further and sought refuge in the Western countries that accepted to receive them. According to the Federal Office of Migration and Refugees (BAMF, 2016), Germany received 186,644 asylum seekers in 2017, following much higher numbers in the previous years, namely, 280,000 people in 2016 and 890,000 in 2015.

Despite the benefits the refugees receive in the Western countries, especially those countries committed to the 1951 Geneva Refugee Convention (UNHCR, n.d.), as compared to the difficult situations they face in the Middle-East, the stressors connected to being displaced into a country whose language and culture differs vastly from their own has its impact on the adjustment and the well-being of the refugees (UNHCR, 2017).

Therefore, it was important to study the factors that help the Syrian refugees adjust and move forward in their host country as well as the factors that hinder their successful adjustment. The variables that were chosen for this study build on previous research mainly done on immigrants. Therefore, this study aimed to investigate the relationship between the different variables, mainly, host language acquisition, age, gender and acculturation strategy on one hand, and sociocultural adjustment and psychological well-being on the other hand.

The context of the study is the city of Stuttgart, which hosts 56 different nationalities. According to the World Population Review (2017), a total of 600,068 people resides in Stuttgart. Based on the latest demographics report produced on the 31 January of 2018 by the Social Security Office of Stuttgart, a total of 7250 refugees reside in Stuttgart in 116 refugee establishments, 27% of which are Syrians.

The literature used to support the hypotheses of this study comprised mostly of psychological research done on immigrants, as well as a small portion that studied the experiences of refugees. Therefore, it is important to keep in mind the common as well as the different experiences that immigrants and refugees pass through before, during, and after their settlement in the host culture. Immigrants on the one hand decide to move following poor economic or political situations in their countries, while refugees are forced to move as a response to the violence and danger they face. Both groups face similar adjustment challenges, but it is important to keep in mind that the different motives might influence the responses and attitudes that immigrants and refugees have in the host country.

The process of cultural changes that take place once a person comes in contact with a foreign culture is called "acculturation". The bi-dimensional model proposed by Berry in 1974, suggests two independent dimensions associated with acculturation, the degree to which individuals maintain or reject their culture of origin, and the degree to which they adopt or reject the host culture. Crossing these two aspects together produces four distinct acculturation strategies: integration, assimilation, separation and marginalisation, where an individual who adopts integration seeks to maintain the culture of origin while adapting and connecting to the host culture; one who adopts assimilation seeks connecting and adapting to the host culture while disconnecting from the culture of origin; separation implies seeking to hold on to the culture of origin while rejecting the host culture; and marginalisation rejects connecting with both, the culture of origin and the host culture (Yu & Wang, 2011).

According to Ward and Kennedy (1999), cross-cultural adaptation can be divided into two aspects, the psychological adaptation and the sociocultural adjustment. Psychological adaptation implies the personal well-being and mental health of the individual and therefore, it is connected to one's emotions, affect, and life satisfaction. However, sociocultural adjustment refers to the ability of the individual to function in the new culture, in managing daily life tasks and is more related to the social skills acquired in the new society. Therefore, based on the above, this study examined each of these two concepts, mainly psychological well-being and sociocultural adaptation, in relation to the different variables age, gender, host language acquisition and the acculturation strategies.

The failure to reach sociocultural adjustment and psychological well-being months and years after arrival in the host country poses a real danger for refugees as their lingering depression and PTSD symptoms might develop into more life-endangering suicidal thoughts as well as substance abuse and criminal behaviour. This is a real challenge for the countries that have received masses of refugees, especially that the number of counsellors and clinical psychologists is vastly disproportionate to the number of individuals needing psychological care and sociocultural support (Bazargan-Hejazi et al., 2011). It is therefore the task of counsellors and psychological health experts to innovate creative guidance and counselling approaches that reach the masses of people who are in dire need for it.

Studies have shown the impact of learning the host language on the sociocultural adjustment of immigrants in the host country, where higher levels of language acquisition correlated with better sociocultural adjustment and where host language acquisition was one of the main predictors of adjustment (Al Jebawi, 2015; Esser, 2006; Kang, 2006; Raijman, Semyonov, & Geffen, 2015; Watkins, Razee, & Richters, 2012).

Studies carried out by Janssen-Kallenberg et al. (2017), Agrawal and Jaiswal (2013), Noorbala et al. (2017), Reid, Rakhilin, Patel, Urry, and Thomas (2017), Detzner, Senyurekli, and Xiong (n.d.), and Polek, Van Oudenhoven, and Ten Berge (2008), have shown that depression symptoms are correlated with older age, especially when age stressors combine with migration stressors and dealing with a new culture and having to learn new skills.

Studies have also shown that female immigrants experience more depression than males and therefore, experience lower well-being in the host country than their male counterparts (Feyera,

Mihretie, Bedaso, Gedle, & Kumera, 2015; Göregenli, Karakuş, & Gökten, 2016; Janssen-Kallenberg et al., 2017; Najam & Hussain, 2015; Wilson, 2011; Noorbala et al., 2017).

Concerning the acculturation strategies and their relationships with sociocultural adjustment and psychological well-being, it was found that integration correlated with better psychological well-being (Abu-Rayya, 2007; Kim, 2006; Kim, 2009; Schmitz & Schmitz, 2012) as well as better sociocultural adjustment (Berry, Phinney, Sam, & Vedder, 2006; Eshel & Rosenthal-Sokolov, 2000; Kosic, 2002). Moreover, studies have shown that assimilation correlated with low psychological well-being especially with larger cultural distances where assimilation then requires higher levels of acculturative stresses (Asvat & Malcarne, 2008; Göregenli et al., 2016; Oh, Koeske, & Sales, 2002) and assimilation was also found to be correlated with better sociocultural adjustment (Kosic, 2002). Finally, separation was related to lower psychological well-being (Abu-Rayya, 2007; Kim, 2006) and lower sociocultural adjustment, for it leads to the isolation of the individuals from their host society (Berry et al., 2006; Eshel & Rosenthal-Sokolov, 2000; Kosic, 2002). Marginalisation in this study was discarded as a separate factor following factor analysis. Therefore, based on the above, we hypothesised the following:

Hypothesis 1: Higher levels of German language proficiency are positively correlated with higher levels of sociocultural adjustment

Hypothesis 2: Age and symptoms of depression are positively correlated

Hypothesis 3: Syrian female refugees experience depression more than men

Hypothesis 4: A: integration is related to better psychological well-being & sociocultural adjustment; B: assimilation correlated with low psychological well-being especially with larger cultural distances & better sociocultural adjustment; C: separation was related to lower psychological well-being & sociocultural adjustment.

Materials

The questionnaire package comprised of the participant consent form followed by the demographics questionnaire and the experience in Germany questionnaire developed by the researcher. Although no hypotheses were constructed around these questions, they were later found to be useful in the interpretation of results. Moreover, three psychological tests were filled by the participants: The Acculturation Attitudes Scale (AAS-16), the revised Sociocultural Adjustment Scale (SCAS-R), and the Mental Health Inventory (MHI-18). All the materials used in this study were translated into Arabic and then back translated into English.

Acculturation Attitudes Scale (AAS-16)

According to Kim (2009), the AAS was developed originally by Kim in 1988 in English and Korean to study the acculturation of Korean Canadians. It comprised of 14 different areas of life with 56 questions. It was used by Kim (2009) in an attempt to study the acculturation of 78 Korean Americans and the Cronbach's alpha retrieved were 0.84 for Integration, 0.84 for Assimilation, 0.77 for Separation, and 0.72 for Marginalisation. Kim (1988) had already established construct, concurrent, and convergent validities of the measure.

According to Schmitz and Berry (2011), the Acculturation Attitudes Scale was used again as a measurement tool in the International Comparative Study of Ethnocultural Youth, this time comprising of 24 items. The AAS-24 was administered on 1799 individuals in Germany, of which about half were immigrants and the other half were German citizens. The results showed that AAS had good internal consistency. The Cronbach's alphas obtained from the immigrants group were 0.70 (Integration), 0.78 (Assimilation), 0.72 (Separation), and 0.62 (Marginalisation). Factor analysis showed the low correlation between the four acculturation attitudes and therefore their independency, and the AAS was found to be effective when used with various cultural backgrounds.

According to Schmitz and Schmitz (2012), the shorter German version of the AAS which comprised of 16 items, touching on tradition maintenance, friends, social activities, marriage, music, and language was administered on 414 immigrants who had been living in Germany for varying number of years. The correlation between emotional intelligence and choice of acculturation styles as well as other factors were examined in this study. The study yielded interesting results and showed again that the AAS-16 has high internal consistency, with Cronbach's alphas ranging from 0.62 to 0.88.

Revised Sociocultural Adjustment Scale (SCAS-R)

According to Ward and Kennedy (1999), the Sociocultural Adjustment Scale was inspired by Furnham and Bochner in 1982 and developed by Searle and Ward in 1990 into a 16-item scale when studying the cross-cultural transition of Malaysian and Singaporean students in New Zealand. The questionnaire required the participants to indicate the amount of difficulty experienced when performing certain activities or in certain social areas. The study indicated good internal reliability of SCAS with alpha values ranging from 0.75 to 0.91. Evidence of construct validity was also found by the significant correlations between sociocultural adjustment and psychological adjustment (0.38), as measured by the Zung Self-rating Depression Scale (ZSDS).

The Revised version of the Sociocultural Adjustment Scale was developed by Wilson (2013), a 21-item self-report inventory, measuring 5 factors of sociocultural adjustment, where the participants needed to indicate their level of competency in a certain social area or behaviour rather than their difficulty in that area. The study carried out by Wilson involved 316 participants living in New Zealand. A 54-item pool was generated and 21 items came out after factor-analysis was run. The internal consistency of these factors was found to be relatively high and the Cronbach alphas of the different subscales are designated here: Interpersonal Communication (0.89), Academic/ Work Performance (0.86), Personal Interests & Community Involvement (0.76), Ecological Adaptation (0.71), and Language Proficiency (0.90). The overall internal consistency of SCAS-R was 0.92. Construct validity tests were also administered and showed a high and negative correlation between the original SCAS and SCAS-R. A positive correlation with SWLS (The Satisfaction with Life Scale) and a negative correlation with ZSDS was also found.

Mental Health Inventory (MHI-18)

The MHI was developed in 1983 by Veit and Ware for the Rand Health Insurance Experiment in the United States. The MHI-18 is comprised of 18 questions about the emotional experience of the participant in the past four weeks. It covers a wide range of positive and negative emotions. The MHI-18 has 4 subscales and one total score, where higher scores indicate better mental health.

According to Ritvo et al. (1997), the MHI-18 administered to 130 Multiple Sclerosis (MS) patients produced very low scores as compared to the normative population scores produced in 1983 by Veit and Ware. The MHI-18 has been refined since its development in 1983 through a series of reliability and validity studies. During the National Health Insurance Study, the MHI was administered to around 5000 individuals from different cities in the US. It was found to correlate highly with other mental health assessment tools.

According to Meybodi et al. (2011), the Farsi version of the MHI-18 was administered to 300 students from the University of Tehran and was tested for reliability and validity. It was found to correlate highly with the General Health Questionnaire. The Cronbach's alpha coefficients for the sub-scores and the total score were also tested and the results were the following: 0.84 (anxiety), 0.83 (depression), 0.63 (behavioural control), and 0.85 (positive affect), and that of the total score was 0.93 (split-half method). These results indicated that the MHI-18 was internally consistent and valid to be used in the Iranian population as an indicator of psychological well-being.

Method

Participants

The participants chosen for this study were Syrian refugees who had come to Germany following the Syrian war that started in 2011. The study did not include other refugees from other nationalities or Syrians who have come for economic reasons over 6 years ago to Germany. More specifically, the sample was a purposeful convenient sample as it targeted only Syrians residing in the city of Stuttgart in Germany. A total of 214 Syrians participated in the study. A detailed demographic description of the participants can be seen in Table 1.

Procedure

The participants were approached and invited to participate in this study through the help of social workers at the governmental refugee establishments in the city of Stuttgart. After the researcher received permission from the administration of each of the refugee residences, Syrians were approached and briefed about the purpose of the study after which they chose either to participate or not. The fact that the researcher and the participants come from neighbouring countries, Syria and Lebanon, and share a common language helped to open the way for the biggest number of those approached to give their consent and respond with hospitality and openness. Only around five people refused to participate because they had prior engagements. Some participants asked if their answers would affect their permission to stay in Germany, but the clarity in the purposes of the study and the assurance they got from the researcher helped them to open up and express

Table 1. Frequency and percentages of demographics ($N = 214$).

Variable	*F*	%
Gender		
Male	129	60.3
Female	85	39.7
National identity		
Arab	185	86.4
Kurdish	29	13.6
Religion		
Muslim	189	88.3
Christian	5	2.3
Yazidi	2	0.9
None	18	8.4
Marital status		
Single	72	33.6
Married	131	61.2
Divorced	5	2.3
Widowed	6	2.8
Place of residence		
Refugee establishment	146	68.2
Private	68	31.8
Age groups		
14–17	14	6.5
18–25	60	28
26–35	60	28
36–45	51	23.8
46–55	25	11.7
>56	4	1.9
Time span in Germany		
<10	15	7
11–20	20	9.3
21–30	137	64
31–40	31	14.5
>41	11	5.1

their feelings and experiences in Germany. The meetings with the participants comprised of filling out the surveys, but also of opening up and expressing the pains, losses and fears they have in their new environment. This gave a chance for the researcher to provide some Counselling and to act as a cultural liaison in explaining some of the confusing matters that the refugees experience in Germany. The researcher met all 214 participants in 12 different refugee establishments, two German language schools, in private houses, and through random street encounters.

Data analysis

Descriptive statistics was first run to get a primary overview of the gathered data. This was followed by running a factor analysis, reliability checks, correlation analyses, and t-tests to study the various hypotheses.

Correlation analysis was done to examine how the level of German language attained related to the sociocultural adjustment of the participants. Correlation analysis was also used to study the relationship between age and depression symptoms, where depression is a subscale of the mental health inventory (MHI-18). Moreover, a t-test was carried out to study how depression varies as a function of gender. The relationships between the various acculturation subscales and sociocultural adjustment and mental health scores were studied through correlation analyses to reach conclusions about the stated hypotheses. Additional correlation analyses, t-tests, and multiple regression analyses were performed.

Ethical considerations

Before administering the study, the researcher applied for IRB clearance from the Ethics Committee at the University where she studies and was granted approval to proceed. Moreover, prior to entering any refugee establishment, the researcher approached the social workers and shared with them the purpose of the study as well as the necessary needed explanatory documents. Finally, participants were asked to fill a consent form before filling out the questionnaires.

Results

The purpose of this study was to examine a set of independent variables, namely, age, gender, language proficiency and acculturation strategies in relation to two separate dependent variables, sociocultural adjustment and psychological well-being among the Syrian refugees in Stuttgart, Germany.

Scale properties

Factor analysis conducted for the AAS-16 scale divided the items of the Acculturation Attitudes Scale into 5 factors, instead of 4, based on the emerged loadings. The clear factors were integration, assimilation, and separation, while the other two factors comprised of arbitrary items from the subscales. Therefore, the items for Marginalisation did not constitute a separate factor. This is in line with a previous study by Schwartz and Zamboanga (2008) who conducted a psychological experiment with 436 Hispanic Americans and their results yielded 6 factors. Integration, assimilation, and separation were clearly represented, but marginalisation was not. Del Pilar and Udasco (2004) also examined the lack of validity in the marginalisation scale and questioned the very concept of it, where they challenged the idea that a minority group in a host country can be totally devoid of any cultural influence, whether it be their own or that of the host culture. This idea was also supported by Fox, Merz, Solórzano, and Roesch (2013).

Reliability testing

The reliability coefficients were calculated for each subscale and scale used in this study and the results are presented in Table 2. The Cronbach's alpha of integration reached 0.725 after items AAS4 and AAS11 were eliminated to improve reliability, and that of separation reached 0.506 following the elimination of item AAS3. The low Cronbach alpha of the separation subscale has to be taken into consideration while interpreting the data.

Hypotheses testing

Hypothesis 1: Higher levels of language proficiency are positively correlated with higher levels of sociocultural adjustment. A Pearson correlation was calculated to examine the relationship between German language proficiency level and sociocultural adjustment. A significant positive correlation was found between the two variables, which confirmed the hypothesis as seen in Table 3.

Hypothesis 2: Age and symptoms of depression are positively correlated. A Pearson correlation was computed to examine the relationship between age and depression. Results showed no correlation between age and depression, and therefore this hypothesis was not confirmed as can be seen in Table 3.

Hypothesis 3: Syrian female refugees experience depression more than men. An independent *t*-test was administered to compare the mean depression levels of males and females in this sample. With depression means of $M = 14.78$ (SD = 4.662) and $M = 14.47$ (SD = 4.839) for males and females, a t value of $t(212) = 0.461$ and a significance value of 0.646 indicated that the difference in the depression levels is not significant between males and females, and hence, this hypothesis was not confirmed.

Hypothesis 4: A: integration is positively correlated with sociocultural adjustment and psychological well-being; B: assimilation is positively correlated with sociocultural adjustment and negatively correlated with psychological well-being; C: separation is negatively correlated with sociocultural adjustment and with psychological well-being. A Pearson correlation was computed to examine the relationship between integration, sociocultural adjustment, and well-being. The results showed that integration was positively and significantly correlated with sociocultural adjustment and well-being, which confirms part A of the fourth hypothesis. Assimilation was found to be positively and significantly correlated with sociocultural adjustment and negatively but insignificantly correlated with mental health, therefore, part B of this hypothesis was only partially confirmed. Finally, results showed that separation was negatively and insignificantly associated with sociocultural adjustment and negatively and significantly correlated with mental health, which also confirms part C of the hypothesis only partially. All these results are presented in Table 3.

Table 2. Cronbach's alphas of the various scales and subscales.

Scale or sub-scale	Cronbach's alpha
AAS	–
AAS_Integration	0.725
AAS_Assimilation	0.668
AAS_Separation	0.506
SCAS_Total	0.889
SCAS_Interpersonal Communication	0.732
SCAS_Academic Work Performance	0.688
SCAS_Personal Interests & Community Involvement	0.661
SCAS_Ecological Adaptation	0.532
SCAS_Language Proficiency	0.835
MHI_Total	0.907
MHI_Depression	0.849
MHI_Anxiety	0.764
MHI_Behavioural Control	0.671
MHI_Positive Affect	0.740

Table 3 . Correlation Matrix between the various independent and dependent variables: German language level, age, acculturation strategies, sociocultural adjustment, mental health and depression.

		SCAS_Total	MHI_Total	MHI_Depression
German language level reached	Pearson correlation	0.394**	–	–
	Sig. (2-tailed)	0	–	–
	N	214	–	–
Age of the participant	Pearson correlation	–	−0.011	0.046
	Sig. (2-tailed)	–	0.874	0.505
	N	–	214	214
AAS_Integration	Pearson correlation	0.151*	0.136*	0.119
	Sig. (2-tailed)	0.027	0.048	0.083
	N	214	214	214
AAS_Assimilation	Pearson correlation	0.254**	−0.025	−0.097
	Sig. (2-tailed)	0	0.713	0.155
	N	214	214	214
AAS_Separation	Pearson correlation	−0.123	−.141*	−0.102
	Sig. (2-tailed)	0.072	0.039	0.137
	N	214	214	214

*Correlation is significant at the 0.05 level (2-tailed).
**Correlation is significant at the 0.01 level (2-tailed).

Additional findings

Multiple regression analysis was performed to examine the predictability of sociocultural adjustment as a dependent variable. The results are seen in Table 4.

Looking at the Beta values as well as the values of significance shows that the biggest contributors to sociocultural adjustment are the German language level, integration, assimilation, and separation (only negatively). Similarly, another regression analysis was carried out to examine the predictability of mental health as the dependent variable. The results can be seen in Table 5.

The results showed that the biggest contributors to mental health were place of residence, sociocultural adjustment, and experiencing difficulty in adjusting to the new culture.

A set of significant correlations was found between different variables and is presented in Table 6.

An independent *t*-test was conducted to examine the mean difference in German language level between males and females. The results showed a significant difference between the two groups where men attained higher language levels ($M = 3.61$; SD = 1.641) than the females ($M = 1.80$; SD = 1.696). Also, sociocultural adjustment was found to be significantly different between males and females, where males reported higher levels of sociocultural adjustment ($M = 75.47$; SD = 10.932) than females ($M = 68.39$; SD = 12.370). The results are presented in Table 7.

Table 4. Regression coefficients of sociocultural adjustment as the dependent variable.

Model		Unstandardised coefficients		Standardised coefficients		
		B	Std. Error	Beta	*t*	Sig.
1	(Constant)	68.96	11.452		6.022	0
	Age	−0.036	0.074	−0.034	−0.488	0.626
	Length of stay	−0.182	0.09	−0.138	−2.027	0.044
	Education in Syria	0.358	0.211	0.116	1.695	0.092
	German language level	2.022	0.57	0.313	3.549	0
	AAS_Integration	1.154	0.579	0.136	1.994	0.048
	AAS_Assimilation	0.829	0.268	0.208	3.095	0.002
	AAS_Separation	−1.21	0.545	−0.149	−2.222	0.028
	AAS_Marginalisation	−0.568	0.622	−0.066	−0.912	0.363
	No. of German friends	0.232	0.121	0.125	1.92	0.056
	Gender	−3.74	1.731	−0.157	−2.16	0.032
	Place of residence	1.317	1.748	0.051	0.754	0.452
	Work Status	−0.307	1.09	−0.02	−0.282	0.779
	Perceiving discrimination	−0.538	1.333	−0.026	−0.404	0.687
	Cultural distance	−2.257	1.437	−0.097	−1.571	0.118

Table 5. Regression coefficients of mental health as the dependent variable.

Model		Unstandardised coefficients		Standardised coefficients		
		B	Std. Error	Beta	*t*	Sig.
1	(Constant)	8.234	15.963		0.516	0.607
	Gender	3.595	2.337	0.122	1.538	0.126
	Age	0.153	0.102	0.118	1.501	0.135
	Time Span in Germany	−0.177	0.121	−0.108	−1.459	0.146
	Education level in Syria	−0.303	0.291	−0.08	−1.044	0.298
	German language level	−0.051	0.805	−0.006	−0.064	0.949
	Place of residence	6.308	2.372	0.198	2.66	0.009
	Work Status	1.93	1.448	0.102	1.333	0.184
	Perceiving discrimination	−2.207	1.802	−0.085	−1.225	0.222
	Physical and health needs covered	−1.585	1.137	−0.099	−1.395	0.165
	Receiving psychological help	−0.78	2.909	−0.019	−0.268	0.789
	Communication difficulties with Germans	−0.593	2.314	−0.02	−0.256	0.798
	Difficulty adjusting to new culture	8.578	2.179	0.287	3.936	0
	No. of German friends	0.081	0.166	0.036	0.487	0.627
	SCAS_Total	0.404	0.103	0.327	3.924	0
	AAS_Integration	0.673	0.781	0.064	0.862	0.39
	AAS_Separation	0.333	0.752	0.033	0.442	0.659
	AAS_Marginalisation	0.743	0.833	0.07	0.893	0.373
	AAS_Assimilation	−0.563	0.365	−0.116	−1.543	0.125

Table 6. Correlation matrix between age, education level, knowing other languages, German language level, sociocultural adjustment, mental health and depression.

		MHI_Depression	MHI_Total	SCAS_Total	German language level reached
Age of the Participant	Pearson Correlation	0.046	0.017	−.184**	−0.395**
	Sig. (2-tailed)	0.505	0.809	0.007	0
	N	214	214	214	214
Other languages the person uses besides Arabic	Pearson Correlation	0.046	−0.001	.176**	0.292**
	Sig. (2-tailed)	0.506	0.993	0.01	0
	N	214	214	214	214
Grade or level reached in Syria	Pearson Correlation	.141*	0.015	0.122	0.213**
	Sig. (2-tailed)	0.039	0.832	0.074	0.002
	N	214	214	214	214
SCAS_Total	Pearson Correlation	.287**	.327**	1	.394**
	Sig. (2-tailed)	0	0		0
	N	214	214	214	214

**Correlation is significant at the 0.01 level (2-tailed).
*Correlation is significant at the 0.05 level (2-tailed).

Table 7. Independent samples *t*-test comparing the difference in German language level attained and sociocultural adjustment as a function of gender.

	t-test for Equality of Means				
				95% confidence interval of the difference	
	t	df	Sig. (2-tailed)	Lower	Upper
German language level reached	7.802	212	0	1.354	2.27
SCAS_Total	4.401	212	0	3.911	10.258

Furthermore, another independent *t*-test was conducted to measure the relationship between place of residence (refugee establishment or private housing) and mental health. A *t*-value of $t(212) = -2.792$ with a significance value of 0.006 implied that the difference between the means is significant at the 0.05 level. Therefore, there is a significant difference in the means of the mental health calculated, where participants living in private housing reported higher mental health scores ($M = 72.71$; SD = 13.092) than those living in the refugee establishments ($M = 66.44$; SD = 16.203).

Discussion

The purpose of this study was to examine the impact of age, gender, host language acquisition and acculturation strategies on sociocultural adjustment and well-being among Syrian refugees in Stuttgart, Germany.

The first hypothesis stated that the German language level of the refugees in the study would be positively correlated with their reported sociocultural adjustment. This hypothesis was confirmed and it is in line with previous research. For instance, Swami, Arteche, Chamorro-Premuzic, and Furnham (2010) conducted a study on Chinese and Malaysian immigrants living in the UK and concluded that language proficiency was correlated with better sociocultural adjustment level and a better overall experience in the host country. Moreover, Kang (2006) found language competence to be a better predictor of adjustment than acculturation strategies as seen in a variety of Asian groups living in the United States. This is in line with the current study where regression analysis showed that German language levels predicted the sociocultural adjustment of participants by 31%. Watkins et al. (2012) also confirm the critical role that language played in allowing the adjustment of the Burmese refugees in Australia, where language was found to be the biggest barrier to adjustment. It is important here to note that around 40% of the Syrian refugees who participated in the current study reported that language learning is the most difficult obstacle they were experiencing in adjusting to life in Germany. Raijman et al. (2015) noted that higher educational levels of the immigrants was related with better language acquisition levels and better adjustment. This might explain some of the adjustment difficulties faced by the participants, where 20% of them did not receive any schooling beyond Grade 5 and around 50% left school after Grade 9, according to the current study. Finally, according to Esser (2006), living in ethnically homogeneous communities hinders immigrants from learning the host language and experiencing involvement in the host society. This applies to 68% of the Syrians in this study who have lived in refugee establishments with other Arabs and international refugees for more than two years.

The second and third hypotheses stated that older age would be correlated with higher levels of depression and that females would experience higher depression rates than men. These two hypotheses were not confirmed by the current study. The studies which these hypotheses were based upon were mainly conducted on immigrants and not on refugees. One can argue that the refugees' situation differs from that of immigrants who resettle willingly into a new culture, and therefore, other factors could be at work contributing more significantly to the depression and mental health of the refugees, regardless of age and gender. For instance, Smeekes, Verkuyten, Celebi, Acarturk, and Onkun (2017) conducted a study with a total of 361 Syrian refugees living in Turkey. The study revealed that neither age nor gender predicted depression scores of the participants. However, maintaining social contact and social identity after migration was a major factor predicting greater life satisfaction and acting as a protective factor against depression. Moreover, a study by Schweitzer, Melville, Steel, and Lacherez (2006) conducted with Sudanese refugees living in Australia showed that social support from the individual's own ethnic community, family separation, employment status, as well as pre- and post-migration stressors predicted higher depression. The effect of pre- and post-migration experiences on mental health was also stressed by Lacroix and Sabbah (2011).

Moreover, in a study conducted on 443 refugees and asylum seekers in Italy, Aragona, Pucci, Mazzetti, and Geraci (2012) concluded that neither gender nor age played a role in whether the participants showed more or less symptoms of Post-Traumatic Stress Disorder (PTSD); in fact, the levels of post-migration living difficulties experienced in the host country was the biggest factor affecting PTSD. The most common post-migration living difficulty experienced was, having no permission to work (38.6%). Relating this to our study, we can conclude that although the Syrian refugees live on "safe" German soil, they continue to hear the news of war, destruction of property, and death of loved ones even several years after their own displacement. Moreover, a total of 60% of the Syrian refugees, who participated in the current study had jobs in Syria and were responsible for their own income; only 4.5% of the participants are currently employed in Germany. Furthermore, having to learn the language first, puts refugees, and especially men in this case, who were the main source of income in their home country, in a much weaker and vulnerable social status than the one they belonged to in Syria. This can be confirmed by Feyera et al. (2015), who conducted a study on 847 Somalian refugees in Ethiopia. The results showed that depression rates were significantly related to continued socioeconomic difficulties and stressful life conditions in the refugee camps as compared to refugees who resettled into homes in Toronto, Canada. In this context, Somalian women showed higher depression rates than the men in the Ethiopian refugee camps. However, Ethiopian refugee men and women who resettled in Toronto experienced similar rates of depression in comparison, and this was explained due to the drop in the social and economic status and the lack of work opportunities for men in Toronto. Also, it was found that stressors related to the shelter conditions in the host country contribute to mental health conditions. The same can be said about the Syrian refugees in Stuttgart who struggle with lack of private housing. This is in line with our regression analysis results that showed the place of residence to contribute up to 20% to the mental health of the refugees, where those living in private housing enjoyed better mental health than those living in refugee establishments.

Moreover, the regression analysis also showed that "having no difficulty in adjusting to the German culture" contributed by 29% to mental health. And this is in line with a study by Zisberg (2017) that involved recent and veteran Russian immigrants in Israel, as well as Middle-Eastern veteran immigrants, and Israeli locals. The results showed that both recent and veteran Russians experienced more depression than the veteran Middle-eastern immigrants. These results put less weight on age as a predictor of depression and more weight on cultural distance as a stronger predictor, where Russians experience bigger cultural distance living in Israel than Middle-Eastern immigrants. This might also explain the results of this current study where 62% of the participants reported that they perceive the German and the Syrian cultures to be very different, while 36% reported that they can find some similarities, and 1% only reported the two cultures to be similar.

Finally, regression analysis of the current study also showed that sociocultural adjustment contributed up to 32% to the well-being of the participants. Also, the additional findings showed that a significant difference in sociocultural adjustment rates exists between males and females, where males enjoyed higher sociocultural adjustment levels than females. There was likewise. a negative correlation between age and sociocultural adjustment. Therefore, although gender and age were not found to contribute directly to depression and well-being rates, however, they seem to contribute indirectly through their direct relationship with sociocultural adjustment.

Part A of the fourth hypothesis stated that integration is positively correlated with sociocultural adjustment and well-being. Correlation analysis confirmed this first part of the hypothesis where integration was found to be positively and significantly correlated with sociocultural adjustment as well as with mental health. This is in line with numerous previous studies that confirm these findings (Abu-Rayya, 2007; Berry et al., 2006; Eshel & Rosenthal-Sokolov, 2000; Schmitz & Schmitz, 2012). It was also found in the current study that integration was the most favourable mode of acculturation chosen by the participants, and this is again in line with previous studies that show integration to be the most preferred strategy of acculturation, as it requires the least amount of acculturative stress and consequently gives the best psychosocial outcomes (Kim, 2006; Lee & Green, n.d.). It is worth noting here that choosing integration as a strategy of acculturation in fact expresses a desire to "fit in", as worded out by Yu and Wang (2011) but translating this desire into action is affected by the environment and the place of residence. According to Kosic (2002), those who practice integration enjoy higher rates of relationships with the host society, and they mostly live in ethnically mixed communities where they can interact with the host community, according to Berry et al. (2006). Therefore, these results prompt us to advise refugees to adopt integration as an acculturation attitude, however, whether they are able to practice integration in reality depends on their place of residence and their level of contact with the host community.

Part B of the fourth hypothesis stated that assimilation is positively correlated with sociocultural adjustment and negatively correlated with well-being. The results of this study confirmed this part of the hypothesis only partially. Assimilation and sociocultural adjustment were found to be positively and significantly correlated and that is in line with previous studies that showed similar results (Berry et al. 2006). However, the relationship between assimilation and well-being varied between different previous studies and was found not to be significant in this study. Various factors seem to play a role in the mental health consequences of assimilation. One major factor was found to be cultural distance between the host culture and culture of origin, where the greater the cultural distance, the more assimilation requires sociocultural changes by the individual and this exerts more acculturative stress on the person's mental health, and therefore, assimilation in this case is connected with higher depression rates (Asvat & Malcarne, 2008; Göregenli et al., 2016; Stephens, 2016). Sixty-two percent of the Syrian refugees taking part in this study reported that they perceive the German culture to be very different from the Syrian one. Therefore, this prompted us to expect a significant negative correlation between assimilation and mental health. However, the insignificant negative correlation points our focus to other factors that might also be impacting these results, namely, perceiving discrimination from the host society. According to Asvat and Malcarne (2008) and Stephens (2016), perceiving discrimination is another factor that contributes to depression and lower well-being within the assimilation model, due to the fact that getting in close contact with the locals through assimilation gets one to recognise discrimination more clearly. In our current study, only 5% of the participants reported perceiving discrimination from locals. Therefore, this very low perception of discrimination might explain why in this study assimilation correlated negatively but insignificantly with mental health scores.

Moreover, Oh et al. (2002) distinguished between two types of assimilation: one related to language assimilation and interaction with the host society, and one related to identity assimilation. The first one was found to be related to lower depression levels, while the second was found to be related to higher depression levels. In the case of the participants in our current study, language assimilation and contact with the host society is slow because of the residence of the biggest percentage of refugees in the refugee establishments and not among other Germans. Also, identity assimilation is not happening because of the big cultural differences, as well as the religious differences. This might also explain why there was no significant relationship between assimilation and mental health.

Finally, Part C of the fourth hypothesis stated that separation correlates negatively to both sociocultural adjustment and well-being. The results of the study confirmed this part of the hypothesis only partially. A significant negative correlation between separation and mental health was found and that is in line with different studies in the field of acculturation studies, where separation requires the least amount of sociocultural change and therefore it exerts the least amount of stress, but it leaves the individual isolated and experiencing poorer well-being (Abu-Rayya, 2007; Berry et al., 2006; Kim, 2006; Stephens, 2016).

Separation was found to be insignificantly correlated to sociocultural adjustment. The regression analysis that was run on sociocultural adjustment as the dependent variable showed that separation contributed negatively to sociocultural adjustment by 15%, but other factors might be at work that are not clearly presented through the results of this study.

Additional findings

The additional results showed the relationship between age, difficulty of learning the German language and sociocultural adjustment, where age was negatively and significantly correlated with the German language level reached and was also negatively and significantly correlated with sociocultural adjustment. This is in line with a study by Reid et al. (2017) that points out the difficulties in language learning and adjustment to a new culture that older people experience. Additional results also showed that women enjoyed worse sociocultural adjustment than men and generally reached lower German language levels than males, and this is in line with the studies by Watkins et al. (2012). Moreover, results also showed that higher education levels reached in Syria correlated with lower depression symptoms as well as higher German language level acquisition, which is in line with previous research (Esser 2006; Feyera et al. 2015; Polek et al. 2008; Raijman et al. 2015; Yu & Wang 2011).

Finally, a significant difference in mental health rates was found as a function of place of residence in Germany, where those living in private housing experienced better mental health than those living in refugee establishments, and this is in line with a study by Feyera et al. (2015), that showed difference in mental health outcomes between those who lived in camps in Ethiopia and those who lived in private housing in Toronto.

Clinical implications

The results of this study guide us towards screening for psychological disorders for refugees, especially those residing in the refugee establishments, regardless of age and gender. There are already some existing counselling services that are provided for refugees in Stuttgart, namely, the *Jugendamt* which serves children, teenagers as well as families, and organisations like *eva* (The Evangelical Society) which provides counselling and practical help for families and individuals. However, there is a shortage of clinical psychologists who can cater to the big numbers of Syrians who came into the country. Language surely continues to be a barrier between the German counsellors and the refugees receiving the counselling services ("In Germany, Refugees", 2017). We cannot stress enough how important it is to the individual to express themselves and receive counselling in their own mother tongues. Moreover, having a translator who mediates the discussion between the counsellor and the refugee seeking help takes away from the effectiveness of the process (Baxter & Cheng, 1996). We add to that the fact that seeking counselling is foreign to the Syrian culture, therefore, it is important to spread awareness about the normality of seeking counselling and to tone down the thoughts that stigmatise those who seek psychological help. Following this step, more Arabic speaking counsellors are needed to provide their services and have direct contact with the refugees. Another suggestion is to train more lay-counsellors who can provide these services for their peers in Arabic, which is a project already being practiced by some German cities ("Germany turns refugees", 2017).

The Federal Office of Migration and Refugees provides free German classes for the refugees starting with 310 hours for them to reach the B1 level (third level) as well as to finish the one-month long integration course. More hours are provided for those who fail to pass the exams. Language training and friendship circles are also being offered by German volunteers in certain public locations in Stuttgart. However, these are not accessible to all, especially to mothers of young children and elderly who are bound to stay in their accommodations and are not able to freely attend the language circles or the official classes. The suggestion is then to offer these services systematically in the different refugee establishments by local volunteers. More focus on the less educated individuals should be offered as they are a neglected at-risk group. Work options for refugees in a way that uses their skills and inserts them into the society where they can learn the language more readily than when merely sitting in a classroom.

Moreover, since adjusting to the German culture was found to be a main predictor of mental health, community cultural seminars can be held, where local German individuals are available to interact with the refugees. This is a bit difficult to attain as Germans are usually occupied with their education and jobs and there is a shortage of German volunteers who are able and ready to give their free time to befriend and support the refugees. Awareness about the various acculturation strategies and the related acculturative stressors should be spread to the refugees, so as to direct them towards better adjustment and well-being. Moreover, the religious gap between the biggest portion of the refugees and their host society contributes to their isolation and the hindrance of their integration and this is a topic that can be further studied and discussed openly in intercultural circles.

Finally, the refugees experience great stress within the refugee establishments, as they share daily life, including sharing kitchens and toilets with other refugees from other countries. This often causes conflicts within the refugee establishments, and therefore, it is important to hold simple inter-cultural and conflict resolution trainings that help the refugees adjust to their temporary living conditions.

Future research recommendations

We recommend further testing of the available acculturation scales and subscales in an attempt to make available tools with higher internal reliability that can be used in various contexts.

Further studies can be done on differences between immigrants and refugees, to clarify commonalities and differences in the experiences of both groups and in the various factors that impact the sociocultural adjustment and the well-being of each.

Cultural distance and religion seem to have some impact on the willingness and the ability to integrate into a new culture. Deeper studies in this field can help refugees who come from completely different backgrounds integrate in a way that doesn't wipe out their own culture and religious identities, and it would clarify what integration really means for these groups.

Studies on the relationships between length of stay, sociocultural adjustment and well-being show varying results, and therefore, it would be suggested that more studies are conducted to learn more about the progress of adjustment and well-being as a function of time.

Limitations of the study

The first limitation to be mentioned is the weak reliability of the separation subscale that was used in this study. Furthermore, it should be noted that this study was limited to refugees in Stuttgart which lies in the Western Germany, and therefore, results cannot be generalised to Syrian refugees outside Stuttgart, who could have very different experiences in the different contexts. Furthermore, the biggest number of Syrians who participated in the study resided in refugee establishments, and therefore the results are biased towards those living in the refugee establishments. This current study was a quantitative one, however a qualitative study would also be very helpful in guiding counsellors and social workers in the areas that pose the biggest challenges for the refugees in order that they may address their struggles in a more effective way.

Acknowledgments

I would like to thank Dr. Hanine Hoot, my main supervisor, whose guidance and input was vital for the completion of this paper, as well as Dr. Marwan Gharzeddine and Dr. David Tawil for their contributions and valuable feedback.

Disclosure statement

The purpose of publishing this study is to make it available for other researchers in this field, who can further build on the current findings and bring more depth into this rich topic.

References

Abu-Rayya, H. M. (2007). Acculturation, Christian religiosity, and psychological and marital well-being among the European wives of Arabs in Israel. *Mental Health, Religion & Culture, 10*(2), 171–190.

Agrawal, S., & Jaiswal, S. (2013). Anasakti: Stress and coping in old age. *Indian Journal of Gerontology, 27*(4), 665–673.

Al Jebawi, G. (2015, October 22). Syrian refugees in German cities. Retrieved from https://www.sicherheitspolitik-blog.de/2015/10/22/syrian-refugees-in-german-cities/

Aragona, M., Pucci, D., Mazzetti, M., & Geraci, S. (2012). Post-migration living difficulties as a significant risk factor for PTSD in immigrants: A primary care study. *Italian Journal of Public Health, 9*(3), 1–8.

Asvat, Y., & Malcarne, V. L. (2008). Acculturation and depressive symptoms in Muslim university students: Personal–family acculturation match. *International Journal of Psychology, 43*(2), 114–124.

BAMF. Asylum statistics. December 2016: http://www.bamf.de/SharedDocs/Anlagen/DE/Downloads/Infothek/Statistik/Asyl/201612-statistik-anlage-asyl-geschaeftsbericht.pdf;jsessionid=FDCD7933B965145229394C06F576961D.1_cid294?__blob=publicationFile; BAMF, Key Asylum Statistics 2016. https://www.bamf.de/SharedDocs/Anlagen/DE/Publikationen/Flyer/flyer-schluesselzahlen-asyl-2016.pdf?__blob=publicationFile; Federal Government, Reply to parliamentary question by The Left, 21 February 2017, 34.

Baxter, H., & Cheng, L. (1996). Use of interpreters in individual psychotherapy. *Australian & New Zealand Journal of Psychiatry, 30*(1), 153–156. Retrieved from https://www.ncbi.nlm.nih.gov/pubmed/8724340

Bazargan-Hejazi, S., Bazargan, M., Shaheen, M., Teklehaimanot, S., Ahmadi, A., Cooper, J. S., & Teruya, S. (2011). Depression symptoms, acculturation, needing care, and receiving care: A study of adolescents living in California. *Journal of Health Disparities Research and Practice, 9*(3), 45–66.

Berry, J. W., Phinney, J. S., Sam, D. L., & Vedder, P. (2006). Immigrant youth: Acculturation, identity, and adaptation. *Applied Psychology, 55*(3), 303–332.

Del Pilar, J. A., & Udasco, J. O. (2004). Deculturation: Its Lack of Validity. *Cultural Diversity and Ethnic Minority Psychology, 10* (2), 169–176.

Detzner, D. F., Senyurekli, A. R., & Xiong, Z. B. (n.d.). Escape from harm's Way: The experiences of Southeast Asian elders and their families. *Hmong Studies Journal, 9*, 1–31.

Eshel, Y., & Rosenthal-Sokolov, M. (2000). Acculturation attitudes and sociocultural adjustment of soujourner youth in Israel. *The Journal of Social Psychology, 140*(6), 677–691.

Esser, H. (2006, December). Migration, language and integration. Programme on Intercultural Conflicts and Societal Integration (AKI) Social Science Research Center Berlin. doi:www.aki.wz-berlin.de

Feyera, F., Mihretie, G., Bedaso, A., Gedle, D., & Kumera, G. (2015). Prevalence of depression and associated factors among Somali refugee at Melkadida camp, southeast Ethiopia: A cross-sectional study. *BMC Psychiatry, 15*(171), 1–7.

Fox, R. S., Merz, E. L., Solórzano, M. T., & Roesch, S. C. (2013). Further examining berry's model: The applicability of latent profile analysis to acculturation. *Measurement and Evaluation in Counseling and Development, 46*(4), 270–288.

Germany turns refugees into mental health counsellors for their peers. (2017, October). *The Guardian*. Retrieved from https://www.theguardian.com/world/2017/aug/31/germany-turns-refugees-into-mental-health-counsellors-for-their-peers

Göregenli, M., Karakuş, P., & Gökten, C. (2016). Acculturation attitudes and urban-related identity of internal migrants in three largest cities of Turkey. *Migration Letters, 13*(3), 427–442.

In Germany, refugees are being trained as mental health counselors for peers. (2017, September 3). *Haaretz*. Retrieved from https://www.haaretz.com/world-news/europe/in-germany-refugees-trained-to-counsel-peers-1.5447223

Janssen-Kallenberg, H., Schulz, H., Kluge, U., Strehle, J., Wittchen, H., Wolfradt, U., … Dingoyan, D. (2017). Acculturation and other risk factors of depressive disorders in individuals with Turkish migration backgrounds. *BMC Psychiatry, 17* (264), 1–12.

Kang, S. (2006). Measurement of acculturation, scale formats, and language competence: Their implications for adjustment. *Journal of Cross-Cultural Psychology, 37*(6), 669–693.

Kim, E. (2009). Multidimensional acculturation attitudes and depressive symptoms in Korean Americans. *Issues in Mental Health Nursing, 30*(2), 98–103.

Kim, U. (2006). *Acculturation attitudes scale: Development and validation of the scale with Korean and Korean-Canadian samples*. Unpublished Manuscript, College of Business Administration, Inha University, Incheon, Korea.

Kosic, A. (2002). Acculturation attitudes, need for cognitive closure, and adaptation of immigrants. *The Journal of Social Psychology, 142*(2), 179–201.

Lacroix, M., & Sabbah, A. (2011). Posttraumatic psychological distress and resettlement: The need for a different practice in assisting refugee families. *Journal of Family Social Work, 14*, 43–53. doi:10.1080/10522158.2011.523879

Lee, J. K., & Green, K. (n.d.). Acculturation processes of Hmong in Eastern Wisconsin. *Hmong Studies Journal, 11*, 1–21.

Meybodi, F. A., Saeedi, Z., Behjati, Z., Noorbala, F., Dastbaravardec, A., & Enjedany, E. (2011). Reliability and validity of a Farsi version of 18-item mental health inventory. *Procedia – Social and Behavioral Sciences, 30*, 1425–1429.

Najam, N., & Hussain, S. (2015). Gender and mental health in Gilgit-Baltistan, Pakistan. *Journal of Pioneering Medical Sciences, 5*(4), 117–120.

Noorbala, A. A., Bagheri Yazdi, S. A., Faghihzadeh, S., Kamali, K., Faghihzadeh, E., Hajebi, A., … Vafaei, F. (2017). A survey on mental health status of adult population aged 15 and above in the province of Kordestan, Iran. *Archives of Iranian Medicine, 20*(11), 71–74.

Oh, Y., Koeske, G. F., & Sales, E. (2002). Acculturation, stress, and depressive symptoms among Korean immigrants in the United States. *The Journal of Social Psychology, 142*(4), 511–526.

Polek, E., Van Oudenhoven, J., & Ten Berge, J. M. (2008). Attachment styles and demographic factors as predictors of sociocultural and psychological adjustment of Eastern European immigrants in the Netherlands. *International Journal of Psychology, 43*(5), 919–928.

Raijman, R., Semyonov, M., & Geffen, R. (2015). Language proficiency among post-1990 immigrants in Israel. *Journal of Ethnic and Migration Studies, 41*(8), 1347–1371. doi:10.1080/1369183X.2014.982523.

Reid, A. G., Rakhilin, M., Patel, A. D., Urry, H. L., & Thomas, A. K. (2017). New technology for studying the impact of regular singing and song learning on cognitive function in older adults: A feasibility study. *Psychomusicology: Music, Mind and Brain, 27*(2), 132–144.

Ritvo, P. G., Fischer, J. S., Miller, D. M., Andrews, H., Paty, D. W., & LaRocca, N. G. (1997). *Multiple sclerosis quality of life inventory: A user's manual*. The Consortium of Multiple Sclerosis Centers Health Services Research Subcommittee (pp. 28–31).

Schmitz, P. G., & Berry, J. W. (2011). Structure of acculturation attitudes and their relationships with personality and psychological adaptation: A study with immigrant and national samples in Germany. *The International Association for Cross-Cultural Psychology Conferences*, 52–70. Retrieved September 10, 2018, from https://scholarworks.gvsu.edu/cgi/viewcontent.cgi?article=1057&context=iaccp_papers.

Schmitz, P. G., & Schmitz, F. (2012). Emotional intelligence and acculturation. *Behavioral Psychology, 20*(1), 15–41.

Schwartz, S. J., & Zamboanga, B. L. (2008). Testing berry's model of acculturation: A confirmatory latent class approach. *Cultural Diversity and Ethnic Minority Psychology, 14*(4), 275–285.

Schweitzer, R., Melville, F., Steel, Z., & Lacherez, P. (2006). Trauma, post-migration living difficulties, and social support as predictors of psychological adjustment in resettled Sudanese refugees. *Australian and New Zealand Journal of Psychiatry, 40*, 179–187.

Smeekes, A., Verkuyten, M., Celebi, E., Acarturk, C., & Onkun, S. (2017). Social identity continuity and mental health among Syrian refugees in Turkey. *Social Psychiatry and Psychiatric Epidemiology, 52*, 1317–1324.

Stephens, C. S. (2016). Acculturation contexts: Theorizing on the role of intercultural hierarchy in contemporary immigrants' acculturation strategies. *Migration Letters, 13*(3), 333–349.

Swami, V., Arteche, A., Chamorro-Premuzic, T., & Furnham, A. (2010). Sociocultural adjustment among sojourning Malaysian students in Britain: A replication and path analytic extension. *Social Psychiatry and Psychiatric Epidemiology, 45*, 57–65.

UNHCR. (n.d.). *Convention and protocol relating to the status of refugees*. Retrieved from http://www.unhcr.org/3b66c2aa10

UNHCR. (2017). *What is a refugee?* Retrieved from https://www.unrefugees.org/refugee-facts/what-is-a-refugee/

Ward, C., & Kennedy, A. (1999). The measurement of sociocultural adaptation. *International Journal of Intercultural Relations, 23*(4), 659–677.

Watkins, P. C., Razee, H., & Richters, J. (2012). I'm telling you … the language barrier is the most, the biggest challenge: Barriers to education among Karen refugee women in Australia. *Australian Journal of Education, 56*(2), 126–141.

Weaver, M. (2017, March 30). Syrian refugees: More than 5m in neighbouring countries now, says UN. *The Guardien*. Retrieved from https://www.theguardian.com/world/2017/mar/30/syrian-refugee-number-passes-5m-mark-un-reveals

Wilson, G. P. (2011). *Fitting-in: Sociocultural adaptation of international graduate students*. NERA Conference Proceedings 2011, p. 21. Retrieved from http://digitalcommons.uconn.edu/nera_2011/21

Wilson, J. K. (2013). *Exploring the past, present, and future of cultural competency research: The revision and expansion of the sociocultural adaptation construct* (PhD thesis). Victoria University of Wellington.

World Population Review. (2017). *Germany Population*. Retrieved September 10, 2018, from http://worldpopulationreview.com/countries/germany-population/

Yu, W., & Wang, S. (2011). An investigation into the acculturation strategies of Chinese students in Germany. *Intercultural Communication Studies, 20*(2), 190–210.

Zisberg, A. (2017). Anxiety and depression in older patients: The role of culture and acculturation. *International Journal for Equity in Health, 16*(177), 1–10.

A job-seeking competency model for North Korean defectors who are college students in South Korea

Hyung Joon Yoon, Sungsik Ahn and Eun Hee Kang

ABSTRACT
The purpose of this study was to develop a job-seeking competency model for North Korean defectors (NKDs) who are college students in South Korea. This study adopted the Delphi method with a panel of 17 experts, comprising of NKDs who secured their jobs successfully and South Korean field experts who have hired NKDs or assisted them with their employment. Through three Delphi rounds, 18 job-seeking competencies were identified with the definition, behavioural indicators, and competency significance. In addition, the preliminary utility of the competency model was examined. Implications of the study results and future directions for enhancing the validity and utility of the competency model are discussed.

Introduction

As of September 2017, 31,093 North Koreans have defected to South Korea, according to the Ministry of Unification (2017). In addition, approximately 1,500 people on average have been entering South Korea every year since 2012. Korea Hana Foundation (2017a) collected data from 11,914 North Korean defectors (NKDs) who entered South Korea between 1997 and 2015 and who are 15 years or older, by visiting them for three months in 2016. According to the report, the employment rate of NKDs was 55%, compared to 61% of all South Korean citizens. In terms of monthly average salary, NKDs made 1,629,000 Korean Won compared to 2,368,000 Korean Won that South Koreans were making. NKDs stayed with one employer for 23 months on average while South Koreans spent 69 months with one employer. This indicates that NKDs are having difficulties in retaining their jobs compared to South Koreans. As for NKDs' educational history, 65.2% had high school education or below, 17.9% attended or graduated from two-year colleges, and only 16.5% were attending or graduated from four-year universities. The number of NKDs who were attending any form of undergraduate institutions was 1,375, accounting for 11.7% of the respondents (Korea Hana Foundation, 2017a).

Many studies explored NKD college students' campus life adaptation (Kim, 2014; Lee, 2003; Lee, 2014; Lee, 2014; Lim, 2015; Woo, 2008), learning (Choe, 2016; Gim, 2015; Kim, 2013), dropout (Yu, Jo, Kim, & Bae, 2013), and perceptions about their career development (Choi, 2012; Paek & Yoo, 2011; Park, 2011, 2008). However, there has been limited research regarding NKD college students' job-seeking upon graduation. NKDs pursue higher education to secure decent jobs considering employability (Kim, 2016). According to Korea Hana Foundation (2017b), 90.7% of NKD teenagers had a plan to pursue higher education – 64.9% for 4-year universities, 17.3% for graduate schools, and 8.5% for 2-year colleges. They, however, face a variety of challenges after entering colleges, resulting in a higher dropout rate (9.5%) compared to South Korean students (6.4%) (Kim, 2016). They tend to face a higher level of challenges in employment than those of South Korean graduates even after completing their higher education successfully (Ro & Oh, 2016; Yu et al., 2013). The saying, "It is more difficult to get a job in South Korea than to defect to South Korea," reflects the harsh reality in employment for NKD youths (Ro & Oh, 2016).

Challenges of North Korean defectors in college and employment settings

Ko (2011) explored the adaptation of NKDs to the college life in South Korea. Through interviews with 16 NKDs, he found out a number of challenges that they face such as financial difficulties, discriminations against NKDs, the use of North Korean accents, isolation from South Korean communities, worries regarding South Korean's perceptions and attitudes toward them, and learning about English-derived Korean. In terms of their career development, the interviewees reported that they do not have sufficient information about the different majors for career decision making. In general, they chose majors based on one's career goal, role model, their experiences in China (leading them to major in Chinese), hunches, and suggestions from others (Ko, 2011).

Kim, Lee, and Kim (2013) explored success factors and barriers for NKDs' career development through an interview with 25 NKDs. Success factors were having a good human network, selfless attitude, challenging spirit and desire to learn, preparedness to meet the right opportunity, occupational and social adjustment, understanding South Korea, and stable family. Barriers included their North Korean accent, lack of opportunities due to discriminations, lack of support toward NKDs, relationship issues, long-term unemployment, lack of information about job and training options, age, and lack of systematic support for their career development. Kim et al. (2013) further explored competencies that NKDs lack compared to South Korean workers based on 298 employer samples. Of the respondents, 26.2% pointed out interpersonal relationships and teamwork. Other competencies were communication (17.4%), a sense of responsibility and self-efficacy (17.1%), use of information (14.4%), problem solving (9.7%), resource and tool utilisation (7.4%), and self-management (7.7%). Kim et al. (2013) proposed the necessity to develop an employability competency assessment tool and use it for a training and development purpose.

Employability competencies for NKDs and youths in South Korea

Ro and Oh (2016) explored the success factors of NKD youths in employment. They studied four cases of NKDs who graduated from colleges or universities in South Korea within the last three years and secured employment that lasted for over a year. They found seven success factors from their case-study: (1) minimum English score for passing a gateway during job application, (2) experiencing various job-related activities offered for NKD youths, (3) campus life of acculturation and earning human capital, (4) proactive attitude, not depending on anomalous benefits for NKDs, (5) strengths focusing on overcoming experiences from adversity [defecting to South Korea], (6) Chinese language proficiency, (7) strategical application focusing on employers in favour of NKDs.

While the results of Ro and Oh (2016) is valuable, it would be helpful to consider a more comprehensive model geared toward college students in South Korea to guide NKD college students effectively. Go, Lee, Kim, and Byun (2010), through their Delphi study with a panel of 18 experts, identified 20 job-seeking competencies – combinations of knowledge, skills, and attitudes – for high school and college graduates in South Korea. They classified the competencies into four clusters as follows:

- Knowledge: self-understanding (4), understanding the context of preferred career options (5), knowledge about major and field experience (13), and foreign language ability (16), common knowledge for job seeking (20);

- Skills: career decision making (11), job-related information search (12), networking (9), developing documents for a job application (16), and communication for job seeking (10);
- Attitudes: positive worldview (1), challenging spirit (2), global mindset (18), and work ethic (7); and
- Adaptation: job and organisational commitment (14), field performance (8), interpersonal relationship (6), problem solving (3), utilising resources (19), and self-management and development (14).

Numbers in the parentheses above show the rank orders of the importance of competencies agreed by the panel of experts. These competencies could be used as a basis for training programmes for South Korean college students' employment. With customisations, the results of Go et al. (2010) could also be used for NKD college students.

Career development programmes for NKDs

Roh and Jeon (2009) examined the cognitive change of NKDs who were on their entrance to South Korea at an early stage. They developed the programme based on a needs assessment by identifying 17 needs in 5 areas and pilot tested it with 40 NKDs. The instruction of the training was based on the cognitive information processing (CIP) approach of Sampson, Peterson, Lenz, and Reardon (1992). Through pre-and post-tests conducted using the Korean Career Barrier Inventory (KCBI; Kim, 2002), they found out that a career development programme that helped to reduce (1) career indecision including lack of self-clarity, disparity between self and occupation, indecisiveness, and lack of information regarding different occupations and (2) barriers to career exploration including lack of self-clarity, lack of career information, anxiety regarding the future, and physical inferiority.

Jeon (2003) explored how a five-day job-seeking assistant training programme affects NKDs' self-esteem, self-efficacy for job-seeking activities, perceived significance on the unemployed status, and their expectations regarding new job opportunities. Participants to the programme represented very diverse groups in terms of age ranging from 20s to 60s (80.5% were in their 30s and 40s) and final education ranging from elementary school to college (79.2% had high school education or below). The results showed that the participants gained a significant level of self-efficacy and job search skills such as resume writing and job interview. While Jeon (2003) claimed that a generalised programme for all populations is effective and recommended, Roh and Jeon (2009) suggested that a more targeted programme considering their educational background is necessary, as some measures turned out to be affected by the programme for a highly educated group only.

Purpose of research and research questions

The purpose of this research was to develop a job-seeking competency model for NKD college students for their successful employment in South Korea. To fulfil it, we adopted the following research questions:

(1) *RQ1*. What are the employment competencies in the existing model that should be retained?
(2) *RQ2*. What are the employment competencies that should be added to the existing model?
(3) *RQ3*. What is the perceived level of the importance of competencies that reached consensus?
(4) *RQ4*. What is the preliminary evidence of the utility of the competency model?

Method

We adopted the Delphi method to reach a consensus among different stakeholder groups regarding NKD college students' competencies for employment. This method is known to be effective in addressing opinions rather than facts (Schmidt, 1997). In order to ensure the rigour of this study, we followed the methodologic criteria such as reporting the definition of consensus and selecting termination timing, proposed by Diamond et al. (2014). To further guide the Delphi process, we selected the *borrowed-and-tailored* approach to competency modelling (Rothwell & Lindholm, 1999). It was because there was an existing competency study (Go et al., 2010) for South Korean college students, which include the NKD college students.

Participants and recruitment

Using a snowball sampling method, we reached out to individuals who were in contact with us first and formed a Delphi expert group of 18 individuals. They were: (1) 10 South Korean Field Experts (SKFE) who had hired NKDs before or supported NKDs for their employment for at least 2 years and (2) 8 NKDs who secured jobs successfully and maintained their employment for at least two years after completing a university education. One NKD from the pool did not participate in any round. Sixteen participants responded to the Round 1 survey (a response rate of 88.9%), and 17 responded to the Rounds 2 and 3 of the survey (a response rate of 94.4%; see Table 1 for more details).

Definition of consensus

We employed a five-point scale (1 = *Not at all valid*; 2 = *somewhat not valid*; 3 = *mediocre*; 4 = *somewhat valid*; 5 = *very valid*). Using the scale, we calculated mean scores for the competencies, averaging the mean scores of all participants. To determine consensus, 3.75 out of 5 was used as a cut-off score. The rationale was that the 3.75 represents 75% out of 100%, which is minimally on the valid side.

In order to validate our chosen method, we applied the *percent agreement method* shown in Diamond et al. (2014) with the Round 1 data, and it turned out to result in a drastic change – too few or all items were selected – depending on how to treat answers with *mediocre*. In addition, this method was comparable to the RAND/UCLA Appropriateness Method (RAM; Fitch et al., 2001). With the Round 1 data, the results of using the 3.75 cut-off score were the same as applying a median rating of 4 or 5. The method of using median score was less strict compared to the 3.75 cut-off score with Round 3 data. Therefore, we felt confident with using the cut-off score. For "yes" or "no" questions, we retained or deleted items that had 51% or more consensus among the participants. This was applied when making decisions for inclusion and deletion of behavioural indicators for competencies.

Table 1. Demographics of the Delphi expert group.

Group	No.	Work Setting	Academic Background	Work Experience
South Korean field experts (SKFE)	1	Large corporation	Bachelor's degree	7 years
	2	Hana Foundation	Doctoral student	5 years
	3	Business Consulting	Bachelor's degree	9 years
	4	Brand restaurant	Bachelor's degree	3 years
	5	Rainbow Youth Center	Master's student	8 years
	6	Religious organisation for NKDs	Master's degree	12 years
	7	A small sized company	Bachelor's degree	10 years
	8	Social enterprise	Bachelor's degree	4 years
	9	Rehabilitation equipment business	Bachelor's degree	3 years
	10	NKD employment support foundation	Master's degree	6 years
North Korean defectors (NKDs)	11	Trade company	Bachelor's degree	2 years
	12	IT company & kindergarten	Bachelor's degree	2 years
	13	Facility management company	Bachelor's degree	2 years
	14	Non-government organisation	Bachelor's degree	5 years
	15	Non-government organisation	Bachelor's degree	5 years
	16	Hana Foundation	Bachelor's degree	3 years
	17	Hana Foundation	Master's student	3 years

Process

RQ 1 and 2 were answered through the following three rounds of a modified Delphi administration.

Round 1. Since we used the *borrowed-and-tailored* approach to competency modelling (Rothwell & Lindholm, 1999), we adopted both ratings and open-ended questions. In the first section, we asked them to what extent the existing list of 20 job-seeking competencies (Go et al., 2010) are applicable to NKDs. When doing so, we provided the definition and behavioural indicators of the competencies and invited their thoughts or suggestions about them. In the second section, we asked them to make suggestions for new competencies to be added along with their definitions and behavioural indicators. We gave them one week to respond with a follow-up for those who were not able to complete it within the one-week mark.

Round 2. After analysing the data following the consensus criteria and creating mean scores for each group, we developed a survey with three sections. The first section displayed the mean scores from both groups for each of the competencies that satisfied the consensus criteria. Then, we required them to answer the same question using the five-point scale again to facilitate consensus among the panel. In addition, we listed behavioural indicators based on the feedback from Round 1 and asked them whether they are relevant with "yes" or "no." Furthermore, we invited further suggestions for the behavioural indicators. The second section listed suggested competencies along with their behavioural indicators and asked them to rate them in the same manner as the first section. The third section invited them to answer whether or not they agree to remove competencies that did not meet the consensus criteria. Using an open-ended question for each of the competencies, we asked for further input.

Round 3. Based on the answers to the Round 2 survey, we created two sections. In the first section, we listed two competencies that were controversial between the two groups along with qualitative answers and required them to rate the relevance again using the five-point scale, further inviting suggestions. In the second section, we listed all competencies including the two controversial one and asked them to rate the importance using a five-point scale (1 = not very important; 5 = very important). While it was not to check the consensus, gaining their perspectives on the importance of the competencies deemed critical for providing developmental opportunities to NKD college students (RQ 3).

Post-Delphi: Preliminary validation. Using the competency model developed in this study, we developed and offered a training programme for NKD college students to assess the utility of the newly developed competency model (RQ 4). The training was offered through Hana Foundation, which is a governmental entity that provides training for NKDs' settlement in South Korea.

Findings

Competencies retained (RQ 1)

Through Round 1 and 2, we identified competencies to retain and remove, by applying the consensus criteria (see Table 2). One exception was with the *job and organisational commitment* competency. We made the decision to suggest removal because three panels mentioned that this competency is for those who hold jobs currently and is not relevant to college students who typically do not hold employment. Fifteen out of 17 (88%) agreed to remove the competency. The competencies that met the consensus criteria include *self-understanding, understanding the context of preferred career options, career decision-making, job-related information search, networking, developing documents for job application, communication for job seeking, positive worldview, challenging spirit, field performance, interpersonal relationship, problem solving,* and *utilising resources*, totalling 14 competencies.

Two competencies, *foreign language ability* and *common knowledge*, were found to have conflicting viewpoints, partially satisfying the consensus criteria by one group. The mean score for *foreign language ability* obtained by NKDs in Round 2 was 4.20, exceeding the consensus criteria. In the

Table 2. Results of Round 1 and Round 2 for the existing competencies.

Competency	Decision	Round 1			Round 2		
		Total mean	SKFE mean	NKD mean	Total mean	SKFE mean	NKD mean
1. Self-understanding	Retain	4.13	4.15	4.08	4.56	4.67	4.43
2. Understanding the context of preferred career options	Retain	4.22	4.00	4.58	4.38	4.44	4.29
3. Knowledge about major	Remove	3.59	3.15	4.33	3.40	3.22	3.67
4. Foreign language ability**	Remove	3.19	3.20	3.17	3.71	3.44	4.20
5. Common knowledge**	Remove	3.59	3.40	3.92	3.63	3.78	3.43
6. Career decision making	Retain	4.40	4.30	4.60	4.25	4.56	3.86
7. Job-related information search	Retain	4.07	4.00	4.20	4.06	4.11	4.00
8. Networking	Retain	4.54	4.56	4.50	4.38	4.43	4.29
9. Developing documents for job application	Retain	4.34	4.50	4.08	4.63	4.56	4.71
10. Communication for job seeking	Retain	4.59	4.60	4.58	4.56	4.67	4.43
11. Positive worldview (attitude)	Retain	4.20	4.10	4.40	4.40	4.40	4.43
12. Challenging spirit	Retain	4.19	3.90	4.67	4.33	4.31	4.43
13. Global mindset	Remove	3.13	3.20	3.00	3.13	3.13	3.14
14. Work ethic	Retain	4.37	4.50	4.10	4.80	4.88	4.71
15. Job and organisational commitment	Remove	3.80	3.50	4.40	88% agreement for deletion*		
16. Field performance	Retain	4.09	3.80	4.58	3.81	3.78	3.86
17. Interpersonal relationship	Retain	4.73	4.70	4.80	4.69	4.56	4.86
18. Problem solving	Retain	4.13	4.10	4.20	4.47	4.25	4.71
19. Utilising resources	Retain	3.83	3.65	4.20	4.06	3.78	4.43
20. Self-management and development	Remove	3.90	3.80	4.10	3.67	3.63	3.71

Note: * Based on suggestions indicating that job and organisational commitment is not a competency for job-seeking college students, we asked participants whether they would agree to delete it regardless of the total mean, which is above 3.75. ** These competencies were asked again in Round 3 as one of the group's average rating was higher than 3.75.

case of *common knowledge*, on average, NKDs rated 3.92 in Round 1 whereas SKFEs rated 3.78 in Round 2, both of which exceeded the consensus criteria. To close the gap and make sure they indeed need to be removed, we included these two competencies in the Round 3 survey. As a result, NKDs rated 3.71 and SKFEs rated 3.67 for *foreign language ability*, making the total mean of 3.69. As for *common knowledge*, NKDs rated 3.71 and SKFEs rated 3.25, making the total mean of 3.47. Both confirmed that these competencies need to be removed.

Competencies added (RQ 2)

In Round 1, we asked the participants what competencies should be added along with relevant behavioural indicators. As a result, four competencies – *stress management, receptiveness to cultural difference, communication,* and *commonly-used South Korean vocabulary* – are identified with three to four behavioural indicators for each. Round 2. Applying the consensus criteria, all four competencies are retained (see Table 3). All of the behavioural indicators listed achieved the agreement rates of 70.59% to 100%, meeting the consensus criteria.

Perceived level of importance of the competencies (RQ 3)

Through the Round 3 survey, participants were asked about their perceived levels of importance of the identified competencies identified through Round 1 and 2 (see Table 4). Considering data from

Table 3. Mean scores for newly suggested competencies from Round 2.

Competency	Decision	Overall (N = 17)	SKFE (*n* = 10)	NKD (*n* = 7)
1. Stress management	Retain	4.38	4.44	4.29
2. Receptiveness to cultural difference	Retain	4.47	4.63	4.29
3. Communication	Retain	4.53	4.63	4.43
4. Commonly used South Korean vocabulary	Retain	3.87	3.88	3.86

Table 4. Final list of competencies with importance.

	Overall ($N = 17$)		SKFE ($n = 10$)		NKD ($n = 7$)	
Competency	M	SD	M	SD	M	SD
1. Positive worldview (attitude)	4.59	.51	4.60	.52	4.57	.53
2. Work ethic	4.59	.71	4.60	.70	4.57	.79
3. Self-understanding	4.52	.62	4.60	.52	4.43	.79
4. Job interview	4.45	.62	4.60	.51	4.29	.76
5. Interpersonal relationship	4.49	.62	4.40	.52	4.57	.79
6. Communication+	4.49	.72	4.40	.84	4.57	.53
7. Understanding the context of preferred career options*	4.46	.51	4.20	.42	4.71	.49
8. Developing documents for job application	4.44	.62	4.30	.48	4.57	.69
9. Challenging spirit	4.35	.86	4.40	.84	4.29	.95
10. Problem solving	4.30	.69	4.30	.82	4.29	.49
11. Career decision making	4.27	.66	4.10	.57	4.43	.79
12. Networking	4.25	.66	4.20	.79	4.29	.49
13. Job-related information search	4.17	.60	3.90	.57	4.43	.79
14. Stress management+	4.17	.70	3.90	.74	4.43	.53
15. Receptiveness to cultural difference+	4.15	.70	4.00	.82	4.29	.49
16. Field performance*	3.95	.70	3.60	.52	4.29	.76
17. Utilising resources	3.81	.53	3.90	.57	3.71	.49
18. Commonly used South Korean vocabulary+	3.79	.81	4.00	.82	3.57	.79

Note: * Competencies that showed a statistically significant difference between the two groups. + Competencies newly added for NKD college students.

both groups, top five important competencies for NKD college students appeared to be *positive worldview, work ethic, self-understanding, job interview,* and *interpersonal relationship.*

While the two groups appeared to have similar viewpoints in general, there were some noticeable differences in their perceptions. As a follow up, we ran an independent samples t-test and found out that there was a statistically significant difference between the groups for *understanding the context of career options* ($M = 4.20$, $SD = .42$ for SKFEs; $M = 4.71$, $SD = .49$ for NKDs), $t(15) = -2.32$, $p = .035$) and for *field performance* ($M = 4.28$, $SD = .76$ for SKFEs; $M = 3.60$, $SD = .52$ for NKDs), $t(15) = -2.23$, $p = .041$).

Preliminary evidence of the utility of the competency model

The competency model with the 18 competencies served as a guideline to develop a one-day training programme offered by Hana Foundation. Because we had a limited time of eight hours, addressing all of the competencies in the training programme was impossible. To address this issue, we identified competencies that could be developed via a one-day training. For example, we eliminated the top-ranked competency – *positive worldview* – as it may take a long time to build this quality. Another way to cope with the time constraint while addressing all of the competencies was to convert the competency modelling results into an assessment and administer it. Applying these ideas, we identified seven modules – (1) competency assessment and review, (2) self-understanding, (3) developing documents for job application, (4) job interview, (5) professional ethics and interpersonal relationship, (6) networking and understanding career options, and (7) developing a competency development plan. The behavioural indicators were used for the assessment as well as for developing training contents. In addition, we developed and distributed a short guidebook with 24 pages, listing all of the competencies, their definitions and behavioural indicators, and ideas and resources to develop the competencies.

A total of 12 NKD college students participated in the training programme. While the target population was college students, there were three recent college graduates, one prospective student, seven current students, and one unknown. Evaluation data were collected in two ways. First, a reaction survey was distributed at the end of the training programme. Second, one month after the programme, we contacted the participants and asked about their experience with the training programme.

The effectiveness of the programme: survey responses

Nine out of 12 participants filled out a reaction evaluation survey. In terms of helpful topics for them, we calculated the responses on a five-point scale. *Job interview* was ranked highest (4.62), and the second one was *competency assessment and review* (4.44). *Professional ethics and interpersonal relationships, networking and career options,* and *developing a competency development plan* received 4.25, respectively. *Self-understanding* received 4.00 and *Developing documents for job application* received 3.11. The overall satisfaction with the programme was 4.33, out of 5 points. As for the question, whether or not they will recommend this programme, 66.7% answered *highly recommend* and 33.3% answered *recommend.* Regarding the question, to what extent this programme would be helpful for NKDs' job search, 66.7% answered *very helpful* and 33.3% answered *helpful.*

Qualitative answers from the participants on the reaction survey reflect the ratings for the topics. Five individuals made comments on the helpfulness of the *job interview* module, for example, "*I learned about the necessity of being strategic for job interviews, applying the STAR technic*" and "*It was good to know about my weaknesses through a mock interview.*" Three participants pointed out the usefulness of the competency model, for example, "*It was helpful to gain various information about different competencies*" and "*Knowing about the competencies was effective in developing my goals.*" Two participants commented on *developing a document for a job application,* for example, "*It was helpful to learn about criteria for developing a cover letter and how to make it attractive*" and "*I learned the importance of developing a core message when translating my thoughts into words.*" Others mentioned about the overall helpfulness of the training programme, excellence of the instructors, the programme's effect on career decision-making, and a new perspective in understanding oneself.

The effectiveness of the programme: phone interview responses

Nine participants responded to the phone interview conducted one month after the training. Seven participants (77.8%) pointed out the use of the competency model in the form of assessment. One participant noted,

> I vaguely knew about necessary skill sets for job search. I was amazed by the existence of the 18 competencies assessment. I think that we need to share this with NKDs. In addition, knowing about the differences in perceptions between NKDs and South Korean employers was beneficial.

Other comments included "Identifying and assessing competencies were most impressive in the programme. I was able to reflect upon my major in relation to the competencies," "This training allowed me to explore specific resources including books to develop the competencies," and "This is the third training programme that I attended. This programme was special to me as I was able to understand myself especially my competencies further."

Six participants (66.7%) commented on cover letter and job interview preparation. One participant only discussed job interview preparation while four mentioned both of them. Some comments include "*After the training, I have been using the STAR technic to develop cover letters effectively*" and "*I gained confidence in writing a cover letter after learning about the STAR technic. Hearing about my interviewing skills from three different evaluators was helpful as well.*" Participants discussed other aspects about the programme including understanding oneself through identifying strengths, knowing about the differences in their perceptions between NKDs and South Korean people, and its influence on one's career decision-making. A response from an NKD who was preparing to enter a college is worth noting:

> I participated in the programme when I was preparing for the college entrance exam. This programme was extremely helpful for my career-decision making. Before attending it, I was only thinking of college entrance without a specific forethought and a sense of reality. I had not thought about graduation and the job search process. This programme provided the opportunity for me to rethink about my career directions. I decided not to pursue the college entrance exam at this moment in order to choose a more suitable career option for me.

One respondent shared his story of job seeking that happened after the training programme. While the content is not directly related to the effectiveness of the training programme, it is worth noting as this represents a career barrier that NKDs needs to overcome in South Korea:

> I was able to pass the first screening with my resume and cover letter. I was successful in the first round of the interview with frontline employees. However, I did not pass the final interview with executives. I heard from the hiring manager that the reason seems to be the fact that I am an NKD. Up until the final interview, I did not reveal the fact that I am an NKD but I told the executives that I am an NKD.

Suggestions for further improvement

While the training programme seemed to be effective, there is room for further improvement. Among seven individuals who left comments, three people asked for more time on individualised, one-on-one feedback. Similarly, three participants felt that it was challenging to cover all of the contents in a day. Lastly, five participants wanted to learn more about specific topics based on their priority such as understanding self, foreign language and certifications, basic work-related skills, and cover letter writing.

Discussion

This study addressed the need to identify and develop NKD college students' competencies for job seeking, which is critical in their successful settlement in South Korea (Kim, 2016; Kim et al., 2013; Ro & Oh, 2016; Yu et al., 2013). Comparing the results of this study to Go et al. (2010)'s study with South Korean youths, the first ranked competency was *positive worldview* in both studies. However, *work ethic* and *self-understanding*, 2nd and 3rd ranked competencies in this study, were ranked 7th and 4th, respectively in Go et al. (2010). This shows the unique need of NKD college students compared to South Korean youths.

The identified competencies, in part, are supported by Kim et al. (2013)'s study with NKD workers in South Korea. Highly ranked competencies in this study such as such as *work ethic* (2nd), *interpersonal relationships* (5th), and *communication* (6th) address the weakest points among NKD workers. Other competencies may represent the unique need of NKD college students compared to NKD workers. For example, among the newly added competencies, *communication* was ranked 6th in Kim et al. (2013), while other competencies such as *stress management, receptiveness to cultural difference*, and *commonly-used South Korean vocabulary* were ranked 14th, 15th, and 18th, respectively.

There has been a call for a more customised training programme for NKD college students (Kim et al., 2013). Utilising the competency model, we further developed an assessment tool and a training programme that address the competencies. Gathering data regarding the effectiveness of the assessment tool and the training programme serves as a mechanism to establish the validity of the competency model. Participants reported that the competency assessment tool helped them to understand their needs for job seeking in South Korea. The training programme relieved some level of anxiety of the participants by providing directions on how to improve the competencies. It also contributed to adjusting unrealistic expectations of NKDs regarding their career development.

Limitations

While this study resulted in a functioning competency model for NKD college students, there is a number of limitations. First, more NKDs could have been represented in the Delphi study to make the number of NKDs equivalent to the number of SKFEs to more strictly balance the opinions of the two groups. Second, the data based on the importance of competencies may not represent the actual importance perceived by the population due to the small sample size. Third, while there was a validation process for the competencies that were identified through Round 2 and 3, there is a possibility that more competencies could be added or removed. For example, while we decided to eliminate foreign language ability, especially English, one of the training participants expressed the need to develop it. Lastly, we did not ask the current NKD college students about their needs in this study, although they are the target population.

Future research

To utilise the competency model with confidence in helping NKD college students about their employment, continuous validation is needed with different groups including NKD college students and employers. It would be ideal to conduct a validation study to further refine the model with a large number of NKD students, NKDs who successfully obtained jobs, and employers who are experienced in hiring NKDs. Examining the differences in perceptions between NKD students and employers would also be beneficial in understanding the needs of each other. In addition, in order to use the competency model as a competency assessment tool, its psychometric properties need to be examined. This study could not do so due to the limited number of training participants. It may be realistic to use training programmes as a way to validate and improve the model because most NKDs are reluctant to reveal their identity before establishing rapport. Furthermore, the importance of the competencies needs to be further examined considering different factors such as job seeking stage, gender, and the type of desired employment. For example, according to Choi (2012), female students perceived *self-understanding* with higher importance than male students did. Examining the importance will aid the provision of customised developmental opportunities.

Future practice

While positive effects of the competency model have been observed, future training programmes employing this competency model could be enhanced by addressing the following. First, the competency model could be turned into a more robust competency assessment tool that can assess the needs of each individual as well as the group. The current practice was to use the assessment tool for self-assessment only. Second, the data based on the importance of the competencies can be used to determine the priority of the competencies when a training programme is offered with limited time. Third, the competency assessment results could be used to develop the action plans to further develop the lacking competencies at the individual level. Finally, if a group assessment takes place prior to offering a training programme, more tailored training content can be developed.

This study can serve as a good example of adapting an existing competency model to a specific population that migrated to a new country. Immigrants from different countries and cultures exhibit unique needs as well as common needs with job seeking. Career and guidance practitioners are urged to explore whether there is an existing competency model within the country and find out a way to make it relevant to the immigrant group. Selecting a specific target group, as featured in this study, within the entire immigrant group may increase the effectiveness of training and counselling interventions. If there is no prior competency study from which you can modify, a tailored approach to competency modelling (Rothwell & Lindholm, 1999) should be used. While there are different ways to identify and utilise a competency model, it is desired to involve different stakeholders for data gathering. At least, employers in the country and successful immigrants need to participate in the identification process in order to produce a well-balanced outcome. When determining a need for the target population based on a competency model, the target population must participate in the needs assessment process.

Disclosure statement

No potential conflict of interest was reported by the authors.

References

Choe, Y. (2016). The effects of Pre-service English teachers' tutoring on the English language learning of North Korean refugee college students. *The Journal of the Korea Contents Association, 16*(4), 770–779. Retrieved from http://www.riss.kr/link?id=A101854947

Choi, G. (2012). *A study on the understanding about the careers of university students from North Korea* (Unpublished master's thesis). Sookmyung Women's University, Seoul. Retrieved from http://www.riss.kr/link?id=T12857832

Diamond, I. R., Grant, R. C., Feldman, B. M., Pencharz, P. B., Ling, S. C., Moore, A. M., & Wales, P. W. (2014). Defining consensus: A systematic review recommends methodologic criteria for reporting of Delphi studies. *Journal of Clinical Epidemiology, 67*(4), 401–409. doi:10.1016/j.jclinepi.2013.12.002

Fitch, K., Bernstein, S. J., Aguilar, M. D., Burnand, B., LaCalle, J. R., Lazaro, P., & Kahan, J. P. (2001). *The RAND/UCLA appropriateness method user's manual*. Santa Monica, CA: RAND. Retrieved from https://www.rand.org/pubs/monograph_reports/MR1269.html

Gim, D. (2015). *The current and causes of difficulties in reading and writing of North Korean students in South Korea* (Unpublished master's thesis). Ewha Womans University, Seoul. Retrieved from http://www.riss.kr/link?id=T13819412

Go, J., Lee, G., Kim, S., & Byun, J. (2010). A study on defining the concept and estimating the weight of employment competency for the youth. *The Journal of Vocational Education Research, 29*(2), 17–42. Retrieved from http://www.riss.kr/link?id=A82400527

Jeon, Y. (2003). *A study on the effects of employment support program for North Korean refugees* (Unpublished master's thesis). Korea University of Technology and Education, Cheonan. Retrieved from http://www.riss.kr/link?id=T9377267

Kim, E. (2002). A study for the development and validation of the Korean college students` career barrier inventory. *The Korean Journal of Counseling and Psychotherapy, 14*(1), 219–240.

Kim, H., Lee, Y., & Kim, M. (2013). *Study on enhancing competency for employability of North Korean refugees (basic research No. 2013–19)*. Seoul: Korea Research Institution for Vocational Education and Training. Retrieved from http://www.riss.kr/link?id=M13473327

Kim, J. (2014). *A qualitative study on the university adjustment of North Korean refugees living in Daejeon city* (Unpublished master's thesis). Korea University, Seoul. Retrieved from http://www.riss.kr/link?id=T13542274

Kim, S. H. [Sung Hwan]. (2013). *A study on the English learning of Saeturmin [North Korea Defectors] students in a Korean university* (Unpublished master's thesis). Chongshin University, Seoul. Retrieved from http://www.riss.kr/link?id=T13232321

Kim, S. H. [Sung Hwan]. (2016). *A study on the improvement of North Korean defectors' adaptability to university life in the Republic of Korea*. Seoul: Korea Hana Foundation. Retrieved from http://www.riss.kr/link?id=M14481613

Ko, G. (2011). *Study on the adjustment of North Korean refugee students to college life* (Unpublished master's thesis). Kyung Hee University, Seoul.

Korea Hana Foundation. (2017a). *2016 Bughan-italjumin jeongchagsiltaejosa [The status of settlement of North Korean defectors in South Korea in 2016]*. Seoul: Korea Hana Foundation. Retrieved from http://kiss.kstudy.com/public/public2-article.asp?key=50895266

Korea Hana Foundation. (2017b). *2016 Talbuk-chungsonyun siltaejosa [The status of North Korean teenage defectors in South Korea in 2016]*. Seoul: Korea Hana Foundation. Retrieved from http://www.riss.kr/link?id=M14481550

Lee, C. Y. (2014). *Effects of acculturative stress and resilience on depression of college students from North Korea* (Unpublished master's thesis). Yonsei University, Seoul. Retrieved from http://www.riss.kr/link?id=T13444577

Lee, E. (2014). *Cultural adaptive aspects of the university students defected from North Korea and their community experiences* (Unpublished master's thesis). Ewha Womans University, Seoul. Retrieved from http://www.riss.kr/link?id=T13388714

Lee, H. K. (2003). *A study on the university life experience of North Koreans defectors in South Korea* (Unpublished master's thesis). Ewha Womans University, Seoul. Retrieved from http://www.riss.kr/link?id=T8586508

Lim, B. (2015). *Psychological problems of female university students that have defected from North Korea during the acculturation to South Korean society* (Unpublished master's thesis). Myongji University, Seoul. Retrieved from http://www.riss.kr/link?id=T13865686

Ministry of Unification. (2017). *Choegeunhyeonhwang [Recent statistics]*. Retrieved from http://www.unikorea.go.kr/unikorea/business/NKDefectorsPolicy/status/lately/

Paek, Y. O., & Yoo, J. P. (2011). *How North Korean refugees experience college: Implications for policy and institutional support*. Seoul: Korea Hana Foundation.

Park, S. (2011). *A qualitative study on carrier barriers perceived by college students who are the North Korean defectors* (Unpublished master's thesis). Sookmyung Women's University, Seoul. Retrieved from http://www.riss.kr/link?id=T12288360

Park, S. Y. (2008). *North Korean immigrant youth's life strategies in the career search process* (Unpublished master's thesis). Yonsei University, Seoul. Retrieved from http://www.riss.kr/link?id=T11220530

Ro, E., & Oh, I. (2016). A case study on employment success factor of North Korean youth defector graduated from universities in South Korea. *The Research Institute of Korean Education, 34*(4), 235–264. Retrieved from http://www.riss.kr/link?id=A103231943.

Roh, K., & Jeon, Y. (2009). The research on the effectiveness of a short-term career development program for North Korean defectors with early stage in their entrance: Focus on the career cognitive change of learners. *Unification Policy Studies, 18*(1), 245–277. Retrieved from http://www.riss.kr/link?id=A99890657

Rothwell, W. J., & Lindholm, J. E. (1999). Competency identification, modelling and assessment in the USA. *International Journal of Training and Development, 3*(2), 90–105. doi:10.1111/1468-2419.00069

Sampson, J. P., Peterson, G. W., Lenz, J. G., & Reardon, R. C. (1992). A cognitive approach to career services: Translating concepts into practice. *The Career Development Quarterly, 41*, 67–74.

Schmidt, R. C. (1997). Managing Delphi surveys using nonparametric statistical techniques. *Decision Sciences, 28*(3), 763–774.

Woo, Y. (2008). *A Study of North Korea Students` Adjustment to South Korean College Life* (Unpublished master's thesis). University of North Korean Studies, Seoul. Retrieved from http://www.riss.kr/link?id=T11559282

Yu, S., Jo, M. S., Kim, K., & Bae, H. (2013). *A study on measures and the problem of the drop-out rate of North Korean refugee university students*. Seoul: Korea Hana Foundation. Retrieved from http://www.riss.kr/link?id=M13944595

Appendix. Final outcome: A list of competencies.

Table AI. List of competencies, definitions, and behavioural indicators for NKD college students.

Competency	Definition This competency is to ...:	Behavioural Indicators
1. Positive worldview (attitude)	Keep a positive attitude in a given situation and to keep performing one's job	• Be aware of the current and past situation in a positive way. • Use positive language in daily talks. • Keep a positive attitude in daily tasks.
2. Work ethic	Keep basic work ethics and appropriate attitude as a professional	• Complete tasks proactively. • Understand and apply regulations and work ethics. • Understand the contribution of my work to the organisation and society. • Meet deadlines responsively. • Differentiate official relationship from private in the organisation and behave appropriately. • Work with integrity and sincerity.
3. Self-understanding	Be aware of traits and circumstances of oneself objectively in choosing the first occupation	• Identify occupations that fit oneself through job experiences. • Increase self-awareness using career assessments (interest, ability, values, etc.). • Understand family and financial circumstances objectively. • Understand strengths and weaknesses of my physical traits. • Identify my level of readiness for job seeking compared to other students. • Understand my psychological and emotional conditions.

(*Continued*)

Table AI. Continued.

Competency	Definition This competency is to ... :	Behavioural Indicators
4. Job Interview	Understand various situation during interviews and express my intention/ idea clearly	• Understand the meaning and intention of interviewer's questions and answer coherently. • Be able to give self-introduction and presentations confidently. • Be able to express and present clearly in different situations. • Identify someone who can help me with a mock interview and provide feedback. • Be able to speak English during an interview if necessary. • Be able to give a summary of my resume or cover letter during an interview. • Understand desired attitude, etiquette, gesture, etc. for an effective interview. • Build a self-image with appropriate attires and make-up to impress interviewers.
5. Interpersonal relationship	Manage human relationships effectively at work	• Understand etiquette and keep it daily. • Introduce myself first when meeting coworkers for the first time. • Identify and use official titles of coworkers in the organisation. • Listen, question and cooperate with coworkers for an amicable working relationship. • Persuade and lead team members to perform well. • Seek help from coworkers in a polite manner. • Recognise conflicts sensitively and resolve it appropriately. • Assert my idea or opinion with respect. • Understand how to respond to problems of internal and external customers and respond appropriately.
6. Communication	Communicate effectively with others	• Understand other's intention before I say. • Communicate with others rationally, not emotionally. • Reject other's requests gently without hurting them. • Express my opinion or idea indirectly rather than directly.
7. Understanding the context of preferred career options	Collect and understand information of target occupations and industries	• Identify and understand information of target occupations, employers and industries via online searching or networking. • Identify and understand information of various employers in the target industry. • Identify requirements of target occupations or employers.
8. Developing documents for job application	Write resumes and cover letters for target occupations	• Be competent in writing resumes and cover letters for target occupations and employers. • Identify someone to help me with revising resumes and cover letters. • Identify the process of target employers to submit resumes and cover letters. • Identify and write required contents for cover letters. • Identify and write about the specific experience as an NKD for the required tasks. • Develop a career portfolio to present my strengths and uniqueness.
9. Challenging spirit	Address challenging situations proactively and keep trying without fear of failing	• Keep proactive and confident attitudes in a job. • Keep trying to complete difficult tasks with persistence.

(*Continued*)

Table AI. Continued.

Competency	Definition This competency is to . . . :	Behavioural Indicators
		• Understand common difficulties for new employees and keeping trying to overcome those. • Keep challenging oneself despite prior failures or mistakes. • Be proactive in human relationships and tasks in the organisation.
10. Problem solving	Understand problems and solve them	• Ask help from supervisors or coworkers to find best solutions when facing a problem. • Be proactive to find solutions when facing a problem. • Define the causes of a problem in a logical and reasonable manner. • Identify and suggest creative solutions for problem solving. • Choose and implement a solution in a logical and reasonable manner. • Identify my role in the process of problem solving and be proactive in my role.
11. Career decision-making	Explore and choose a career option to pursue one's career goal	• Set specific career goals by searching for various information. • Identify options for career goals by collecting information. • Evaluate and choose feasible options for each career goal. • Evaluate one's employability based on the chosen goals and options.
12. Networking	Build and utilise the human network for job-seeking activities	• Understand the nature and utility of human networking. • Identify individuals to contact for networking (professors, seniors, recruiters, relatives, etc.). • Keep in touch with whom can provide job- or career-related information. • Collect information for job seeking from my network.
13. Job-related information search	Explore, evaluate, and utilise information about occupations and recruitment	• Identify locations or persons for occupational or recruitment information. • Identify and utilise various information resources. • Collect job-related information through effective searching. • Evaluate the reliability and appropriateness of collected job-related information. • Apply appropriate information to oneself considering one's situation.
14. Stress management	Manage and reduce one's stress	• Identify my own ways to reduce stress. • Manage my stress to ensure my performance at work. • Recognise the time when I am under stress. • Reduce my stress in order not to affect others.
15. Receptiveness to cultural difference	Be receptive to different cultures than mine	• Understand and be receptive to a different culture, circumstance, or values than mine. • Accept the differences between others and me. • Coordinate different opinions and values between others and me.
16. Field performance	Perform actual tasks of the target occupation	• Experience job-related tasks through club activities, field practicum, volunteering, internship, etc. • Experience job-related task after understanding the target occupation.

(*Continued*)

Table AI. Continued.

Competency	Definition This competency is to ... :	Behavioural Indicators
		• Experience job-related tasks with a diverse population (especially people born and raised in South Korea) • Experience job-related tasks beyond qualification or English tests.
17. Utilising resources	Choose and utilise resources such as computers and devices for work	• Be competent in using basic office software (Word, Powerpoint, Excel, etc.) and search online. • Understand devices related to my work, and choose, and utilise them. • Identify various information media, and choose and utilise them for work.
18. Commonly used South Korean vocabulary	Use South Korean vocabulary for smooth communication in South Korea	• Understand and use commonly used South Korean vocabulary. • Understand and use South Korean vocabulary that is commonly used in the target occupation. • Understand and use commonly used foreign words and internet terms. • Understand and use foreign words and internet terms that are commonly used in the target occupation.

Families left behind at the source of migration: implications for career guidance practitioners

Sachin Kumar

ABSTRACT

Issues surrounding migration are receiving unprecedented attention at the global, regional, as well as national levels. However, a review of the literature shows that there is more focus on international migration compared to internal migration. Further, there is more emphasis on issues related to the migration destination rather than those at the source of migration. Using the cultural preparation process model as a framework, this paper aims to understand the career and livelihood planning needs of those who are left behind. The left-behind families of pine resin tappers in the Changar region of the Indian Himalayas are presented as a case study to draw the attention of career guidance and counselling professionals to this unattended population.

Introduction

Puruba se aai reliya pachhun se jahajiya
Piya ke ladi lei gai ho.
Reliya hoi gai mor sabatiya piya ke ladi lei gai ho
Reliya na bairi jahajiya na bairi uhai paiswai bairi ho
Deswa deswa bharmai waiuhai paiswai bairi ho
(The train came from the east and the ship came from the west
and took my husband away.
Railway has become my co-wife who has taken my husband away.
Rail is not my enemy, ship is not my enemy, money is my enemy
which makes my husband go from country to country.)
An excerpt from a folk song in Bhojpuri dialect of the Hindi
language heard from the wives of migrant workers quoted in Nārāyaṇa, 2017, p. 31

Migration is a part of human history. But the twenty-first century has been termed as a century of people on the move: a century of migrants (Guterres, 2008, June 16). As a consequence, issues surrounding migration are under the spotlight at the global, regional, as well as national levels. A review of migration studies points out that there is more focus on international migration compared to internal migration to the point that the term *migration* is used interchangeably with *international migration* (King & Skeldon, 2010). By contrast, temporary, seasonal, circular and short-term migrants have not attracted enough attention. Also, there is more emphasis on issues at the migration destination than those at the source of migration. Further, while the rights of and support services for migrant workers are extensively discussed now (e.g. Baruah & Cholewinski, 2006; Hickey, Narendra, & Rainwater, 2013), the discussion on situation of those who are left behind is a relatively recent phenomenon (e.g. Rajan, 2013). From the career guidance and counselling perspective, the assumptions of contemporary career theory and practice do not seem to adequately address the career development needs experienced by migrants (Bimrose & McNair, 2011). While a few guidance and counselling practitioners and researchers have reported their work with and studies of international migrants (e.g. Cohen, Arnold, & O'Neill, 2011), guidance support services and interventions for those who are left behind remain largely unreported. The paper aims to understand the career and livelihood planning needs of those who are left behind. The opening section of this paper sums up the magnitude of internal, temporary, and seasonal migration, largely in the Indian context and highlights the issues of those who are left behind. The paper proposes the cultural preparation process model (Arulmani, 2011, 2014a) as a framework to understand issues at the migration source. Taking the seasonal migration of male members of the families in the Changar region of the Indian Himalayas as case study, the next section draws attention to some of the issues faced by the families left behind at the source of migration. The proposition that climate-change induced migration disrupts the community's cultural preparation status equilibrium (Arulmani, 2011) is explored. The final section of the paper proposes a livelihood planning perspective with an advocacy approach that guidance and counselling professionals could draw upon to address issues at the migration source and point the community towards a new equilibrium.

Internal, temporary, seasonal migration and left-behind families

There were 763 million internal migrants in the world in 2013, three times the number of international migrants (Bell & Charles-Edwards, 2013). In the context of the developing world, internal migration has been found to be a particularly important phenomenon in terms of both the potential benefits and associated challenges (de Wind & Holdaway, 2005, October 25–26). In the Indian context as well, migration in search of livelihoods, as a survival strategy is pervasive. Based on census data from the last three consecutive rounds the recent Economic Survey (Government of India, 2017) shows that the number of migrants stating economic reasons as the reason for migration rose from 26 million in 1991 to 51 million in 2011 which was 8.1% and 10.5% of the total workforce respectively. Male migration for economic reasons rose from 9.6% in 1991 to 12.7% in 2011 while female migration for economic reasons increased from 4.4% to 5.7% during this period. Interestingly, during 1991–2001 the annual growth rate of the work force and growth rate of migrant workforce remained identical at 2.4% while during the next decade the growth rate of migrants almost doubled at nearly 4.5% but the workforce growth rate actually started to fall. New estimates based on railway passenger traffic data reveal annual work-related migration of about 9 million people after 2011. Various estimates have been made using direct and indirect evidence (e.g. Deshingkar & Akter, 2009; Mazumdar, Neetha, & Agnihotri, 2013). The share of migrants in the workforce is estimated to lie between 17% and 29%. It is further estimated that there are 10 million workers who can be characterised as short-term or seasonal migrant workers who reside in rural India which is over 5.5 times the number of people who move permanently on account of work every year (Chandrashekhar, 2017). It also means that an equivalent number of families are left to live on their own. The left-behind are a much larger group than the migrant group (Toyota, Yeoh, & Nguyen, 2007). Hence, the first key imperative to draw attention to these populations derives from the sheer magnitude of their numbers.

On the other hand, the rates of temporary and seasonal migration have been found to be high in remote rural areas with low agro-ecological potential, poor access to credit and other prerequisites for occupational diversification (Bird & Deshingkar, 2009). Seasonal migration is adopted as a survival strategy by people in chronic poverty who are largely illiterate and belong to the "lower" castes: scheduled castes (SCs), scheduled tribes (STs), and Muslim communities, the people at the margins of society (e.g. Bird & Deshingkar, 2009; Deshingkar & Akter, 2009; Keshri & Bhagat, 2011). Scheduled castes and tribes, because of their extremely disadvantaged status, are listed in the constitution of India as populations for whom special privileges are to be provided (Government of India, n.d.). Hence, the second key imperative derives from the need for an unambiguous social justice agenda for guidance and counselling practitioners (e.g. Ivey & Collins, 2003). There have been repeated calls as well for an inclusive vocational psychology grounded in social action with a focus on the marginalised (e.g. Blustein, 2015).

Migration of men in search of livelihood has been found to have both positive and negative impacts on the left-behind families (e.g. Démurger, 2015) especially on women (e.g. Desai & Banerji, 2008; Jetley, 1987; Ullah, 2017) and children (e.g. Antman, 2013; Roy, Singh, & Roy, 2015). Evidence from different parts of India including the states of Kerala (Gulati, 1993), Bihar (Datta & Mishra, 2011), Odisha (Agasty & Patra, 2014), Rajasthan (Aajeevika Bureau, 2006) and Himachal Pradesh (Kishtwaria, Thakur, & Rana, 2007) shows that while on the one hand, women's autonomy and independence increased in a few instances, work burdens increased and difficulties of basic survival were compounded. Distinctions have been made between migration for accumulation of wealth and migration for survival (e.g. Deshingkar & Start, 2003; Smita, 2007) where the former is resorted to for extra income and latter is generally distress-driven. It is evident from the literature that seasonal and temporary migration are not helping the family come out of a subsistence level existence and they are barely able to survive (Mishra, 2016). It is important that this very significant segment of the population, which is huge in number yet invisible from the eyes of practitioners and policy makers, is given voice and visibility so that their issues can be adequately addressed.

The cultural preparation process model: A theoretical reference point

While a wide range of factors contribute to the push and pull that affect migration, the literature has repeatedly shown intrinsic links between culture and migration (e.g. Sam & Berry, 2010), particularly with reference to career and livelihood planning. Hence, this paper takes a cultural approach and uses Arulmani's (2011, 2014a) cultural preparation process model as a theoretical reference point to view career and livelihood planning issues at the source of migration. Over the last few years this model has informed the development of culturally grounded interventions for various aspects of career guidance (e.g. social cognitions: Arulmani & Abdulla, 2007; career decision making: Arulmani, 2010; assessment and testing: Arulmani, 2015). Of particular relevance to this paper is the recent application of this model to develop culturally sensitive approaches to serve the career development needs of refugees and immigrants in the international context (Arulmani, 2016). This paper extends the model to understand issues at the source of migration as well because it "... contextualizes career interventions for local contexts" (McMahon, 2014, p. 23). The observation that culture, through a complex and enduring process, prepares individuals and groups to engage with work, occupation, and career in a certain manner, lies at the heart of the cultural preparation process model. The model rests upon a set of 5 inter-related propositions (Arulmani, 2011, 2014a) which are paraphrased as follows. Macro global trends (e.g. changes in social orientations, economic cycles, political upheavals, technological transformations, and natural disasters such as climate change or drought) form the backdrop against which people's engagement with work is defined. The socialising forces of enculturation engender a cultural preparation status equilibrium in relation to work orientations. In other words, enculturation brings about an equipoise in the manner in which an individual or a group engages with work roles. This equilibrium is influenced by three key factors: patterns of social organisation along the individualism-collectivism continuum, patterns of value attribution, and the processes of role allocation. The model further proposes that human beings' unique ability for cultural learning enables the internalisation of lessons accrued through the interaction between the individual and the group, ultimately leading to a state of equilibrium. A set of ideas, opinions, and convictions about career and career development processes, which have been termed as career beliefs (Arulmani & Nag-Arulmani, 2004), foster the maintenance of this equilibrium. The model points out that with various macro changes come the forces of acculturation requiring the individual and/or the group to change and align themselves to a new way of engaging with work. Acculturative forces may be consonant or dissonant with the existing equilibrium. While consonant acculturative forces further stabilise the existing career preparation status equilibrium, dissonant forces disrupt this equilibrium. Given its focus on local cultural realities, the cultural preparation process model offers a theoretical vantage point from which to view cultural processes underlying career and livelihood and was selected to be the framework within which the present study was conducted.

The study: the case of left-Behind families of pine-resin tappers in the Changar region of India

Background

Changar region: the locale

Changar is located in the rain shadow area of inner Shiwalik range of the Indian Himalayas (the state of Himachal Pradesh, India). Changar is commonly associated with remoteness, scarcity, and a rugged-degraded terrain. Although rapid road construction in recent years has improved access to the region, water scarcity and degradation of the natural resource base have been aggravated over the years due to a steady increase in human and livestock populations as well as dwindling social mechanisms to regulate the use and protection of natural resources. A lack of convergence of the government's developmental activities and rigid hierarchical community relationships within villages impede development initiatives (GTZ, 2006; Kotru, n.d.; Planning Commission & UNDP, 2003). As a result of limited irrigation coverage and the degraded nature of the land, agriculture is no longer a viable and sustainable livelihood option in this region (GTZ, 2006; Planning Commission & UNDP, 2003). Working together, these factors have culminated in massive employment related migration.

Migration for pine resin tapping from Changar region

Forced by the environmental exigencies listed above, men migrate out of their homes in search of livelihoods. The uniqueness of migration from this region is the fact that men seasonally migrate as semi-skilled pine resin tappers. Some migrate a few kilometres away in the same district, others go more than a thousand kilometres to Nepal and Bhutan, crossing international borders for better remuneration. One of the most important non-timber forest products, resins are metabolic by-products of plant tissues and used as food and medicine. They are also an important export commodity (Giri, Prasad, Pandey, Prasad, & Baboo, 2008). People from Changar are known for their pine resin tapping skills and hence they are much sought after. Men from about 100 families go out each year for 8–10 months leaving behind the women, children, and the elderly. Despite their hard work the nature of their work does not meet the criteria of decent work as defined by the ILO (1999). Their income is meagre, the working environment is unsafe, collective representation is absent, and social security coverage is negligible.

Propositions

As mentioned in the opening section, this paper aims at understanding career and livelihood planning needs of those who are left behind at the source of migration in the particular context of families of pine resin tappers in the Changar region on Indian Himalayas. Based on the available literature, the description of the Changar region and push–pull factors related to seasonal migration for pine resin tapping, the following propositions guide this study:

- Climate change induced seasonal migration for pine resin tapping by the men of the Changar region causes a dissonant disturbance in the cultural preparation status equilibrium of those left behind at the source of migration.
- This disturbance has resulted in adverse consequences for left-behind families in terms of increased economic and physical hardships, weakening family cohesion, emotional deprivation, and sub-optimal utilisation of benefits being provided by the government.

- Career and livelihood practitioners could become a consonant acculturative force to help the left-behind families attain a new cultural preparation status equilibrium and thereby ameliorate their life situation.

Method

A case study approach is recommended when the research does not manipulate the behaviour of those involved, when it aims at covering contextual conditions, the boundaries are not clear between the phenomenon and the context, and when the aim is to understand the "hows" and "whys" of the phenomenon under study (Baxter & Jack, 2008; Yin, 2003). Since the present study fits the above criteria, a case study approach was taken. The approach was explorative and descriptive with the unit of analysis being the disturbance of the cultural preparation status of the left-behind families of pine resin tappers. The study drew upon the methods of focus group discussion and individual, one-on-one interviews. The data were recorded in the form of field notes and a reflexive journal. The interactions were held in Hindi, the local language. In all cases, participants were informed about the purpose of the study and were given the option of withdrawing. As the primary researcher, I conducted the study in two phases during September-October, 2016. I have been a college lecturer to students from the mountain regions of Himachal Pradesh (the province in which this study was conducted) as well as a voluntary development practitioner in these regions for nearly two decades. I hold an M.Phil. in Career and Livelihood Planning and have been a part of various career development initiatives at national and regional levels. I developed partnerships with development organisations working in the region and through them, with headmen of the village panchayats (a unit of local self-governance at the village level). Together this group constituted a panel of key informants for this study. The data for the various sections of this study emerged both from primary and secondary sources. Table 1 presents a summary of data sources and methods used.

In the first phase, along with a desk review of government and other reports (e.g. GTZ, 2006; Planning Commission & UNDP, 2003) I consulted the key informants to identify villages that recorded the highest number of left-behind families. Six villages were selected based on this information. Next, I visited these villages over the period of a week. The objectives of this phase were to understand: the environmental context, occupational dynamics of pine resin tapping, and the issues and concerns of the left-behind families of the pine resin tappers. Based on my prior knowledge of the region and consultations with the key informants I developed a semi-structured interview schedule. A total of 15 questions were formulated pertaining to the reasons (e.g. Why do people migrate from this region for pine resin tapping?), the process (e.g. How and when do they migrate?), and the consequences (What are the advantages and disadvantages of this migration for the family?) of migration for pine resin rapping. One focus group discussion (FGD) was held in each village and the same questions were asked in all six discussions. Each group comprised pine resin tappers and their family members and were recruited by the partner voluntary organisation. Each FGD lasted for about 60–90 min and was concluded once a point of data saturation was achieved. It was possible to triangulate the information obtained through the FGDs, through an in-depth interview with the former headman of one of the villages and a telephonic interview with an ex-labour contractor in the

Table 1. Data sources and methods.

Section	Data source	Method
Internal, temporary, seasonal migration and left -behind families	Secondary	Literature review
Environmental context of Changar region	Secondary + Primary	Literature review + Interviews with key informants
Migration for pine resin tapping	Primary	Focus Group Discussion
Key themes	Primary	Interviews

pine resin tapping business. This phase of study helped to understand the locale and context and consequences of pine resin tapping in this region.

In the second phase, data were collected from two main sources: PS, a 55-year-old male development practitioner and, the left-behind family of BM, a 40-year-old, male pine resin tapper. The results and discussion section of this paper largely draws from the data collected during this phase of study. I interviewed PS who heads a non-governmental organisation (NGO) working with families of pine resin tappers. The interview lasted approximately 90 min in PS's field office in Changar. PS's work involved connecting pine resin tappers' families with government schemes and creating alternate sources of income for them. He provided valuable information pertaining to the altered role of women as the head of the family when the men folk were away and the prevailing interface between policy and implementation of support services. Secondly, keeping the case study approach in view, one family was selected for more in-depth interactions. In consultation with the key informant panel, the following criteria was set up for selection of the most suitable family: left-behind family of a pine-resin tapper belonging to the tribal and/or minority community entitled to benefits of welfare schemes of the government; willingness and enthusiasm to be a part of the study; experience of at least one instance of denial of a benefit due to the absence of male head of household. BM, a Muslim Gujjar was recommended by the key informants since this family fulfilled the above criteria. I engaged with the family over a period of three days. BM's family comprises his mother SB (63 years), his wife BB (37 years), his daughter MB (13 years), and his son KU (11 years). Conversations and interviews were held over the three days. The questions expanded on the semi-structured interview format used in Phase 1 and focused on problems encountered and the ways this family dealt with them. Examples of questions include: What has been your traditional occupation and why did you leave that? What made the men in your family choose pine resin tapping as a profession? What have been the benefits and drawbacks of this occupation? What problems/hardships do you face in the absence of men in your family? How do you cope with the problems?

Data analysis

The data comprised interview transcripts, field notes, and reflexive journal maintained by the author. The data were subjected to thematic analysis. I worked through the entire data set to identify themes in the data that contributed to the research propositions. Both open and axial coding were used. With a view to establish the validity of the findings, I iteratively presented emerging themes and trends in the data to PS for his feedback, comments, and validation.

Results and discussion

The one family selected for the in-depth study belonged to the Gujjar Muslim community and my interaction with the family provided information related to the context of this community in this region. Gujjars are one of the tribal communities of Himachal Pradesh (Negi, 1976). Traditionally they have been nomadic pastoralists engaged in buffalo rearing. They gradually became semi-sedentary in different parts of Himachal Pradesh practicing agriculture on small land holdings during the season and travelling with their buffaloes during rest of the months. But for the last 6–7 decades or so, they have settled around the Changar region. While they have continued buffalo rearing and supplying milk to the residents of the local community (the host community), they also work on their farms to cultivate wheat and maize. Hence, it can be said that a certain cultural preparation status equilibrium related to their livelihood did persist despite the change of locations. But once grazing grounds started to dwindle due to weather exigencies and weed infestation, this equilibrium was disrupted. As a result, Gujjar men began to emulate members of the host community, by seasonally migrating for pine resin tapping. Going back to the cultural preparedness model it could be said that the Gujjar community was enculturated to follow a blend of a pastoral as well as an agricultural life style. They experienced the equilibrium of earning their livelihoods by supplying milk and cultivating crops. The global trend of weather changes caused a loss of livelihood and therefore a disruption of their cultural preparation status equilibrium. At the same time they experienced the acculturative influence of the host culture whose members practiced pine resin tapping.

The key themes that emerged from the analysis of the data are now presented and discussed.

Erosion of traditional livelihood base

The people in the Changar region have been practicing agriculture and animal husbandry for many centuries. Gujjars are recent settlers in this region and as discussed above, they have traditionally been a pastoral-agricultural ethnic group across generations and are skilled in the rearing of buffaloes. Despite change of locations, they continued their traditional occupations. But over the last decade, due to the degradation of pasture land, this traditional occupation has been severely affected. For example, SB says: "We do rear buffaloes because it is part of the tradition. But it is more of a burden and no longer supports our livelihoods."

At the same time, as PS, the development practitioner explains: "Weather extremes, deteriorating soil quality, weed infestation, and crop destruction by monkeys have made agriculture almost impossible. Agriculture is no longer the mainstay of people in this region."

These climate induced macro environmental changes have contributed significantly to the alteration of the cultural preparedness status equilibrium related to the livelihood of the Gujjars.

Pine resin tapping: intergenerational replacement of traditional community occupation

Due to the pernicious erosion of the traditional livelihood base, options such as seasonal migration for pine resin tapping seem to have emerged as a key survival strategy. In the case of Gujjars, they have shifted to this occupation over the last three generations. This alteration has not only disturbed traditional occupational patterns but has also pulled younger male members of the family away from their traditional occupation toward pine resin tapping. As SB says, "Earlier my father used to go along with my uncles for pine resin tapping. Then my brother and husband started going. Now, my son follows the same footsteps." While the consonance-dissonance value of this change in livelihood equilibrium could be argued, the fact remains that this occupational shift is not a temporary move, but one that seems to have been transmitted across at least three generations.

Debt trap

Typically a pine resin tapper such as BM is paid an advance against the agreed upon total amount from the labour contractor before he goes out for pine resin tapping. The remaining amount is paid when the tapper returns at the end of the season. A part of the advance amount is given to the family for its expenses. However as BB, the wife of BM says: "The salary is paid for a duration of nine months, but is spent within three to four months for running the household." The family is forced to avail more loans from local money lenders, banks, and friends. Therefore by the time someone like BM returns, the family is already in debt. The remaining money from his salary is insufficient to pay off the debts. BM has no other option other than to take another advance and go out pine resin tapping once again. Hence, an occupation such as this places families in cyclic debt traps. So, while the available literature says that the families of migrant workers enjoy better financial health due to regular remittances (e.g. Adams, 2011; Démurger, 2015), in the case of BM and other pine resin tappers migrants from Changar region, this does not hold ground.

Economic hardships: consequences for women

A further outcome of this disturbance in equilibrium is the expansion of the traditional role of the woman of the household from homemaker and caregiver, to worker. BM's wife BB has to take up odd jobs as a daily wage worker in order to support the family financially and to repay debts. SB says:

> Women have to supplement family income. Earlier I used to go too but now my daughter-in-law goes as a daily wage earner. Other women of the extended family work as maid servants, daily wage labourers on construction sites, or gather minor forest produce.

This double burden of work and role expansion affects the well-being of the left-behind. With a personal income and control over spending the transition from homemaker to worker seems empowering at first, this empowerment seems notional even in the short run.

Physical burden

Other than financial hardships, the migration of the males in the community sets in motion a chain of events affecting the physical and the emotional health of those who are left behind and the erstwhile cultural preparation status equilibrium for them too is disturbed. In the absence of the men of the house, SB's daughter in-law BB has to take care of the livestock, arrange for fodder, milk them, supply the milk, and take care of their health and hygiene. In many instances, rearing livestock does not seem to be a profitable activity and it is becoming increasingly difficult to arrange fodder for the animals. Taking care of livestock is an extremely tedious and time consuming task, adding burden to the woman's health and well-being. On the agricultural side, farms are left uncultivated because of erratic rainfall, shortage of farm workers, uncontrollable weed growth, and pest menaces. It seems, therefore, that traditional role allocation, despite being patriarchal and stereotypical, did adhere to the principle of division of labour and being left to fend for themselves implies that women related to the men who migrate, are overburdened with household chores, care work, and part time wage earning responsibilities. Furthermore, the children also are required to share some of the burden of the women of the family. For example, they arrange water for the family and the animals, carrying 20–30 l head loads from water sources away from the village. PS observes: "Children in early adolescence become care-givers to their younger siblings or elderly people. They even start working at a very young age to augment family income."

Emotional privations

Other than economic and physical hardships, families of pine resin tappers, including that of SB's family suffer from obvious psychological privations owing to the long term absence of the male members. The emotional vacuum left behind by BM seems to be debilitating for the entire family. As BB says, "I wish my husband would have worked locally- even as a daily wage earner. At least he would have come by evening and could have been with the family." Family members feel bereft of a companion or a guardian for the most part of their lives. While fear and anxiety seem to be the most dominant emotions, loneliness and helplessness can also be discerned. The fact that the working camps of resin-tappers are located in jungles outside communication coverage, family members can never be sure about their men's safety.

Inability to access government provisions

Government of India and the government of Himachal Pradesh have launched a number of initiatives for the development of disadvantaged and marginalised communities such as tribals, low income families, women, and minorities. PS, the development practitioner observes:

> Different government agencies do offer a number of schemes for the poor and disadvantaged people who are living at the bottom of the pyramid. But lack of awareness about these provisions and initiatives becomes a hurdle for the families in Changar region.

Enlightened and committed community workers like PS do try to inform people about these opportunities regularly but many a times, the predicament in which families of seasonal migrants find themselves prevent them from accessing these benefits. For example, government disburses scholarships to students from designated castes and tribes. SB's granddaughter MB was also shortlisted for this scholarship but she could not avail this opportunity because claim forms needed to be signed by the father who was away tapping pine trees! By the time he would return, the deadline for applying for the grant would have passed. Clearly, the processes of claiming benefits are not women-friendly. It becomes even more difficult in a context where stepping out of home is not the norm for women in these cultures. Negotiating with government officials to claim benefits is indeed a struggle for them. Using the language of the cultural preparedness model, a new equilibrium has emerged amongst those who are left behind but it is a dissonant equilibrium, affecting wellbeing rather than restoring it.

The themes that have emerged from this analysis inform us that the concerns of pine resin tappers and their families largely remain unacknowledged and unaddressed. They are not able to benefit from the various schemes and programmes initiated by the government for ameliorating the conditions of disadvantaged and marginalised communities because the mechanisms for claiming these benefits are gender insensitive. At the same time, it is evident that families of pine resin tappers face both emotional as well as economic crises. Other than experiencing an emotional void created due to long absences of the dear ones, they also find themselves entangled in a vicious debt trap. Overall, it seems the alteration of cultural preparation status equilibrium tilts toward dissonance rather than consonance for those left behind at the source of migration.

Bringing the equilibrium back: role of counselling professionals

It goes without saying that the issues at the source of migration need urgent, coordinated, and concerted efforts by a spectrum of professionals who could act as positive sources of acculturation by developing interventions that would bring about a new and positive equilibrium. While the notion of career development as it is interpreted in urban, middle class contexts may not be directly relevant to the needs of the left behind, guidance and counselling professionals do need to acknowledge that such client groups also need to be served. Initiatives that aim to bring a consonant livelihood preparation status equilibrium back into the lives of migrants and their families could be considered. For career guidance and counselling professional who intend to work for the left behind families, this paper proposes a livelihood planning perspective with an advocacy approach.

As evident from the excerpt of the folk song quoted at the outset of this paper, the search for a sustainable livelihood pushes people to search for opportunities outside their regions. If people have a secure livelihood, it is unlikely that they would leave their homes. While migration has been found to be desirable for global and regional growth (e.g. Alonso, 2011; Goldin & Cameron, 2011, Dec. 20) and for poverty reduction (e.g. Adams & Page, 2005), the experiences of people from Changar and similar regions show this assertion in less favourable light, pointing instead to the necessity of perhaps curtailing this form of migration. The facilitation of sustainable livelihoods is known to have improved the economic and social conditions of disadvantaged communities and households (e.g. Bisht & Dastidar, 2012). Hence, creating livelihood options and helping a household develop a livelihood portfolio become a key strategy for checking migration from a given region. Policies and projects are needed to strengthen the livelihood base through interventions in labour markets, agricultural innovations, ensuring access to formal credit, and improving the public distribution system. These are examples of actions that could be taken to give people a reason not to migrate (Mishra, 2016). Tools and frameworks are available to design sustainable livelihood interventions (e.g. Datta, Kandarpa, & Mahajan, 2014).

From a guidance and counselling perspective, Arulmani (2014b) has introduced the idea of livelihood planning. He describes a livelihood counsellor as a specialised career guidance practitioner equipped with " … skills to allow the context to define the meaning of career along with the capability to understand and optimise traditional occupational structures for modern work environments" (Arulmani, 2014b, p. 11). This formulation has a number of corollaries for practitioners that could be linked to career guidance activities. Two specific career guidance themes are outlined in the following section.

Firstly, it is important that a livelihood counsellor understands the cultural and economic features that characterise the livelihood of a household and community, its context and practical livelihood promotion approaches. Livelihood is a multidimensional and complex construct connoting more than a means of living. As Baumgartner and Hogger (2004) point out, contexts do not merely define livelihood orientations, they also shape them. Therefore, a deep understanding of the context is essential for the accurate situating of a livelihoods intervention. For example, the Mountain Specificities Framework (Jodha, 1992) is very useful for situating and understanding any developmental project in a mountainous ecosystem. In the context of Changar region, a number of natural resource based occupations particularly those based on non-timber forest produce could be explored and supported for which cultural preparedness has also been discerned. In the context of Gujjar community, dairy farming still remains a viable and culturally accepted option provided essential prerequisites for building a successful enterprise are taken care of.

Secondly, it is equally important that the livelihood counsellor has a culturally resonant tool kit for livelihood promotion, design implementation and evaluation. Critical amongst these tools are methods to address the social cognitions and career beliefs of the target audience. From the labour market perspective, guidance could include methods to develop links between traditional occupations and contemporary markets (e.g. through the modernisation of traditional skills and valorisation of traditional products) and accurate and relevant occupational information (e.g. government schemes, skill development/retraining opportunities) to be passed on to the target group. It is also important to be a part of a network or community of practitioners so that cross fertilisation of ideas may take place and learning can be shared. In India, for example, there are organisations such as Institute of Livelihood Research and Training (http://ilrtindia.org/), ACCESS Development Services (http://www.accessdev.org), and others which provide professional services to support livelihood practitioners.

Livelihood planning perspective must adopt an advocacy approach primarily because the description of issues at the source of migration in the previous section clearly warrants that change is needed at the systemic level as well. Advocacy has been seen as the active component of a social justice approach to counselling (Fickling, 2016). Advocacy counselling has been defined as an " … empowerment stratagem that counselors and psychologists use to fully empathize with their clients to exact social change" (Green, McCollum, & Hays, 2008, p.15). It is evident that in order to ameliorate the conditions of left-behind families, advocacy counsellors need to work with clients and on behalf of clients. They are expected to complement direct services in their centres with indirect forms of helping through other settings and institutions that influence the lives of people (Kiselica & Robinson, 2001). A number of tools and models are available for designing advocacy interventions (e.g. Green et al., 2008; Hof, Dinsmore, Barber, Suhr, & Scofield, 2009). Lewis, Arnold, House, and Toporek (2002) describe a matrix with 43 competencies under six major domains: client empowerment, client advocacy, community collaboration, systems advocacy, public information, and social/political advocacy. The model finds it imperative to start with empowering the client, advocating for removing barriers faced by them, collaborating with the community for understanding systemic influences impacting client/client groups, and advocating change, informing the public about the needs of the client or client groups, and finally advocating for public policy changes. For left behind families, actions need to be taken on multiple fronts. They need to be empowered to take charge of their own lives, deal with their emotions effectively, and learn to negotiate within family and community as well as with the government officials. Policy makers, the community, and the public at large need to be sensitised to the issues of pine resin tappers and their families and bring their issues into main stream policy discourse. A convergence of all the welfare measures taken by the government needs to be ensured. Above all, socio-political advocacy is needed to ensure that the process of claiming government benefits and entitlements is women-friendly.

Concluding thoughts

A growing discourse has emerged among policy-makers, development practitioners and professionals from various fields for provision of adequate support services for migrant workers worldwide. However, discussions do not have the same vigour when it comes to families who are left behind. It is important that efforts are made to bring them into mainstream policy discussions. One set of solutions could focus on using the career guidance tools mentioned above, to guide communities toward sustainable livelihood options locally and thereby potentially avert distress migration does not take place. Another set of solutions could focus on providing support services for the families who are left behind. Making existing provisions easily accessible to women would be the least to be aimed at. In the Indian context, a comprehensive policy on migration is being mooted (Borhade, 2016; Chandrashekhar, 2017). It is an opportune moment to advocate for policies and programmes for left-behind families. At the same time, as argued by the cultural preparedness approach, the diversity of contexts must be accounted for. Possibilities of mutual learning between countries in the global North and the global South and between countries in the global South have been highlighted in the extant literature (e.g. Sultana, 2017). This offers the discipline of guidance and counselling a unique opportunity to adapt the existing advocacy counselling framework and more concretely articulate livelihood planning approaches to address the needs of this hitherto underserved group. Over the years, career guidance as a discipline has reinvented itself in order to respond to emerging challenges. Addressing the disturbed cultural preparedness equilibrium of left-behind families could be a new theme in its overall mission.

Acknowledgment

I am thankful to: the people of Changar region for sharing their life stories; the Friedrich Ebert Stiftung, India office for giving me an opportunity to visit Changar region in connection with production of a short film on migration; the Society for Environment and Rural Awakening (ERA), a community based organisation for facilitating access to the target community; and Gideon Arulmani, Director, The Promise Foundation, Bangalore, India for the detailed discussions I have had with him in the writing of this paper.

Disclosure statement

No potential conflict of interest was reported by the author.

References

Aajeevika Bureau. (2006). *Impact of male migration on women in South Rajasthan: Evidence and prospects for interventions.* Ahmedabad: Author. Retrieved from https://www.unescogym.org/wp-content/uploads/2015/11/COMPRESSED-Impact-of-male-migration-on-women-in-south-Rajasthan.pdf

Adams, R. H. (2011). Evaluating the economic impact of international remittances on developing countries using household surveys: A literature review. *Journal of Development Studies, 47*(6), 809–828.

Adams, R. H., & Page, J. (2005). Do international migration and remittances reduce poverty in developing countries? *World Development, 33*(10), 1645–1669.

Agasty, M. P., & Patra, R. N. (2014). Migration of labour and left-behind women: A case study of rural Odisha. *American International Journal of Research in Humanities, Arts and Social Sciences, 7*(1), 28–33.

Alonso, J. A. (2011). *International migration and development: A review in light of the crisis* (CDP Background Paper No. 11 (E)). New York, NY: United Nations Economic and Social Council. Retrieved from http://www.un.org/en/development/desa/policy/cdp/cdp_background_papers/bp2011_11e.pdf

Antman, F. M. (2013). The impact of migration on family left behind. In A. F. Constant, & K. F. Zimmermann (Eds.), *International handbook on the economics of migration* (pp. 293–308). Cheltenham: Edward Elgar.

Arulmani, G. (2010). *The Jiva approach to career guidance and counselling: An Indian model* (Project Report). Bangalore: The Promise Foundation.

Arulmani, G. (2011). Striking the right note: The cultural preparedness approach to developing resonant career guidance programmes. *International Journal for Educational and Vocational Guidance, 11*, 79–93.

Arulmani, G. (2014a). The cultural preparation process model and career development. In G. Arulmani, A. J. Bakshi, F. T. L. Leong, & A. G. Watts (Eds.), *Handbook of career development: International perspectives* (pp. 81–104). New York, NY: Springer International.

Arulmani, G. (2014b). Career guidance and livelihood planning. *Indian Journal of Career and Livelihood Planning, 3*(1), 9–11.

Arulmani, G. (2015). The question is the answer: The cultural preparedness approach to assessment for career guidance. In M. McMahon, & M. Watson (Eds.), *Career assessment: Qualitative approaches.* (pp. 207–218). Melbourne: Sense Publishers.

Arulmani, G. (2016). *Understanding the career development needs of immigrants through the cultural preparedness framework.* Bangalore: The Promise Foundation.

Arulmani, G., & Abdulla, A. (2007). Capturing the ripples: Addressing the sustainability of the impact of social marketing. *Social Marketing Quarterly, 13*(4), 84–107.

Arulmani, G., & Nag-Arulmani, S. (2004). *Career counselling: A handbook.* New Delhi: Tata McGraw-Hill.

Baruah, N., & Cholewinski, R. (2006). *Handbook on establishing effective labour migration policies in countries of origin and destination.* Vienna/Geneva: Organization for Security and Co-operation in Europe, International Organisation of Migration, International Labour Office.

Baumgartner, R., & Hogger, R. (Eds.). 2004). *In search of sustainable livelihood, managing resources and change.* New Delhi: Sage.

Baxter, P., & Jack, S. (2008). Qualitative case study methodology: Study design and implementation for novice researchers. *The Qualitative Report, 13*(4), 544–559.

Bell, M., & Charles-Edwards, E. (2013). *Cross-national comparisons of internal migration: An update on global patterns and trends* (Population division technical paper no. 2013/1). New York, NY: UN DESA. Retrieved from http://www.un.org/en/ development/desa/population/publications/pdf/technical/TP2013-1.pdf

Bimrose, J., & McNair, S. (2011). Career support for migrants: Transformation or adaptation? *Journal of Vocational Behavior, 78*(3), 325–333.

Bird, K., & Deshingkar, P. (2009). *Circular migration in India* (Policy brief no. 4). Prepared for World Development Report. Overseas Development Institute (ODI). Retrieved from https://www.odi.org/sites/odi.org.uk/files/odi-assets/publications-opinion-files/3381.pdf

Bisht, S. S., & Dastidar, S. G. (2012). AAGAS: A community endeavour for bio-conservation 21 and employment generation. In *Enhancing livelihoods of the poorest of the poor* (pp. 21–38). Delhi: ACCESS Development Services.

Blustein, D. L. (2015). Interview by Anuradha J. Bakshi and G. Arulmani (through email). *Indian Journal of Career and Livelihood Planning, 4*(1), 62–70.

Borhade, A. (2016). Internal labour migration in India: Emerging needs of comprehensive national migration policy. In D. K. Mishra (Ed.), *Internal migration in contemporary India* (pp. 290–336). New Delhi: Sage.

Chandrashekhar, S. (2017, April). Towards a national policy on migration. *Yojana, 61*, 27–29.

Cohen, L., Arnold, J., & O'Neill, M. (2011). Migration: Vocational perspectives on a complex and diverse transition. *Journal of Vocational Behavior, 78*(3), 321–324.

Datta, A., & Mishra, S. K. (2011). Glimpses of women's lives in rural Bihar: Impact of male migration. *Indian Journal of Labour Economics, 54*(3), 457–477.

Datta, S., Kandarpa, R., & Mahajan, V. (2014). *Resource book for livelihood promotion* (4th ed.). Hyderabad: Institute of Livelihood Research and Training/BASIX.

Démurger, S. (2015). *Migration and families left-behind: Families that stay behind when a member migrates do not clearly benefit.* Germany: IZA. Retrieved from https://wol.iza.org/articles/migration-and-families-left-behind/long

Desai, S., & Banerji, M. (2008). Negotiated identities: Male migration and left-behind wives in India. *Journal of Population Research, 25*(3), 337–355.

Deshingkar, P., & Akter, S. (2009). *Migration and human development in India, human development research paper 2009/13.* New York, NY: United Nations Development Programme. Retrieved from https://mpra.ub.uni-muenchen.de/19193/1/MPRA_paper_19193.pdf

Deshingkar, P., & Start, D. (2003). *Seasonal migration for livelihoods in India: Coping, accumulation and exclusion* (ODI working paper 220). Retrieved from http://www.odi.org.uk/publications/working_papers/wp220.pdf

de Wind, J., & Holdaway, J. (2005, October 26–27). *Internal and international migration in economic development.* Paper presented to the fourth coordination meeting on international migration, population division of the UN, New York. Retrieved from http://www.un.org/esa/population/meetings/fourthcoord2005/P11_SSRC.pdf

Fickling, M. J. (2016). An exploration of career counselors' perspectives on advocacy. *The Professional Counselor, 6*(2), 174–188.

Giri, S. K., Prasad, N., Pandey, N. K., Prasad, M., & Baboo, B. (2008). *Natural resins and gums of commercial important: At a glance.* Ranchi: Indian Institute of Natural Resins and Gums. Retrieved from http://ilri.ernet.in/~libraryilri/nrg/nrg.pdf

Goldin, I., & Cameron, G. (2011, December 20). Migration is essential for growth. *European Financial Review.* Retrieved from http://www.europeanfinancialreview.com/?p=2157

Government of India. (2017). *Economic survey 2016-17*. New Delhi: Department of Economic Affairs, Ministry of Finance. Retrieved from http://indiabudget.nic.in/es2016-17/echapter.pdf

Government of India. (n.d.). Constitution of India. Retrieved from https://www.india.gov.in/sites/upload_files/npi/files/coi_part_full.pdf

Green, E. J., McCollum, V. C., & Hays, D. (2008). Teaching advocacy counseling within a social justice framework: Implications for school counselors and educators. *Journal of Social Action in Counseling and Psychology*, *1*(2), 14–30.

GTZ. (2006). *Final evaluation 2006 indo-German changar Eco-development project, India* (Brief Report). Eschborn: Author. Retrieved from https://www.giz.de/en/downloads/gtz2006-en-indien-changar-schlussevaluierung.pdf

Gulati, L. (1993). *In the absence of their men: The impact of male migration on women*. New Delhi: SAGE.

Guterres, A. (2008, June 16). *People on the move: The challenges of displacement in the 21st Century*. International rescue committee UK annual lecture at royal geographical society. Retrieved from http://www.unhcr.org/admin/hcspeeches/48873def4/people-move-challenges-displacement-21st-century-international-rescue-committee.html

Hickey, M., Narendra, P., & Rainwater, K. (2013). *A review of internal and regional migration policy in Southeast Asia* (Migrating Out of Poverty Working Paper, 8). Singapore: National University of Singapore.

Hof, D. D., Dinsmore, J. A., Barber, S., Suhr, R., & Scofield, T. R. (2009). Advocacy: The T.R.A.I.N.E.R. Model. *Journal for Social Action in Counseling and Psychology*, *2*, 15–28.

International Labor Organization (ILO). (1999). *Decent work*. Report of the director-general to the 87th session of the international labour conference. Geneva, Switzerland: Author. Retrieved from http://www.ilo.org/public/english/standards/relm/ilc/ilc87/rep-i.htm

Ivey, A. E., & Collins, N. M. (2003). Social justice: A long-term challenge for counseling psychology. *The Counseling Psychologist*, *31*(3), 290–298.

Jetley, S. (1987). Impact of male migration on rural females. *Economic and Political Weekly*, *22*(44), WS 47–WS 53.

Jodha, N. S. (1992, August 1–4). *Mountain perspective and its utility: A framework for development strategies*. Paper presented in the workshop on 'Approaches to sustainable development of Indian Himalayas', Manali, Himachal Pradesh. Retrieved from http://www.nepjol.info/index.php/HR/article/viewFile/2408/2148

Keshri, K., & Bhagat, R. B. (2011). Temporary and seasonal migration: Regional pattern, characteristics and associated factors. *Economic and Political Weekly*, *47*(4), 81–88.

King, R., & Skeldon, R. (2010). 'Mind the gap!' integrating approaches to internal and international migration. *Journal of Ethnic and Migration Studies*, *36*(10), 1619–1646.

Kiselica, M. S., & Robinson, M. (2001). Bringing advocacy counseling to life: The history, issues, and human dramas of social justice work in counseling. *Journal of Counseling and Development*, *79*(4), 387–397.

Kishtwaria, J., Thakur, S., & Rana, A. (2007). Migration-Its multidimensional impact on mountain women. *Studies of Tribes and Tribals*, *5*(1), 25–28.

Kotru, R. (n.d.). *Participatory appraisal, improvement and management of grassland resources in Himalayan watersheds*. Retrievedfrom:http://www.fao.org/waicent/Faoinfo/Agricult/Agp/agpc/doc/pasture/peshawarproceedings/participatory.pdf.

Lewis, J. A., Arnold, M. S., House, R., & Toporek, R. L. (2002). *ACA advocacy competencies*. Retrieved from https://www.counseling.org/Resources/Competencies/Advocacy_Competencies.pdf

Mazumdar, I., Neetha, N., & Agnihotri, I. (2013). Migration and gender in India. *Economic and Political Weekly*, *48*(10), 54–64.

McMahon, M. (2014). New trends in theory development in career psychology. In G. Arulmani, A. J. Bakshi, F. T. L. Leong, & A. G. Watts (Eds.), *Handbook of career development: International perspectives* (pp. 13–27). New York, NY: Springer.

Mishra, D. K. (2016). Seasonal migration from Odisha: A view from the field. In D. K. Mishra (Ed.), *Internal migration in contemporary India* (pp. 263–290). New Delhi: Sage.

Nārāyaṇa, B. (2017). *Culture and emotional economy of migration*. Abingdon: Routledge.

Negi, T. S. (1976). *Scheduled tribes of Himachal Pradesh: A profile*. Meerut: Raj Printers.

Planning Commission & UNDP. (2003). *Successful governance initiatives and best practices: Experiences from Indian states*. New Delhi: Authors. Retrieved from http://planningcommission.gov.in/plans/stateplan/bpm-full-mnul.pdf

Rajan, S. I. (Ed.). (2013). *India migration report 2013: Social costs of migration*. New Delhi: Routledge.

Roy, A. K., Singh, P., & Roy, U. N. (2015). Impact of rural-urban labour migration on education of children: A case study of left behind and accompanied migrant children in India. *Space and Culture, India*, *2*(4), 17–34.

Sam, D. L., & Berry, J. W. (2010). Acculturation: When individuals and groups of different cultural backgrounds meet. *Perspectives on Psychological Science*, *5*(4), 472–481.

Smita, S. (2007). *Locked homes empty schools: The impact of distress seasonal migration on the rural poor*. New Delhi: Zubaan Publication.

Sultana, R. G. (2017). Futures for career education and guidance in the Mediterranean? In R. Sultana (Ed.), *Career guidance and livelihood planning across the Mediterranean* (pp. 419–437). Rotterdam: Sense Publishers.

Toyota, M., Yeoh, B. S. A., & Nguyen, L. (2007). Bringing the 'left behind' back into view in Asia: A framework for understanding the 'migration–left behind nexus. *Population, Space and Place*, *13*, 157–161.

Ullah, A. A. (2017). Male migration and 'left–behind' women: Bane or boon? *Environment and Urbanization ASIA*, *8*(1), 59–73.

Yin, R. K. (2003). *Case study research: Design and methods* (3rd ed.). Thousand Oaks, CA: Sage.

Learning Engagement as a target for interventions: a qualitative study of first-generation migrant adolescents in Finnish secondary education

Linda Molin-Karakoc and Minna Ikola

ABSTRACT

Engagement is considered key in measuring student development, offering valuable clues into the adaptation, motivation and participation of students. This article sheds light on the multifaceted construct of engagement and its implications for first-generation migrant adolescents. Participant interviews and observations were conducted to investigate student experiences of engagement and the utility of engagement in intervention designs. Identified determinants of engagement consist of cultural capital, school norms and values, teacher-student relationships and relevance of support services. The results show that engagement goes beyond individual dispositions and achievement and includes learning environments and resources. Keeping in mind the vulnerable position of migrants and the need to ensure equal educational opportunity, a reshaping of engagement-related support services, interventions and school practices is needed.

Introduction

Student engagement is regarded as one of the keys to addressing problems such as low achievement, boredom, alienation and high dropout rates (Fredricks, Blumenfield, & Paris, 2004). Similarly, engagement is often thought to reflect the degree of adaptation among migrant students as the school offers a proximal context in which a large share of the student's time is spent and the social, political and cultural values of the host country are fostered (Chiu, Pong, Mori, & Chow, 2012; Suarez-Orozco, Suarez-Orozco, & Todorova, 2008).

The potential of engagement as a target for interventions has been suggested in the literature and carried out in practice, yet without challenging characterisations of the concept *per se*. This may be due to disagreements regarding what engagement stands for and the variation in engagement subtypes in the field. Whereas some scholars prefer to focus on engagement as unidirectional, in which students are engaged according to normative understandings of engagement (e.g. Tuominen-Soini & Salmela-Aro, 2014), others consider engagement as a multidirectional process reflecting the goodness-of-fit between the school, the student and variables influencing that fit (e.g. Appleton, Christenson, Kim, & Reschly, 2006; Wonglorsaichon, Wongwanich, & Wiratchai, 2014). Traditionally, engagement has been measured quantitatively through a division of engagement into subtypes (Appleton et al., 2006; Chiu et al., 2012; Willms, 2003 Wonglorsaichon et al., 2014;). Qualitative interpretations of engagement, expanding the concept in a practically applied school context, are, on the other hand, missing. Hence, in contrast to existing research relying on quantitative data to substantiate categories and predefined conceptualisations, we approach engagement through the lived experiences of students. The study seeks to elaborate on engagement as a meta-construct and investigate if and how engagement is applicable in interventions among migrant students.

What is engagement?

Engagement: definitions in the literature

Engagement has long confused researchers, not least because of the lack of consensus regarding the concept. In an attempt to distinguish engagement from other similar concepts, some scholars (Appleton et al., 2006; Fredricks et al., 2004) have defined engagement as the "energy in action, the connection between person and activity" (e.g. Appleton et al., 2006, p. 428). Closely-related concepts such as motivation and participation have been described as "the direction, intensity, and quality of a student's energy" (*motivation*, Appleton et al., 2006, p. 428) and "an activity which has the intent or effect of influencing or achieving public good" (*participation*, Greco Morasso, 2012, p. 313). Still, uses of engagement infrequently become synonymous with either motivation or participation when the link between the two is missing. In addition, the tendency among scholars (Adelman & Taylor, 2010; Reyes, Brackett, Rivers, Elbertson, & Salovey, 2011; Wonglorsaichon et al., 2014) to accentuate mostly personality or the relationship between learner and environment is apparent in the terminology used (*school engagement* and *student* engagement). In such studies, the impact of extra-personal factors such as learning resources, power structures or communities of support (Taylor & Parsons, 2011) therefore becomes lost.

Engagement as a multifaceted construct

Apart from issues of terminology, subtypes of engagement appear equally restrictive. While a growing number of scholars are invested in research on engagement as related to achievement (Wonglorsaichon et al., 2014; Tuominen-Soini & Salmela-Aro, 2014), others have explored different contextual factors which may account for underlying psychological processes among disengaged students (Appleton et al., 2006; Fredricks et al., 2004). In so doing, researchers have generally resorted to subtypes of engagement such as cognitive and emotional (Chiu et al., 2012); cognitive, psychological and behavioural (Appleton et al. 2006; Furlong & Rebelez-Ernst, 2014) or cognitive, academic and affective (Fredricks et al., 2004; Reyes et al., 2011; Fredricks & McColskey 2011). The most exhaustive list by far is found in Taylor and Parsons (2011), who demonstrate that engagement includes academic, cognitive, intellectual, institutional, emotional, behavioural, social and psychological dimensions. On the one hand, such uses of categories or subtypes may help in conceptualising and measuring an otherwise complex construct. On the other hand, the interrelatedness of macro vs. microstructures, social relations and ecological systems impacting the engagement of individuals cannot be gauged when stale categories are used. Considerations of engagement beyond immediate micro-contexts have been called for (Appleton, Christenson, & Furlong, 2008; Chiu et al., 2012), however, to our knowledge, no attempts have been made to address this issue nor the lack of qualitative studies.

Engagement and its applicability in interventions

The construct of engagement is said to capture the gradual process by which students disconnect from school (Finn, 1989). Consistent with the understanding that dropping out of school is not an instantaneous event, but a process that unfolds over time, engagement serves as a means for understanding and intervening when initial signs of students' disconnection with school and learning are observed (Appleton et al., 2006; Finn, 1989; University of Minnesota, 1990). Students with a stronger sense of belonging and motivation are said to have fewer psychological health and social problems, such as diminished rates of delinquency, social rejection, depression, drop-outs and drug use (Anderman, 2003; Finn, 1989). Furthermore, higher participation, seen in attendance rates and completion of homework, is said to make students more likely to achieve better academically or, simply, complete school (Willms, 2003).

Current intervention models (e.g. University of Minnesota, 1990) are designed to intervene when students' motivation and/or participation deteriorate. In *Check & Connect*, engagement is defined as commitment to and investment in learning, as well as identification with and belonging at school. Engagement is associated with desired academic, behavioural, cognitive and affective outcomes, such as persistence in school and graduation (University of Minnesota, 1990). Whereas *Check & Connect* is based on four subtypes of engagement as argued by Appleton et al. (2006) and includes partnership with families, the model falls short on cross-cultural considerations or providing bottom-up approaches to engagement. In our view, the utility of engagement in interventions demands further critical analyses that move beyond personality pathology.

Our study: aims, scope and research questions

The predominant emphasis on *indicators* of engagement (e.g. motivation, participation or achievement) as opposed to *facilitators or obstructers* of engagement (e.g. learning materials, school context, communities of support) is witnessed in the preference of the passive form "to be engaged" instead of the active form "to engage" in current scholarship. Similarly, current engagement models provide personalised, timely interventions, yet lack a comprehensive analysis of extra-personal factors. In our study, therefore, we set out to challenge standardised definitions of engagement and investigate if and how a whole-society approach can work in engagement interventions. As the emphasis is on migrant learners, our study seeks to bring forth qualitative understandings of engagement and shed light on engagement in cross-cultural contexts. Considering our interest in expanding conceptualisations and uses of engagement, the research questions posed for the study are:

(1) What are the qualitative interpretations of engagement among migrant students?
(2) Can engagement be a target for interventions in culturally diverse classrooms and if so, how?

Although some of the potential differences in engagement between host society students and migrant students have been probed (see, e.g. Chiu et al., 2012), due to their quantitative nature, neither cross-cultural comparisons nor suggestions for intervention policy and practice can be deduced from these studies. We propose that engagement should be approached holistically; therefore the term learning engagement, as opposed to student or school engagement, has been adopted. Such an encapsulation of "engagement" shifts responsibility from the individual, his/her disposition (see, e.g. Willms, 2003) to the reciprocity of people, learning environments and learning resources.

Theoretical framework for the study of engagement

Engagement amidst migrant students is said to portray both their short-term adaptation to school and their long-term adaptation to society (Suarez-Orozco & Suarez-Orozco 2001; Chiu et al., 2012). That said, such adaptation should take into consideration that relationships between learners, environments and resources are both dynamic and reciprocal. Based on resources available, a person reacts to his or her environment and in doing so alters the environment. Behaviour or human psychology should therefore never be examined in a vacuum but according to contextual variables (Scheffer, 2005).

The theoretical ensemble chosen for this study underlines the role of context and resources more than the individual. By adopting a whole-of-society approach, the theories advance our understandings of engagement and the centrality of resources, connections and relationships in discussions of engagement among migrant learners.

The ecological systems theory

An effective framework for gauging reciprocal influences between learners, environments and resources is provided by Bronfenbrenner's ecological systems model (1992). Bronfenbrenner's ecological systems describe contexts of development that are divided into five systems: the immediate environment (micro-system), connections (meso-system), the indirect environment (exo-system), social and cultural values (macro-system) and development over time (chrono-system). Through this system, fluctuations in learning engagement can be explained by changes in environment, time and resources. A lack of resources or a missing connection in one or many of the systems implies a decreased chance of realising full human potential and brings about an evolutionary process which may hinder development.

In previous studies, the impact of micro-, meso- and exo-levels on engagement has mainly been addressed in form of incongruences between the home and the school or parent-student, parent-teacher relationships (Appleton et al., 2006; Chiu et al., 2012). In the case of migrant students, parental education and the influence of the parents' educational backgrounds on achievement (not engagement) have been stressed (Suarez-Orozco et al., 2008). The effect of all ecological systems, including macro- and chrono-levels, on engagement, on the other hand, has neither been stressed nor researched. Hence, we posit that values in society are meaningful for the engagement of migrant students as learning a new land entails learning to navigate the education system and prevailing norms. We postulate that a holistic, multidirectional portrayal of the challenges and problems arising in the ecological systems can thus address engagement among migrant students more comprehensively.

The theory of capital

Bourdieu's theory of capital provides a means to explaining symbolic and material resources, relationships between resources and their impact on individuals and larger groups. Whereas Putnam theorises social capital as advantageous to society promoting civic engagement and connections, Bourdieu's theory of capital is one of reproducing inequalities in society, especially with regard to the maintenance of privileges for people from dominant classes (Bourdieu, 1986). According to Bourdieu, power relations and power structures are perpetuated through the possession of networks and mutual recognitions of legitimate languages, knowledge and relationships (Bourdieu & Waquant, 1992). How schools determine their curriculum and instruction ties school knowledge, linguistic and cultural knowledge with the dynamics of class, gender and race. The mastery of dominant languages and social relations becomes a form of symbolic capital, affording its masters symbolic power (Bourdieu & Waquant, 1992).

Non-dominant classes, migrants in particular, who do not inherit recognisable social or cultural capital from their parents are negatively affected by power structures, having their previous social, cultural and linguistic knowledge invalidated. Educational capital, i.e. educational material commodities such as diplomas and formal education, may hence be seen as an alternative opportunity in upward mobility among non-dominant classes (Bourdieu, 1986). Parental education or positive attitudes towards schooling may help motivate a student to navigate the murky waters of education and make them strive harder academically. Educational capital, however, is dependent on skills in the dominant language as it is through the dominant language that the migrant students are introduced into the dominant culture, its norms and values and find essential connections and resources. Therefore, investments in the dominant language mean an active aspiration to gain symbolic and material resources that will in turn improve other forms of capital (Bourdieu, 1986). Symbolic power is unlikely to be given to other non-dominant languages and cultures when there is a political agenda to promote a mono-cultural, mono-linguistic state (Bourdieu, 1986). The role of capital has largely been overlooked in research on engagement and more attention should henceforth be paid to the inequalities produced by the dispersal of capital and how this imbalance affects those at a disadvantage in an achievement driven society.

The socio-cultural learning theory

Vygotsky's theories stress the fundamental role of social interaction in the development of cognition and that community plays a central part in the process of meaning-making. For Vygotsky, the environment in which children grow up will influence how they think and what they think about as cognitive development stems from social interactions learned as a child (Vygotsky, 1978). The Zone of Proximal development (ZDP) is the area where the most sensitive instruction or guidance should be given and allows the child to develop skills they will then use on their own. Cognitive functions, even those carried out alone, are influenced by the beliefs, values and tools of intellectual adaptation of the culture of origin and are therefore socio-culturally determined (Vygotsky as stated in McLeod, 2018).

As argued by Vygotsky (1978), culturally relevant input is a prerequisite for cognitive development and affects engagement levels amidst students. As schools may uphold largely mono-cultural values and norms, intercultural sensitivity amongst teachers and education professionals coupled with culturally relevant learning resources are crucial for improving the accessibility of ZDP in culturally diverse learning environments. For instance, tools used by students for enhancing memory may differ - some may find note-taking culturally relevant, whereas for others, collecting pebbles, or the repetition of names of ancestors are equally employable memory-enhancing strategies (McLeod, 2018). Should culturally relevant material be unavailable or learning activities stand in conflict with previously learned ways of knowing, students may experience considerable cognitive difficulties to complete tasks and become demotivated over time.

Methods and materials

The selection of methodology and ethical concerns

Quantitative studies on learning engagement have emphasised the correlation between levels of achievement (such as grades/scores, attendance rates, truancy, etc.) and cognitive, behavioural and emotional aspects of students (e.g. Fredricks et al., 2004; Tuominen-Soini & Salmela-Aro, 2014; Wonglorsaichon et al., 2014). Such methodologies accommodate presumptions about engagement by not directly involving the subjects of research, i.e. the students. More recently, however, researchers have begun involving students and teachers in measurements of engagement by means of individual interviews (Hammar Chiriac, 2014), focus groups (Senior & Howard, 2015) and comments on research designs (Appleton et al., 2008). The aforementioned studies however do not include children or adolescent learners nor learner expositions of the construct.

For the sake of qualitative data, i.e. rich, detailed accounts of a phenomenon, semi-structured interviews and participant observations were selected as methods for this study. The selection of solely qualitative methods was based on the premise that quantitative measures are overrepresented in the field and do little to capture the essence of engagement as experienced by the students. In order to ensure validity and reliability of the study, all four of Lincoln and Guba's (1985) evaluative criteria were met in the selection and application of our research: credibility (prolonged engagement, persistent observation and member-checking), transferability (thick description), dependability (external audit) and confirmability (triangulation). Our positions as trainees at the facility allowed for ample contact with the students over an entire academic year, possibilities to carry out observations on a weekly basis, conduct inter-researcher member-checks, undertake double coding procedures and an external audit by our supervisor. Potential researcher bias was identified in the form of power relations (students vs. teacher trainees) and presumptions about migrant students as opposed to native students in the angle of this study (e.g. cultural connotations of engagement). However, power relations and potential researcher bias were dealt with by confirming that no coercion was felt on part of the students, reflecting on our positions, discussing our research and planned methodology with colleagues and supervisor, carrying out frequent member-checks and employing a qualitative mixed-method approach for the triangulation of data. Familiarity and rapport between researchers and participants eased the formation of trust prior to commencing research. Information about the research project was provided and informed, voluntary consent was sought only after a student's careful consideration and comprehensive understanding of the purpose, scope and implications of the project. To avoid any negative impact due to participation in the study, we chose to anonymise names of participants and the school.

Participants and locale

Participants in the study consisted of twenty-one (21) migrant students in the ninth grade, i.e. their final year of secondary school. They were 16-18-year-old first-generation migrants, all of whom had lived in Finland for less than 10 years, and the majority had come to know only the Finnish education system. The participants, six male and 15 female students representing 10 different countries of origin, had used two or more support services (e.g. supported teaching, second language classes, native language tuition, counseling services, SEN classes). The reason for migration or socio-economic status were not sought after in this study to avoid stigmas or misrepresentations of the participants' legal migration status.

Data collection and analysis

Prior to the interviewing process, the researchers observed the participants and recorded field notes from 22 lessons during the academic year. The length of each lesson varied between 45 and 75 min. The subjects ranged from Geography, Math, IT and native language tuition to second language or SEN classes. One-on-one interviews with the participants were carried out towards the end of the school year. Each interview spanned 30–32 min in duration, resulting in 643 min of interview material. The interviews and observations were coded and analysed using a thematic analysis approach (Braun & Clarke, 2006). The interviews were first audio-recorded, transcribed, coded and re-coded to search for meaning and patterns. The field notes of both researchers were compared for meaning and double-coded. Both sets of data were coded until saturation point, which in the case of interviews was after the 17th interview. After grouping codes, they were linked to overarching themes, selected based on commonalities in codes emerging from both the interview data and observation data.

Findings

Five themes emerged from the analysis with significance for a restructuring of engagement and engagement interventions. The themes appeared across the sample and stood out as highly relevant for migrant students and for what has *not* been taken into account in engagement-related research. The themes were:

(1) Cultural capital (micro/macro-level influence)
(2) School norms and values (macro-level influence)
(3) Teacher-student relationship (micro-level/chrono-level influence)
(4) Student resources in the home and school (meso-level influence)
(5) Relevance of support services (micro/exo-level)

Cultural capital (micro/macro-level)

Participant concern with second language skills as an enabler of engagement permeated all participant discussions. Much like previous studies about the importance of cultural capital, of which linguistic capital is a form (e.g. Chiu et al., 2012; Devine, 2005), competence in the dominant language was directly associated with sustenance in school work and feelings of belonging at school:

> I feel engaged at school since I know Finnish very well, it easy to study. (Girl, 18)
>
> Finnish is not my native language, studying here is hard and I am not in the least bit
>
> motivated/ (Boy, 17)
>
> I struggle with Finnish. It will be tough to finish school. (Girl, 16)

The participants held the idea that only Finnish was essential for educational attainment and formation of friendships. Correspondingly, lack of self-esteem and apathy concerning schoolwork was evident in students who did not yet master the Finnish language. Participants might have been aware that their cultural capital and, as a result, symbolic power can only increase along with their acquisition of Finnish. Similarly, as native languages or cultures did not seem to possess "legitimate power" (Bourdieu, 1986; Devine, 2005), participant disregard for native languages confirms a "minority complex" (see Suarez-Orozco, 2001):

> I do not see the point in studying my mother tongue. I will not need it for anything here. (Boy, 17)

A depreciation for native languages could indicate the participants' wish to acquire educational capital to compensate for lost cultural capital (Bourdieu, 1986). At the same time, some awareness of inequalities existed:

> At school we learn about other cultures e.g. by organizing a bake sale for French class.
>
> The school could learn more about the students' [home] culture[s]. (Girl, 16)

Our observations in the school reinforce that multicultural/intercultural education was only superficially implemented in the curriculum in the form of events emphasising European cultures and languages.

School norms and values (macro-level)

The school values and norms were associated with engagement among the participants. Disengaging variables pertained to the emphasis on rigour in Finnish education and a paucity of play-based schoolwork:

> In Finland, subjects are so carefully studied ... it was different in [the participant's country of origin]. I was more into school there. (Girl, 18)
>
> Learning should not only be serious but fun too. (Boy, 17)
>
> Nicer [*sic*] teachers should not focus on serious study so much but letting our hair down more. (Girl, 17)

Similarly, limited appreciation for spoken as opposed to written production was lamented:

> We want to speak more but the teachers don't want to listen. (Girl, 17)
>
> I am not a good writer so I wish we could have oral exams, or at least do more speaking activities. (Girl, 18)

Our observations confirm such experiences, as many of the participants were not as immersed in activities stressing rigour or written production as when multimodal forms of learning such as speech and signing were encouraged. Kinesthetic exercises or audio-visual content creation using ICT were seen as highly motivating for the participants and talked about in a positive manner with teachers and peers. According to our observations, when the topic or task appeared burdensome or tedious, the participants engaged in alternate activities and teacher reprimands or referrals to SEN classes or other support services were in such cases frequent. In the same vein, learning resources were discussed in light of values projected by the school. Culturally relevant material was identified as integral for sustaining engagement amidst the participants. As one participant reminisces:

I really liked the movie [*Bend it Like Beckham*], it was the first [one] I could relate to. (Girl, 16)

Culturally relevant material, such as a film on intercultural encounters, produced higher levels of motivation and participation such as more time spent on task, renewed interest in the subject and continued discussions of the material in other learning contexts. Changes to the environment (new teacher, new syllabus) or learning resources (student-oriented classes, knowledge construction using ICT) were noticeably welcomed by the participants, characterised by their renewed efforts to find personal meaning in tasks and initiations of new relationships with the teacher.

Teacher-student relationship (micro-level/chrono-level)

Participants' feelings of alienation or lack of energy when carrying out school activities were in the majority of cases linked to the teacher. Teacher misjudgments, such as mistaking cognitive abilities for behavioural misconduct, was found as particularly detrimental to the engagement of the participants:

They [teachers] do not notice that I don't know even if I try, they think that I don't focus. (Girl, 17)

The teachers should explain more in class, try to see things the way we do. (Girl, 18)

In participant depictions of disengaging teachers, the paucity of emotional (e.g. inspiration, affection or empathy) and behavioural (e.g. demonstrating interest in different cultures and fair treatment of students) role modelling was recurrent. Engaging teachers, on the other hand, were characterised as providers of ample encouragement and affirmative action:

When I raise my hand, the teacher pick[s] me and encourage[s] me. (Girl, 17)

I feel connected when they give me speaking turns and help. (Girl, 18)

Our observations demonstrated that positive, caring relationships between participants and teachers had little influence on engagement over time as this variable tended to change based on lesson, teacher or social situation, supporting the findings of Taylor and Parsons (2011). However, how the participants' innate mechanisms were reciprocated in times of adversity (e.g. perpetual misjudgments by the teachers and removal of student due to perceived misconduct) were highly influential in reducing participant engagement overall for extended periods of time, signalling chrono-level effects.

Student resources in the home and school (meso-level)

A misallocation of resources was seen as an indicator and obstructer of engagement by the participants. Conflicts arising from expectations and responsibilities in the two primary ecosystems placed a heavy toll on the student. As one participant puts it:

None of my parents know Finnish, and I do all the learning and chores at home. (Girl, 16)

On the other hand, consistent with the theories of Bourdieu (1986), parental optimism regarding educational achievement and the provision of mental support in the home were helpful in raising engagement levels:

My parents want me to attend school and do my homework properly … they see it as a

chance they never got and I will see to it that I fulfil their dreams. (Girl, 17)

I am inspired in the best possible way by my family. (Girl, 18)

Super and Harkness (1999) contend that parental attitudes to the child's situation and abilities are vital to the child's opportunities for participation and advancement. Setting high expectations for their children, parents demonstrate a belief in social mobility and indirectly renders the school and educational attainment attractive for the migrant students (Chiu et al., 2012; Suarez-Orozco et al., 2008). Children are normally wired to please their parents, yet such aspirations were not matched by the school in our study. As one participant complains:

> The teachers should take us more seriously. We want to achieve but there are many problems in our way, like language. (Girl, 17)

Participants were compelled to navigate expectations and, according to our observations, shortcomings of communication in the meso-system prevailed. In particular, tangible supports or resources available to the students in the home or at the school were not very effectively communicated between the two parties, leading to some participants "falling through the cracks".

Relevance of support services (micro/exo-level)

While the participants mentioned parents, elder siblings as well as teachers as their chief source of support, the significance of support measures (counseling, native language tuition, peer learning, etc.) at school was either ignored or dismissed:

> I do not see support services as useful. (Boy, 17)

> Supported teaching is good, as well as Finnish as a second language classes, but I do not need other support services. (Girl, 18)

> I do not see the point in studying my mother tongue. I will not need it for anything here. (Boy, 17)

Indifference shown towards support services might reflect culture-specific understandings of mental, emotional or academic support (Brar-Josan & Yohani, 2017). Throughout the interviews, participants demonstrated unawareness of whom support services were intended for and avoided deep-seated discussions of the use of such services. Supported teaching is habitually given by the subject or homeroom teacher, and hence the supportive role of the teacher as highlighted by the participants might represent a distrust in other school professionals. During our observations, unconventional articulations for support (attention-seeking and behavioural misconduct during class), albeit directed at the teacher, could in our view have been more qualitatively tended to by other professionals such as counselors or teaching assistants. However, without the teachers' acknowledgement of right forms of support, participants acting up were typically removed from the class, ignored or referred to SEN classes haphazardly. Shortages in communication between different professionals at school were in these cases evident. Furthermore, many of the participants retracted their requests for help for fear of rejection or leaning too much on the teacher.

Discussion

As confirmed by the results of this study, discussions of engagement demand looking beyond individual dispositions and performances of students. In our heterogeneous sample, experiences of the dominant language, Finnish, as the only tool needed for achievement and social relations and non-dominant languages as redundant confirm Bourdieu's theory of dominant languages as cultural capital through which holders can wield symbolic power (Bourdieu & Waquant, 1992). While Chiu et al. (2012) contend that generally positive migrant attitudes towards school means that a cultural capital view cannot be justified, based on our findings, we would like to argue that in addition to views on schooling as an instrument for social mobility, the importance given to the dominant language as opposed to native languages means that a power hierarchy has been subconsciously adopted by those under the rule of it, in this case participants and their families. As symbolic, invisible power can only be exercised with the complicity of those unaware of their subjection to or reproduction of it (see Bourdieu & Waquant, 1992) this means a loss of equitable educational opportunities for migrant learners as native speakers of non-dominant languages.

It is important to note that being part of the nation-state, schools often seek to uphold the status quo and afford its dominant population symbolic capital by underemphasising non-dominant languages and cultures in curricula (Chiu et al., 2012; Devine, 2005). This socialisation role of schools to preserve privileges of certain groups within the population is also known as the "hidden curriculum" (see, e.g. Suarez-Orozco et al. 2008). For the democratisation of schools, hidden curricula ought to be made explicit, minimised, or reoriented so that all students, despite cultural affiliations, are afforded equal opportunity and enjoyment of learning. Through appraisals of hegemonic values transmitted by schools, education professionals can become more attuned and empathetic to student needs and recognise inconsistencies that add to the academic, social and psychological stress they undergo. Also, as the participants so eloquently point out, learning activities involving non-hegemonic values, i.e. representations beyond White, Western ideals match more democratic principles of learning and simultaneously underpin Vygotsky's (1978) idea of culturally relevant input for student development.

As our finding on school-oriented, normative views of learning and its ill-alignment with participant learning styles shows, more speech and other multimodal forms of learning ought to be implemented in school curricula when migrant learners are concerned. In the Finnish education system and curricula, importance is generally placed on written production (Sahlberg, 2009). Interestingly, however, participant calls for increased recognition of skills beyond written ones stand in line with recent research about the shortcomings of migrant education in Finland (Schleicher, 2012). Whilst recommendations for teachers to induce migrant students to talk longer in order to rehearse language skills are present in Finnish scholarship (Kyttälä & Sinkkonen, 2014), meager attention has been paid to the inclusion of multimodality or alternate forms of meaning-making in the education and assessment of migrant learners. Curricular emphasis on rigour and writing, promoting seriousness at the expense of joy, suggest that standardised norms in Finnish schools may overwhelm the ideas of schooling migrant students have. Student requests for changes to the learning environment carry importance for engagement and learning models promoted by the school as seen in Appleton et al. (2006) and more effort has to be put into comparisons between the students' current and previous education systems with an emphasis on cross-cultural ways of learning and achievement ideologies.

Lived experiences of the teacher-student relationship in this study shows that engagement cannot be understood simplistically in terms of an internal attribution of students but as a social experience in which the teacher, as an attachment figure, provides a security base, i.e. the objectification of a safe haven to explore new settings, obtain comfort and security in a new home land (Bowlby, 1979; Suarez-Orozco et al., 2008). Such a social experience acts as a trigger for the student's innate mechanisms and theories (e.g. "teachers are to be trusted"); yet plays a pivotal role in the revision and reorganisation of theory in light of counter-evidence (e.g. "teachers in the host country do not care about me") (Scheffer, 2005). As the finding regarding the teacher-student relationship reveals, in times of adversities and disengagement, teacher behaviour and disposition played the most crucial role. The lack of emotional and behavioural support demonstrated that trust between the two microsystems could not always be formed, triggering negative feelings among the participants. Feelings of acceptance and affection amidst both teachers and peers were sought by the participants during our observations. The teachers' powerful role as gatekeepers to academic attainment as well as well-being of students, e.g. in terms of self-esteem and self-actualisation (Maslow, 1943), needs to be reviewed to offer more insights into their professional development, especially regarding dealing with the socio-emotional needs of the students. Contrary to the findings of Chiu et al. (2012), our findings revealed that only negative teacher experiences shaped engagement levels over time, indicating a link between micro and chrono-levels. Teacher misjudgments resulting in referrals stand in line with Onchiwari and Keengwe (2008, p. 269) argument that "manifestations of the needs by the immigrant children can be culturally shocking to the [dominant population] and lend themselves to misinterpretation". Prior to SEN referrals, differentiation and pedagogical response should be carried out (Watts-Taffe et al., 2012) and inclusive strategies for meeting diverse needs ought to be more carefully planned and developed in both teacher education and practice to circumvent disengagement as a result of teacher misjudgment.

Enhanced cooperation between the school and the home has previously been addressed by scholars (Adelman & Taylor, 2010; Chiu et al., 2012; Suarez-Orozco et al., 2008; Taylor & Parsons, 2011); yet our findings indicate that meso-level difficulties become increasingly transparent when student voices are heard. Parental optimism, high expectations for educational achievement and the provision of support in the home were considered benign in raising engagement levels whereas the lack of recognition of such efforts by the school rendered parental expectations and student efforts fruitless. In other cases, exo-level influences such as parents' shortcomings in the dominant language or employment skills made educational attainment onerous for the students (cf. Ochniwari et al. 2008; Suarez-Orozco et al., 2008). As our study demonstrates, investigations into communication and the dispersal of resources between the school and the home must include student voices to ensure the effects on learning engagement can be fully accounted for.

Support services were not paid focal attention by the participants of this study. Limited interest in support services could be explained by a distrust in mental health professionals and/or parental cultural identities or community beliefs (i.e. exo-level influences) mediating values related to abilities, disabilities and support services sought by the students (Brar-Josan & Yohani, 2017; Super & Harkness, 1999). Restricted access to information about the range of support services available could constitute an alternative factor (Suarez-Orozco et al., 2008). The participants' preference for supported teaching, provided by the teacher, as well as appreciation of parents, siblings and teachers as sources of motivation and encouragement emphasised the inclination of participants to approach familiar, trusted sources of support. Similarly, retractions of requests in the classroom indicate that certain caution for seeking help was exercised by the participants. The typical image of migrant children as hard-working, respectful towards elders and authorities and anxious to please (Devine, 2005) might in many cases have repercussions for their equity of opportunity and supports. Socio-culturally determined behaviour aiming at recognition and more individualised help could thus, quite paradoxically, result in a lack of attention and not getting help at school (Devine, 2005). Mismatches between the supports the students sought and the complexity of their needs call for more investigation into how support services could be better tailored and applied to fit different belief systems and the challenging situations of migrant learners. A clarification of support services, their aims and target group in order for increased access and appreciation of such resources amid students and their families could be a starting point, followed by professional development for teachers, guidance and counseling professionals and other mental health professionals to extend current, Westernised interpretations of mental health support, e.g. via the use of cultural brokers.

Conclusions

Learning engagement in the case of migrant learners entails more than dispositions and performance. It stands for the compatibility of people (student, teachers, peers, parents and other professionals), learning environments (school, home, communities) and resources (different forms of capital, cultural relevance, sources of support, access to support services). This multidirectional network has a direct influence on the engagement of individuals in which sustained motivation and participation among migrant learners in particular are defined by reciprocity (e.g. school-home, teacher-student, dominant culture-non-dominant culture and support services-communities) and systemic functionality or wellbeing (micro-meso-exo-macro-chrono).

In the study, five themes applicable to engagement were found: (1) cultural capital, (2) school norms and values, (3) teacher-student relationship, (4) student resources in the home and school and (5) relevance of support services. The themes reveal that learning engagement can be considered both a process (e.g. negotiating understandings of engagement between teacher and students) and an outcome (e.g. the acquisition of the dominant language or school optimism in the home). Cultural capital and the socialisation role of schools lead to unequitable opportunities for migrant learners and a focus on skills defined by dominant discourses. By making "hidden curricula" more explicit and including non-dominant discourses, the social positions of migrants at school can be improved. Similarly, implementing multimodalities into the curriculum helps support different learning styles and may ease migrant learners' transition between education systems.

The teacher-student relationship was seen as most impactful in relation to the engagement of migrants. The role of teachers in linking ecological systems, developing culturally relevant learning resources as well as cultivating student wellbeing and sense of belonging appeared focal and detrimental effects were seen particularly in cases where a mismatch in expectations prevailed. Professional development undertaken in cross-cultural teaching contexts hence deserves more attention, especially regarding meeting the socio-emotional needs of migrant students.

Communities of support and home-school expectations regarding learning engagement have previously been studied but more research should be devoted to learner voices. More specifically, exo-level influences on engagement such as parental adjustment struggles may be overlooked if student voices are excluded from home-school cooperation research. Our study showed that responsibilities carried out at home carry weight for the students' sustenance in schoolwork and that conflicting expectations can alter both motivation and participation. Also, a reshaping of support services for migrant learners does not merely entail increased access or ensuring that sufficient information is available to make services culturally attractive. It means an inclusive, holistic approach to help match the complex, dynamic needs of culturally diverse student populations still unprivileged and underserved in education systems today.

Interventions focused on personality and performance are insufficient in the case of migrant learners. For the effective design of preventive support measures, more attention needs to be paid the extra-personal enablers and disablers of engagement outlined in this study. Whilst indicators of engagement, such as performance, can guide engagement identification, the double minority position of migrant students, typically not as well equipped socially or academically as their peers, has to be recognised and efforts need to be made to alleviate that position in future intervention designs. In the words of Furlong and Rebelez-Ernst (2014):

> Student engagement is part of a larger pattern that reflects whether a child is experiencing supportive and nurturing developmental contexts (school being one critical developmental context) ... When this system works synergistically with what is experienced at home and in the community, engagement lays the foundation of positive experiences for a lifelong pattern of living a meaningful and satisfying life. (Furlong & Rebelez-Ernst, 2014, p. 1)

Human development should never be analysed in a vacuum and categorisations rarely provide a holistic picture of any phenomenon under study. It is our hope that future studies in guidance and counseling focus more on social ecologies, nurturing developmental contexts in addition to personalised service, comparing different student populations longitudinally to help arrive at further conclusions about engagement and support services. As this study has sought to underline, the recognition of diversity as well as the inclusion of learners in the design of services ought to permeate such studies and remain a priority in education.

Disclosure statement

No potential conflict of interest was reported by the authors.

ORCID

Linda Molin-Karakoc http://orcid.org/0000-0002-7907-6993

References

Adelman, H. S., & Taylor, L. (2010). *Mental health in schools: Engaging learners, prevention problems, and improving schools.* Thousand Oaks, CA: Corwin Press.

Anderman, L. (2003). Academic and social perceptions as predictors of change in middle school students' sense of school belonging. *The Journal of Educational Experimentation, 72*(1), 11–21.

Appleton, J. L., Christenson, S. L., & Furlong, M. (2008). Student engagement with school: Critical conceptual and methodological issues of the construct. *Psychology in the Schools, 45*(5), 369–386.

Appleton, J. L., Christenson, S. L., Kim, D., & Reschly, S. L. (2006). Measuring cognitive and psychological engagement: Validation of the student engagement instrument. *Journal of School Psychology, 44*(2006), 427–445.

Bourdieu, P. (1986). The forms of capital. In J. Richardson (Ed.), *Handbook of theory and research for the sociology of education* (pp. 241–258). Westport, CT: Greenwood.

Bourdieu, P., & Waquant, L. C. D. (1992). *An invitation to reflexive sociology.* Cambridge: Polity Press.

Bowlby, J. (1979). *The making and breaking of affectional bonds.* London: Psychology Press.

Brar-Josan, N., & Yohani, S. C. (2017). Cultural brokers' role in facilitating informal and formal mental health supports for refugee youth in school and community context: A Canadian case study. *British Journal of Guidance and Counselling, 2017*(1), 117–130.

Braun, V., & Clarke, V. (2006). Using thematic analysis in psychology. *Qualitative Research in Psychology, 3*(2), 77–101.

Bronfenbrenner, U. (1992). Ecological systems theory. In R. Vasta (Ed.), *Six theories of child development: Revised formulations and current issues* (pp. 133–145). London: Jessica Kingsley.

Chiu, M. M., Pong, S. I., Mori, I., & Chow, B. W. (2012). Immigrant students' emotional and cognitive engagement at school: A multilevel analysis of students in 41 countries. *Journal of Youth and Adolescence, 41*(11), 1409–1425.

Devine, F. (Ed.). (2005). *Rethinking class: Culture, identities and lifestyles.* New York, NY: Palgrave MacMillan.

Finn, J. (1989). Withdrawing from school. *Review of Educational Research, 59*(2), 117–142.

Fredricks, J. A., Blumenfield, P. C., & Paris, A. H. (2004). School engagement: Potential of the concept, state of the evidence. *Review of Educational Research, 74*, 59–109.

Fredricks, J. A., & McColskey, W. (2011). Measuring student engagement in upper elementary through high school: A description of 21 instruments. Retrieved from https://ies.ed.gov/ncee/edlabs/regions/southeast/pdf/REL_2011098.pdf

Furlong, M., & Rebelez-Ernst, R. (2014). School and student engagement. In Greydanus, D. E., Pratt, H. D. & Patel, D. R. (2013). Health Promotion: Adolescent Well Being. In A. Michalos (Ed.), *Encyclopedia of quality of life and well-being research* (pp. 2735–2743). Netherlands: Springer.

Greco Morasso, S. (2012). Learning as a precondition of migrants' interest and engagement. *Human Affairs, 22*(3), 313–324.

Hammar Chiriac, E. (2014). Group work as an incentive for learning – students' experiences of group work. *Frontiers in Psychology, 5*, 558–568.

Kyttälä, H. M., & Sinkkonen, M. (2014). Experiences of Finnish teachers working with immigrant students. *European Journal of Special Needs Education, 29*(2), 167–183.

Lincoln, Y. S., & Guba, E. G. (1985). *Naturalistic inquiry.* Newbury Park, CA: Sage.

Maslow, A. H. (1943). *A theory of human motivation. Psychological Review, 50*(4), 370–396.

McLeod, S. (2018). *Lev Vygotsky.* Retrieved from https://www.simplypsychology.org/vygotsky.html

Onchiwari, A.-O., & Keengwe, J. (2008). Teaching the immigrant child: Application of child development theories. *Early Childhood Education Journal, 36*(3), 267–273.

Reyes, M. R., Brackett, M. A., Rivers, S. E., Elbertson, N. A., & Salovey, P. (2011). Classroom emotional climate, teacher affiliation, and student conduct. *Journal of Classroom Interaction, 46*, 27–36.

Sahlberg, P. (2009). A short history of educational reform. Retrieved from file:///C:/Users/Alp/AppData/Local/Temp/AshorthistoryofeducationalreforminFinland.pdf

Scheffer, R. H. (2005). *Key concepts in developmental psychology.* London: SAGE.

Schleicher, A. (2012). Helping immigrant students succeed. Retrieved from https://www.oecd.org/education/Helping-immigrant-students-to-succeed-at-school-and-beyond.pdf

Senior, C., & Howard, C. (2015). The state of the art in student engagement. *Frontiers in Psychology 6*, 355. doi:10.3389/fpsyg.2015.00355

Suarez-Orozco, C., Suarez-Orozco, M., & Todorova, I. (2008). *Learning a new land: Immigrant students in American society*. Cambridge: Harvard University Press.

Suarez-Orozco, M. (2001). Globalization, immigration, and education: The research agenda. *Harvard Educational Review*, *71*, 345–366.

Super, C., & Harkness, S. (1999). *Parents' cultural belief systems: Their origins, expressions and consequences*. New York, NY: The Guildford Press.

Taylor, L., & Parsons, J. (2011). Improving student engagement. *Current Issues in Education* 14(1). Retrieved from http://cie.asu.edu/

Tuominen-Soini, H., & Salmela-Aro, K. (2014). Schoolwork engagement and burnout among Finnish high school students and young adults: Profiles, progressions, and educational outcomes.. *Developmental Psychology*, *50*(3), 649–662.

University of Minnesota. (1990). *Check & Connect*. Retrieved from http://checkandconnect.umn.edu/research/default.html

Vygotsky, L. S. (1978). Mind in society: The development of higher psychological processes. In M. Cole, V. John-Steiner, S. Scribner, & E. Souberman, (Eds.) (pp. 19–100). Cambridge, MA: Harvard University Press.

Watts-Taffe, S., Laster, P., Broach, L., Marinak, B., Connor McDonald, C., & Walker-Dalhouse, D. (2012). Differentiated instruction: Making informed teacher decisions. *The Reading Teacher*, *66*(4), 303–314.

Willms, J. D. (2003). Student engagement at school: A sense of belonging and participation. Retrieved from http://www.oecd.org/education/school/programmeforinternationalstudentassessmentpisa/33689437.pdf

Wonglorsaichon, B., Wongwanich, S., & Wiratchai, N. (2014). The influence of students school engagement on learning achievement: A structural equation modeling analysis. *Procedia - Social and Behavioral Sciences*, *116*, 1748–1755.

A comparison of mental health literacy, attitudes, and help-seeking intentions among domestic and international tertiary students

Bonnie A. Clough, Sonia M. Nazareth, Jamin J. Day and Leanne M. Casey

ABSTRACT

Limited research has examined distress or help-seeking knowledge and attitudes among international students. The aim of this study was to examine psychological distress, mental health literacy (MHL), and help-seeking attitudes and intentions among a sample of domestic and international tertiary students. The sample comprised 357 domestic and international tertiary students. Participants completed an online questionnaire package, with measures relating to distress, MHL, help-seeking attitudes, and help-seeking intentions. International student status was predictive of lower scores on MHL, help-seeking attitudes, and help-seeking intentions for suicidal ideation. Student group was not predictive of help-seeking intentions for emotional problems or psychological distress, but international students had lower help-seeking intentions for suicidal ideation. Educational interventions targeting MHL and help-seeking attitudes and intentions among international students may be required to improve help-seeking behaviours.

Many studies have documented the various psychosocial, academic, and financial challenges in the university environment (Adlaf, Gliksman, Demers, & Newton-Taylor, 2001; Furnham, Cook, Martin, & Batey, 2011; Palmer & Puri, 2006; Ryan, Shochet, & Stallman, 2010). Such challenges appear more marked for international students, due to the additional stressors of transitioning to a new culture and social and learning environment (Khawaja & Dempsey, 2007, 2008; Lu, Dear, Johnston, Wootton, & Titov, 2013; Mori, 2000; Reavley & Jorm, 2010). There have been many terms in the literature developed to explain the adjustment difficulties of international tertiary students, including "foreign student syndrome" (Ward, 1967), "acculturative stress" (Berry, Kim, Minde, & Mok, 1987), and "uprooting disorder" (Tsang, 2001). A number of studies report that international students experience high levels of psychological distress, including helplessness, social withdrawal, loneliness, homesickness, irritability, and even hostility (Sandhu, 1995; Sawir, Marginson, Deumert, Nyland, & Ramia, 2008). An important aspect of understanding these mental health needs is examining whether these difficulties are unique to the experience of being an international student and whether there are differences between international and domestic students in understanding of and attitudes toward mental health problems.

A number of theories have been proposed to understand the experiences of international students. Broadly, contemporary theories have focused on the cognitive, social and behavioural, and affective adaptation of the individual to their new environment (Zhou, Jindal-Snape, Topping, &

Todman, 2008). For example, social identification theories typically focus on the cognitive changes associated with cultural adaptation, which may include changes to one's self-identity (Deaux, 1996). This change process may be associated with increased mental health concerns. However, across these theories, the links between adaptation and psychological functioning require further research. For example, successful adaptation may not necessarily lead to better psychological functioning if the individual still feels guilt or loss for the transition. There is a need for greater research examining the psychological processes, including reactions to distress (e.g. help-seeking intentions and attitudes), among international students.

Psychological distress among university students

Psychological distress is common among university students (Cooke, Bewick, Barkham, Bradley, & Audin, 2006; Khawaja & Dempsey, 2007; Lu et al., 2013; Stallman, 2010). However, despite substantial research conducted on the psychological well-being of university students, relatively little research has been carried out on the psychological well-being and distress levels of international students (Khawaja & Dempsey, 2007, 2008; Lu et al., 2013). Previous research has found that when compared to domestic students, international students have higher psychiatric morbidity rates (Janca & Hetzer, 1992) and experience additional difficulties unique to their situation (Toyokawa & Toyokawa, 2002).

A number of studies have compared psychological wellbeing, distress, or psychiatric morbidity between international and domestic students, with results largely mixed as to whether differences exist between the two groups on indicators of mental health (e.g. Fritz, Chin, & DeMarinis, 2008; Janca & Hetzer, 1992). To the authors' knowledge, only one study has been conducted in the Australian context comparing the psychological well-being of domestic and international tertiary students. Khawaja and Dempsey (2008) compared the two groups of university students on psychological variables such as psychological distress, social support, mismatched expectations, academic stress, and dysfunctional coping strategies. When compared to domestic students, international students had higher mismatched expectations of university life with their actual experience, had less perceived social support, and utilised more dysfunctional coping strategies. However, contrary to hypotheses, international students reported similar levels of psychological distress in comparison with domestic students. Overall, this study highlighted that the distress was equivalent between the two student populations but international students tended to have lower levels of social support and poorer coping mechanisms to deal with this distress when compared with their domestic counterparts. The international students were more likely to adopt coping strategies such as avoidance and repression of their difficulties instead of accessing suitable services. However, help-seeking intentions and factors that influence these intentions were not examined.

Help-seeking behaviours among university students

Despite evidence suggesting a higher level of mental health problems among university students, the utilisation of mental health services by this population is relatively low. Among an American sample, up to 84% of university students who screened positive for anxiety or depression had not accessed treatment services for the disorder (Eisenberg, Golberstein, & Gollust, 2007). In a survey of 1168 students across three Australian universities, Stallman and Shochet (2009) found that 83.9% of students experienced elevated psychological distress, out of which only 34.3% had engaged in help-seeking behaviours. Similar to the general tertiary student population, there is an observable trend of underutilisation of mental health services among international student populations (Morgan, Ness, & Robinson, 2003; Nilsson, Berkel, Flores, & Lucas, 2004; Raunic & Xenos, 2008; Yakushko, Davidson, & Sanford-Martens, 2008). In particular, a survey of Chinese-speaking international students in Australia identified that 54% of the students reported high psychological distress, with only 9% engaging with a mental health service for assistance (Lu et al., 2013). In addition to low help-seeking rates among domestic and international students, a number of studies have examined differences in help-seeking rates between the two student populations and found that international students demonstrate lower service use compared to their counterparts (Hunt & Eisenberg, 2010; Khawaja & Stallman, 2011; Morgan et al., 2003; Nilsson et al., 2004). Despite these differences, there remains a lack of research in this population examining factors that may be influencing such disparities in help-seeking intentions.

Mental health literacy

A factor that has been widely discussed as a facilitator of help-seeking is mental health literacy. Jorm et al. (1997) coined the term "Mental Health Literacy (MHL)" which can be defined as "knowledge and beliefs about mental disorders which aid their recognition, management or prevention" (p. 182). A number of studies have indicated that levels of knowledge about mental health and available help-seeking options is less than optimal in the university student community, and particularly so within the international student community (Ang & Liamputtong, 2008; Lu et al., 2013; Raunic & Xenos, 2008; Reavley, McCann, & Jorm, 2012; Shea & Yeh, 2008). In the previously mentioned survey of Chinese-speaking international students attending an Australian university, common barriers to seeking professional help for mental health problems were reported as being limited knowledge of available mental health services, the perception that their distress was not severe enough to access treatment, and the lack of knowledge of symptoms of psychological distress (Lu et al., 2013). However, much of this research has been descriptive or qualitative in nature. There is a need for more precise measurement of MHL in this field, using quantitative and psychometrically robust methods (O'Connor & Casey, 2015; O'Connor, Casey, & Clough, 2014).

The current study

Given the increasing numbers of individuals choosing to study abroad, it is vital to understand their psychological well-being while at university. The purpose of the current study was to examine potential differences in mental health and related constructs, such as MHL and help-seeking attitudes, between domestic and international students in Australia. Though this study was primarily exploratory in nature, based on the prior studies reviewed above we expected to observe lower MHL and poorer help-seeking attitudes and intentions among international students. Furthermore, based on recent examination of mental health differences between domestic and international students in an Australian context (Khawaja & Dempsey, 2008), we expected to observe similar overall levels of psychological distress between the two student groups.

Method

Participants

A power analysis was conducted using G*Power 3.1 (Faul, Erdfelder, Buchner, & Lang, 2009) to determine the minimum sample size required for the between-groups analysis. The power analysis indicated that 128 participants (64 in each group) were required, based on a power level of .80, and an estimated medium effect size ($d = .5$), when employing the traditional .05 criterion for statistical significance.

Data were obtained from a total of 357 domestic and international students from an Australian university and associated tertiary college. These students included undergraduate, post-graduate, and tertiary preparation (such as diploma) students across all study areas. The sample comprised 148 domestic students and 209 international students. Among the domestic students, 26 were male and 122 female, with ages ranging between 17 and 59 years ($M = 25.5$, $SD = 9.46$). Among the international students, 79 were male and 130 were female, with ages ranging between 17 and

52 years ($M = 23.0$, $SD = 5.47$). The characteristics of the two student populations are further explored as part of the main statistical analyses.

Design

The study was a between-groups (two levels: international or domestic) cross-sectional survey design. Data were examined in an exploratory fashion for potential differences between groups on the dependent variables of psychological distress, MHL, and help-seeking attitudes and intentions.

Materials and measures

Demographics

All participants were asked to provide demographic information, including: age, gender, student status (i.e. international student or not), ethnicity, length of time lived in Australia, educational qualifications or current degree, years of university completed, and previous use of mental health services (MHSs).

General psychological distress

The Kessler-10 (K-10; Kessler et al., 2003) is a 10-item questionnaire that provides a global measure of psychological distress based on questions about the level of anxiety and depressive symptoms in the most recent four-week period. Total scores range from 10 to 50, with higher scores indicating higher levels of psychological distress. Internal consistency in the current study was high ($\alpha = .91$).

Help-seeking attitudes

Attitudes towards help-seeking were assessed using the Inventory of Attitudes toward Mental Health Services (IAMHS; Mackenzie, Knox, Gekoski, & Macaulay, 2004). The 24-item measure has three subscales: psychological openness, help-seeking propensity, and indifference to stigma. In the current study, the full scale demonstrated high internal consistency (Cronbach's alpha coefficient = .86).

Help-seeking intentions

Intentions to seek help for mental health problems were measured by the General Help-Seeking Questionnaire (GHSQ; Wilson, Deane, & Ciarrochi, 2005). The scale consists of two subscales, one for each type of problem: suicidal problems and personal-emotional problems. A higher score indicates greater intentions to seek help. Internal consistency in the current study was acceptable for the emotional problems scale ($\alpha = .72$) and for the suicidal problems scale ($\alpha = .77$). In the current study, as intentions to seek professional help were of primary interest, a variable labelled *highest help-seeking intention*, was created for both suicidal and emotional problem subscales. Each participant was allocated the highest score they gave to any one professional help source from the three included in the measure (mental health professional, phone helpline, doctor/GP). As described in Smith and Shochet (2011), this scoring method is preferable to an average score of the professional sources as an individual need only be willing to seek help from one particular professional source in order to receive appropriate assistance.

Mental health literacy

MHL was assessed using the Mental Health Literacy Scale (O'Connor & Casey, 2015), which measures knowledge about mental health and related issues. Responses are summed to produce a total score, with higher scores indicating greater MHL. In the current study internal consistency was high (Cronbach's alpha = .92).

Procedure

Ethical approval was granted from the university's human research ethics committee. Participants were recruited by posters placed across the university campus, posts on social networking sites (e.g. Facebook), and recruitment emails sent to all students through the university's internal email system. As an incentive, all participants were entered into a draw to win one of four $50 shopping gift cards for participation. Additionally, first year psychology student participants (13.45% of sample) received 1-hour course credit for participation. Consent, demographics, and questionnaire data was collected through the online survey programme LimeSurvey (https://www.limesurvey.org/).

Results

Analyses were conducted using SPSS version 22.0 (IBM, 2013). Examination of the data indicated that the assumption of normality was violated for several variables, and as such transformations were conducted. However, as transformations did not change the significance or interpretation of any analyses, only untransformed data is presented. Missing data was observed across variables. Little's Missing Completely at Random Test (MCAR; Little, 1988) was significant (χ^2 (444) = 499.86, $p = .034$), indicating that systematic failure to respond to one or more items occurred. The highest rate of missing data occurred for the demographic item relating to field of study, with most of the missing data occurring among the international student sample (51.67% of international students non-responding, 14.19% of domestic students non-responding). It was hypothesised that this item may not have been worded clearly for participants whose first language was other than English. Although imputation was considered for this variable, as it was not intended for use in the primary hypotheses and because the rate of non-responding was differential between the groups, field of study was removed from subsequent analyses. Descriptive data for the variable is, however, contained in Table 1. Removal of the variable returned a non-significant result on the MCAR test (χ^2 (444) = 483.11, $p = .097$), indicating that remaining data was missing completely at random. Listwise deletion by analysis was used to handle remaining missing data.

Preliminary analyses

Chi-square and t-tests were conducted to investigate whether the international and domestic student populations were significantly different on demographic variables, as displayed in Table 1. Compared to domestic students, international students were more likely to be male (χ^2 (1, N = 357) = 13.46, $p < .001$, $V = .20$), younger (t (236) = 2.77, $p = .01$, $d = .03$), have been studying at university for less time (χ^2 (7, N = 357) = 41.60, $p < .001$, $V = .34$), and have no previous use of MHSs (χ^2 (1, N = 357) = 51.37, $p < .001$, $V = .39$).

As the study contained a quasi-experimental independent variable (whereby random allocation to the two groups was not possible), it was not surprising that differences emerged between the two groups on key demographic variables. To control for the potential influence of these demographic variables on the outcome variables, a series of hierarchical regressions was conducted. More specifically, demographic variables found to be non-equivalent between the international and domestic student samples were first entered into the model (Model 1). These included gender (0 = male, 1 = female), age, previous use of MHSs (0 = no, 1 = yes), and years at university (dummy coded 0–7). To determine whether group differences existed after accounting for sampling differences in the previous step, student group (0 = domestic, 1 = international) was entered into Model 2 and difference in model fit examined, to indicate whether student status accounted for variance in the outcome variable above and beyond that of the demographic variables.

Table 1. Descriptive Statistics for international and domestic students across demographic and psychological variables.

	Domestic M (SD) / *n* (%)	International M (SD) / *n* (%)
Age	25.34 (9.32)	23.02 (5.41)
Gender		
Male	30 (19.1%)	75 (37.5%)
Female	127 (80.9%)	125 (62.5%)
Years at university		
None	–	34 (17.0%)
Currently in first year	60 (38.2%)	78 (39.0%)
Currently in second year	24 (15.3%)	28 (14.0%)
Currently in third year	23 (14.6%)	18 (9.0%)
Currently in fourth year	18 (11.5%)	5 (2.5%)
Completed bachelor's	5 (3.2%)	4 (2.0%)
Currently postgraduate	25 (15.9%)	28 (14.0%)
Completed postgraduate	2 (1.3%)	5 (2.5%)
Years in Australia		
<3 months	–	57 (28.5%)
3–6 months	–	38 (19.0%)
6–12 months	1 (0.6%)	33 (16.5%)
1–3 years	3 (1.9%)	50 (25.0%)
> 3 years	153 (97.5%)	22 (11.0%)
Study Discipline		
Psychology	34 (26.8%)	13 (12.9%)
Other health-related	26 (20.5%)	18 (17.8%)
Other	67 (52.8%)	70 (69.3%)
Previous use of MHSs		
Yes	91 (58.0%)	41 (20.5%)
No	66 (42.0%)	159 (79.5%)
Psychological distress	20.71 (8.03)	19.33 (6.91)
Mental health literacy	132.41 (13.12)	113.12 (15.54)
Help-seeking attitudes	67.54 (15.53)	57.90 (12.43)
Psychological openness	21.10 (6.02)	16.21 (5.93)
Help-seeking propensity	24.12 (5.31)	21.43 (5.91)
Indifference to stigma	22.34 (7.54)	20.30 (6.53)
Highest Help-seeking intentions (E)	5.74 (1.31)	5.25 (1.45)
Highest Help-seeking intentions (S)	5.89 (1.38)	5.29 (1.70)

Note: E = emotional problems; S = suicidal thoughts.

Main analyses

Descriptive statistics for international and domestic students' scores on the measures of psychological distress, MHL, help-seeking attitudes, and help-seeking intentions are displayed in Table 1.

Psychological distress

As described above, hierarchical multiple regressions were conducted with psychological distress as the response variable. Model 1 (Table 2) accounted for a small but significant amount of variance in

Table 2. Hierarchical multiple regression of demographic variables and student group on psychological distress.

	Model 1				Model 2			
Variable	B	β	sr^2	*p*	B	β	sr^2	*p*
Gender: Female	0.92	0.06	<.01	.305	0.85	0.05	<.01	.347
Age	−0.13	−0.13	.02	.023	−0.13	−0.13	.02	.022
Previous MHS Use	3.19	0.21	.04	<.001	3.02	0.20	.03	.001
Years at University	−0.01	<0.01	<.01	.971	−0.02	−0.01	<.01	.935
Student Group: International					−.51	−.03	<.01	.562
R^2		.06				.06		
F / df		5.00	4325	.001		4.06	5324	.001
ΔR^2						<.01		
ΔF / df						.34	1324	.562

Note: $N = 330$.

psychological distress (approximately 6%). The addition of student group in Model 2 did not significantly improve the amount of variance explained by Model 1, indicating that psychological distress was approximately equivalent between the domestic and international students after demographic differences in samples were accounted for. Age and previous use of MHSs were significant individual predictors in the model, with younger age and having accessed MHSs in the past both predictive of higher psychological distress.

Mental health literacy

A hierarchical multiple regression was conducted to assess the influence of demographic variables and student group on MHL. Model 1 (Table 3) was significant, explaining 26% of the variance in MHL. Model 2 accounted for significantly more variance (41% total) than Model 1, indicating that student group was a significant predictor of MHL after controlling for differences in demographic variables. In order of importance in the final model, being an international student, having no previous contact with MHSs, being at university for less time, and being male were associated with poorer MHL. Age was a significant predictor in Model 1, but became non-significant in Model 2, indicating that at least some of the variance in the response variable originally accounted for by age was better explained by student group.

Help-seeking attitudes

The IAMHS total score was used as the response variable to indicate help-seeking attitudes. Model 1 (Table 4) was significant, and showed that 40% of the variance in help-seeking attitudes was explained by the demographic variables entered. Model 2 was also significant, indicating that international student status explained a significant amount of variance beyond that of the demographic variables (45% total). In the final model, the most important predictor was student group with international student status being associated with poorer help-seeking attitudes. Age and gender were

Table 3. Hierarchical multiple regression of demographic variables and student group on MHL.

	Model 1				Model 2			
Variable	B	β	sr^2	p	B	β	sr^2	p
Gender: Female	6.40	0.17	.03	.003	4.65	0.12	.01	.016
Age	0.25	0.12	.01	.046	0.17	0.08	.01	.126
Previous MHS Use	11.56	0.33	.10	<.001	6.37	0.18	.03	.001
Years at University	1.45	0.17	.03	.003	1.37	0.16	.02	.002
Student Group: International					−14.85	−.43	.15	<.001
R^2		.26				.41		
F / df		22.55	4257	<.001		36.09	5256	<.001
ΔR^2						.15		
ΔF / df						67.07	1256	<.001

Note: $N = 262$.

Table 4. Hierarchical multiple regression of demographic variables and student group on Help-seeking Attitudes.

	Model 1				Model 2			
Variable	B	β	sr^2	p	B	β	sr^2	p
Gender: Female	6.02	0.19	.03	.001	5.27	0.16	.03	.002
Age	0.37	0.20	.03	.001	0.35	0.18	.03	.001
Previous MHS Use	5.42	0.18	.04	.001	3.22	0.11	.01	.065
Years at University	0.49	0.07	<.01	.240	0.41	0.07	<.01	.317
Student Group: International					−6.29	−.21	.04	<.001
R^2		.40				.45		
F/ df		14.61	4305	<.001		15.05	5304	<.001
ΔR^2						.04		
ΔF/ df						14.27	1304	<.001

Note: $N = 310$.

also significant predictors in the final model, such that younger age and being male were also associated with poorer help-seeking attitudes.

Help-seeking intentions for emotional problems

Model 1 (Table 5) of the hierarchical regression for help-seeking intentions for emotional problems was significant (7% of variance explained). The addition of student group in Model 2 did not explain significantly more variance than that already explained by the demographic variables (8% total). In the final model, previous use of MHSs and age were significant predictors, such that previous use and older age were associated with more positive help-seeking intentions for emotional problems.

Help-seeking intentions for suicidal thoughts

Model 1 (Table 5) explained a significant amount of variance in help-seeking intentions for suicidal thoughts (approximately 7%). Model 2 explained significantly more variance than Model 1 (8% total), indicating that student group accounted for variance above and beyond that already accounted for by the demographic variables. Student group was the most important individual predictor, with international student status being associated with poorer help-seeking intentions for suicidal thoughts. The only other significant predictor in the final model was years at university, with greater years of study being associated with more positive help-seeking intentions for suicidal thoughts.

Discussion

Consistent with calls for more research examining mental health needs and service use among international students (Raunic & Xenos, 2008), the aim of the present study was to examine the constructs of psychological distress, MHL, and help-seeking attitudes and intentions among international and domestic students. The study was quasi-experimental in nature due to the non-random allocation of participants to groups (domestic or international). Unsurprisingly, demographic differences were found between the two student groups. However, consistent with our hypotheses, differences between the two student samples still emerged once the potential influence of these demographic

Table 5. Hierarchical multiple regression of demographic variables and student group on Help-seeking Intentions.

		Model 1				Model 2			
	Variable	B	β	sr^2	p	B	β	sr^2	p
Emotional Problems	Gender: Female	<0.01	<0.01	<.01	.988	−0.03	−0.01	<.01	.869
	Age	0.03	0.15	.02	.020	0.03	0.15	.02	.027
	Previous MHS Use	0.53	0.19	.03	.004	0.44	0.16	.02	.025
	Years at University	0.01	0.01	<.01	.842	0.01	0.01	<.01	.859
	Student Group: Int					−0.26	−0.09	<.01	.158
	R^2		.07				.08		
	F / df		5.00	4254	.001		4.41	5253	.001
	ΔR^2						.01		
	ΔF / df						2.00	1253	.158
Suicidal Thoughts									
	Gender: Female	−0.23	−0.07	<.01	.292	−0.28	−0.08	.01	.203
	Age	0.02	0.08	.01	.224	0.01	0.07	<.01	.295
	Previous MHS Use	0.49	0.15	.02	.018	0.33	0.11	.01	.124
	Years at University	0.11	0.14	.02	.037	0.10	0.13	.02	.039
	Student Group: Int					−0.44	−0.14	.02	.037
	R^2		.07				.08		
	F/ df		4.48	4254	.002		4.51	5253	.001
	ΔR^2						.02		
	ΔF/ df						4.38	1253	.037

Note: $N = 259$ for both analyses, Int = International.

differences had been controlled. Specifically, international students reported lower help-seeking intentions for suicidal thoughts, and greater barriers to help-seeking, including lower mental health literacy and less favourable attitudes towards seeking help.

Psychological distress

Previous research examining psychological distress and wellbeing between international and domestic students has been mixed (Fritz et al., 2008; Hechanova-Alampay, Beehr, Christiansen, & Van Horn, 2002; Janca & Hetzer, 1992; Rajapaksa & Dundes, 2002). In the current sample, no differences were found between the two student groups in terms of psychological distress, consistent with other recent studies conducted in Australia (Khawaja & Dempsey, 2008; Stallman, 2010). Regardless of group membership, the students in the current study reported moderate levels of distress, which supports previous findings in which 75% of the tertiary students assessed reported moderate levels of distress (Pierceall & Keim, 2007). It is possible that international students studying in Australia do not experience the same degree of emotional distress and concerns as international students studying in other countries. However, nearly 40% of the international students in our sample had been living in Australia for over one year, thus it is possible that a significant proportion may have adapted and acculturated adequately to the challenges associated with studying abroad. Research has indicated that stressors such as accommodation problems and education system differences tend to be resolved or adjusted to earlier in the transition to university (Khawaja & Dempsey, 2008). Finally, consistent with previous literature (e.g. Stallman, 2010), we also found that being of younger age and having previously accessed MHSs were associated with higher levels of psychological distress. Considered within the context of theories of acculturation, it is possible that the students in the present sample had either engaged in effective cognitive, social and behavioural, and affective adaptation processes, or that engagement in these processes were not predictive of their psychological distress.

Attitudes and mental health literacy

Also consistent with previous research (Fan, 1999; Shea & Yeh, 2008), international students had lower levels of MHL than their domestic counterparts. MHL was also lower among males, students who had been studying for less time, and students who had not previously had contact with MHSs. However, there was a statistically significant difference between domestic and international students on MHL after controlling for these demographic variables, and student group was the strongest predictor of MHL. These results support the proposition that being an international student may be related to additional barriers to accessing appropriate mental health treatment (Lu et al., 2013). It is therefore not surprising that international student status was the strongest predictor of poorer attitudes toward accessing mental health services after controlling for related demographic variables, including younger age and being male. These findings are consistent with previous research demonstrating that concerns about stigma and the usefulness of mental health treatment are common among international students (Khawaja & Dempsey, 2008; Lu et al., 2013), as is underutilisation of support services on university campuses (Mori, 2000). Less positive help-seeking attitudes reported by the international students may be a result of these students being more likely to use avoidance and other passive coping strategies to deal with their distress (Khawaja & Dempsey, 2008; Leong & Lau, 2001). That is, although levels of distress were similar between the two groups, it may be that international students cope with this distress via different mechanisms.

Help-seeking intentions and behaviour

In addition to poorer help-seeking attitudes, international students also reported lower help-seeking intentions (via professional sources) for suicidal ideation. No differences were found between groups for help-seeking intentions for emotional problems. These results are partially consistent with previous literature that suggests lower help-seeking intentions and reluctance to seek help exists among international students (Lu et al., 2013). It has also been postulated that higher MHL levels and positive help-seeking attitudes are associated with higher help-seeking intentions (Smith & Shochet, 2011; Wilson et al., 2005). In support of this notion, all three of these factors were found to be higher among domestic than international students. Years at university was also a significant predictor of help-seeking. International students also reported less previous use of mental health services than domestic students. This finding should be considered within the context of the broader student mental health literature, which typically reports lower help-seeking and use of mental health services by university students, domestic and international, when compared to the general population (e.g. Eisenberg et al., 2007). As such, international students may be considered to be a particularly vulnerable sub-group of a population with already low indicators of help-seeking intentions and behaviours.

Limitations and strengths

Although the current research has provided increased understanding of international students and their needs, some limitations should be noted. First, all participants came from a single Australian institution, suggesting that they may not adequately represent the average tertiary student in Australia. This noted, use of one university also holds constant the university environment, context, and culture, thus enhancing the internal validity of the study. Second, even though some of the scales used in the study have been used previously in cross-cultural settings (e.g. K-10), their validity on the basis of international students has not been evaluated. Furthermore, the relationship between field of study and the variables of interest was unable to be evaluated due to the high rate of missing data among international students for this item. Also, the group of international students were treated as a homogeneous group in the current study, as the purpose was to examine trends within the group as a whole. However, it is likely that differences exist among international students based on culture, gender, and other background and personal variables, which should be considered in future research. Lastly, although the design of the study allowed for a robust analysis by quantitative methods, utilising a mixed methods design would have enabled for a more in depth qualitative analysis to better understand the unique needs and difficulties experienced by this population. Despite these limitations, it should be noted that the current study had several strengths. This study is one of only a few to assess the mental health literacy and help-seeking attitudes and intentions of international students, and in particular, to compare international students to a domestic student sample from the same study environment. Furthermore, the study was well powered and differences between groups were evident after controlling for existing demographic differences.

Summary and future directions

The comparison between the two student groups revealed that although both groups experience similar levels of psychological distress, the two groups differ on MHL levels, help-seeking attitudes, and help-seeking intentions for suicidal ideation. These findings have important implications for the tailoring of suitable interventions that focus on promoting the use of professional mental health services to students. International students may be in need of proactive interventions targeting mental health knowledge and help-seeking attitudes. Future research that includes the use of mixed or qualitative components may provide greater insight into the specific areas to target for interventions among tertiary international students. Such tailored interventions targeting mental health knowledge and attitudes may be beneficial in increasing student engagement with mental health services. These interventions would also provide financial benefit by reducing treatment costs through early intervention. In particular, future research may also be required to investigate the optimal timing and dosage of interventions throughout the acculturation process. Of particular interest for education providers, will be whether low intensity interventions, such as online and digital interventions, may be able to support international students through preventative approaches to improving mental health literacy and help-seeking intentions and attitudes. Such interventions have potential for wide and cost-effective dissemination, and may increase the likelihood of students' future engagement with mental health services, as needed. The development of tailored interventions for this population, digital or in person, will likely provide considerable benefit for international students experiencing mental health difficulties, an issue which is of particular importance given the exponential growth in international study and student populations.

Disclosure statement

No potential conflict of interest was reported by the author(s).

References

Adlaf, E., Gliksman, L., Demers, A., & Newton-Taylor, B. (2001). The prevalence of elevated psychological distress among Canadian undergraduates: Findings from the 1998 Canadian campus survey. *Journal of American College Health, 50*, 67–72.

Ang, P., & Liamputtong, P. (2008). "Out of the circle": international students and the use of university counselling services. *Australian Journal of Adult Learning, 48*(1), 109–130.

Berry, J. W., Kim, U., Minde, T., & Mok, D. (1987). Comparitive studies of acculturative stress. *International Migration Review, 21*(3), 491–511.

Cooke, R., Bewick, B. M., Barkham, M., Bradley, M., & Audin, K. (2006). Measuring, monitoring and managing the psychological well-being of first year university students. *British Journal of Guidance & Counselling, 34*(4), 505–517. doi:10.1080/03069880600942624

Deaux, K. (1996). *Social identification*. In E. T. Higgins & A. W. Kruglanski (Eds.), *Social psychology: Handbook of basic principles* (pp. 777–798). New York, NY: Guilford Press.

Eisenberg, D., Golberstein, E., & Gollust, S. E. (2007). Help-seeking and access to mental health care in a university student population. *Medical Care, 45*(7), 594–601.

Fan, C. (1999). A comparison of attitudes towards mental illness and knowledge of mental health services between Australian and Asian students. *Community Mental Health Journal, 35*(1), 47–56.

Faul, F., Erdfelder, E., Buchner, A., & Lang, A. G. (2009). Statistical power analysis using G*Power 3.1: Tests for correlation and regression analyses. *Behavior Research Methods, 41*, 1149–1160. doi:10.3758/BRM.41.4.1149

Fritz, M. V., Chin, D., & DeMarinis, V. (2008). Stressors, anxiety, acculturation and adjustment among international and North American students. *International Journal of Intercultural Relations, 32*(3), 244–259.

Furnham, A., Cook, R., Martin, N., & Batey, M. (2011). Mental health literacy among university students. *Journal of Public Mental Health, 10*(4), 198–210. doi:10.1108/17465721111188223

Hechanova-Alampay, R., Beehr, T. A., Christiansen, N., & Van Horn, R. K. (2002). Adjustment and strain among domestic and international student sojourners. *School Psychology International, 23*(4), 458–474. doi:10.1177/0143034302234007

Hunt, J., & Eisenberg, D. (2010). Mental health problems and help-seeking behavior among college students. *Journal of Adolescent Health*, *46*(1), 3–10. doi:10.1016/j.jadohealth.2009.08.008. Retrieved from http://www.ncbi.nlm.nih.gov/pubmed/20123251

IBM. (2013). *Ibm statistics for windows (version version 22.0)*. Armonk, NY: IBM Corp.

Janca, A., & Hetzer, J. E. (1992). Psychiatric morbidity of foreign students in Yugoslavia. *International Journal of Social Psychiatry*, *38*, 287–292.

Jorm, A. F., Korten, A. E., Jacomb, P., Christensen, H., Rodgers, B., & Pollitt, P. (1997). "Mental health literacy": A survey of the public's ability to recognise mental disorders and their beliefs about the effectiveness of treatment. *Medical Journal of Australia*, *166*, 182–186.

Kessler, R. C., Barker, P. R., Colpe, L. J., Epstein, J. F., Gfroerer, J. C., Hiripi, E., & Zaslavsky, A. M. (2003). Screening for serious mental illness in the general population. *Archives of General Psychiatry*, *60*(2), 184–189. doi:10.1017/S0033291702006074

Khawaja, N., & Dempsey, J. (2007). Psychological distress in international university students: An Australian study. *Australian Journal of Guidance and Counselling*, *17*(1), 13–27.

Khawaja, N., & Dempsey, J. (2008). A comparison of international and domestic tertiary students in Australia. *Australian Journal of Guidance and Counselling*, *18*(1), 30–46.

Khawaja, N., & Stallman, H. M. (2011). Understanding the coping strategies of international students: A qualitative approach. *Australian Journal of Guidance and Counselling*, *21*(2), 203–224. doi:10.1375/ajgc.21.2.203

Leong, F., & Lau, A. (2001). Barriers to providing effective mental health services to Asian Americans. *Mental Health Services Research*, *3*(4), 201–214.

Little, R. J. (1988). A test of missing completely at random for multivariate data with missing values. *Journal of the American Statistical Association*, *83*(404), 1198–1202.

Lu, S. H., Dear, B. F., Johnston, L., Wootton, B. M., & Titov, N. (2013). An internet survey of emotional health, treatment seeking and barriers to accessing mental health treatment among Chinese-speaking international students in Australia. *Counselling Psychology Quarterly*, *27*(1), 96–108. doi:10.1080/09515070.2013.824408

Mackenzie, C. S., Knox, V., Gekoski, W., & Macaulay, H. (2004). An adaptation and extension of the attitudes toward seeking professional psychological help scale. *Journal of Applied Social Psychology*, *34*, 2410–2433.

Morgan, T., Ness, D., & Robinson, M. (2003). Student's help-seeking behaviours by gender, racial background, and student status. *Canadian Journal of Counselling*, *37*(2), 151–166.

Mori, S. (2000). Addressing the mental health concerns of international students. *Journal of Counselling and Development*, *78*, 137–144.

Nilsson, J. E., Berkel, L. A., Flores, L. Y., & Lucas, M. S. (2004). Utilization rate and presenting concerns of international students at a university counseling center. *Journal of College Student Psychotherapy*, *19*(2), 49–59. doi:10.1300/J035v19n02_05

O'Connor, M., & Casey, L. (2015). The mental health literacy scale (MHLS): A new scale-based measure of mental health literacy. *Psychiatry Research*. doi:10.1016/j.psychres.2015.05.064

O'Connor, M., Casey, L., & Clough, B. (2014). Measuring mental health literacy–a review of scale-based measures. *Journal of Mental Health*, *23*(4), 197–204.

Palmer, S., & Puri, A. (2006). *Coping with stress at university: A survival guide*. London: Sage.

Pierceall, E. A., & Keim, M. C. (2007). Stress and coping strategies Among community college students. *Community College Journal of Research and Practice*, *31*(9), 703–712. doi:10.1080/10668920600866579

Rajapaksa, S., & Dundes, L. (2002). Its a long way home: International student adjustment to living in the United States. *Journal of College Student Retention: Research, Theory & Practice*, *4*(1), 15–28.

Raunic, A., & Xenos, S. (2008). University counselling service utilisation by local and international students and user characteristics: A review. *International Journal for the Advancement of Counselling*, *30*, 262–267.

Reavley, N., & Jorm, A. F. (2010). Prevention and early intervention to improve mental health in higher education students: A review. *Early Intervention in Psychiatry*, *4*(2), 132–142. doi:10.1111/j.1751-7893.2010.00167.x Retrieved from http://www.ncbi.nlm.nih.gov/pubmed/20536969

Reavley, N., McCann, T. V., & Jorm, A. F. (2012). Mental health literacy in higher education students. *Early Intervention in Psychiatry*, *6*(1), 45–52. doi:10.1111/j.1751-7893.2011.00314.x. Retrieved from http://www.ncbi.nlm.nih.gov/pubmed/22182365

Ryan, M., Shochet, I., & Stallman, H. M. (2010). Universal online interventions might engage psychologically distressed university students who are unlikely to seek formal help. *Advances in Mental Health*, *9*(1), 73–83.

Sandhu, D. S. (1995). An examination of the psychological needs of the international students: Implications for counseling and psychotherapy. *International Journal for the Advancement of Counselling*, *17*, 229–239.

Sawir, E., Marginson, S., Deumert, A., Nyland, C., & Ramia, G. (2008). Loneliness and international students: An Australian study. *Journal of Studies in International Education*, *12*(2), 148–180.

Shea, M., & Yeh, C. (2008). Asian American students' cultural values, stigma, and relational self-construal: Correlates of attitudes toward professional help seeking. *Journal of Mental Health Counseling*, *30*, 157–172.

Smith, C. L., & Shochet, I. M. (2011). The impact of mental health literacy on help-seeking intentions: Results of a pilot study with first year psychology students. *International Journal of Mental Health Promotion*, *13*(2), 14–20.

Stallman, H. (2010). Psychological distress in university students: A comparison with general population data. *Australian Psychologist*, *45*(4), 249–257. doi:10.1080/00050067.2010.482109

Stallman, H., & Shochet, I. A. N. (2009). Prevalence of mental health problems in Australian university health services. *Australian Psychologist*, *44*(2), 122–127. doi:10.1080/00050060902733727

Toyokawa, T., & Toyokawa, N. (2002). Extracurricular activities and the adjustment of Asian international students: A study of Japanese students. *International Journal of Intercultural Relations*, *26*, 363–379.

Tsang, E. (2001). Adjustment of mainland Chinese academics and students to Singapore. *International Journal of Intercultural Relations*, *25*, 347–372.

Ward, L. (1967). Some observations on the underlying dynamics of conflict in a foreign student. *Journal of College Health Association*, *10*, 430–440.

Wilson, G., Deane, F. P., & Ciarrochi, J. (2005). Measuring help-seeking intentions: Properties of the general help-seeking questionnaire. *Canadian Journal of Counselling*, *39*(1), 15–28. Retrieved from http://cjc-rcc.ucalgary.ca/cjc/index.php/rcc

Yakushko, O., Davidson, M., & Sanford-Martens, T. C. (2008). Seeking help in a foreign land: International students' use patterns for a US university counseling centre. *Journal of College Counseling*, *11*(1), 6–18.

Zhou, Y., Jindal-Snape, D., Topping, K., & Todman, J. (2008). Theoretical models of culture shock and adaptation in international students in higher education. *Studies in Higher Education*, *33*(1), 63–75.

Conclusion: implications for career guidance and counselling

Füsun Akkök, Deirdre Hughes and Gideon Arulmani

The field of career guidance has long been a cornerstone of education, employability and workforce development. Migration is a complex phenomenon that touches on a multiplicity of economic, social, cultural and political aspects all around the world. Findings from this and other books, articles and data-driven insights on migration have taught us that this phenomenon is not uniform across the world, but is shaped by economic, geographic, demographic and other factors resulting in distinct migration patterns, such as migration "corridors" being developed over many years (MIDEQ, 2023)

Career guidance is defined as:

> *"Services which help people of any age to manage their careers and to make the educational, training and occupational choices that are right for them. It helps people to reflect on their ambitions, interests, qualifications, skills and talents – and to relate this knowledge about who they are to who they might become within the labour market"* (ETF et al., 2021).

In some countries, terms such as "career counselling", "career development", "careers information, advice and guidance", "vocational counselling" or "vocational guidance" are used to refer to the range of activities that are included within the term career guidance.

There are vast differences in approaches and acculturation processes, often referred to as *acculturation stress* (Selcuk et al., 2020). The latter is described as the strain that is associated with navigating away from one's culture of origin to another culture (Berry, 2006). This can have a negative impact not only on adults, but also on children's psychological health (Rogers-Sirin et al., 2014). Factors such as the family's legal status, forced versus voluntary migration and perceived discrimination contribute to acculturative stress which in turn can contribute to child anxiety (Potochnick & Perreira, 2010).

The unprecedented pace of change in geopolitical, environmental and technological spheres has led some analysts and commentators to coin or use phrases such as the "age of accelerations," the "fourth industrial revolution "and the "age of change" (Mauldin, 2018). However, as the global migration crisis intensifies, it is crucial for countries across the world to shift their narratives and policies towards support rather than viewing migrants with suspicions and misgivings.

There are compelling reasons why this paradigm shift is not just ethical but also in the best interests of nations. For example, the global community has a moral obligation to protect vulnerable individuals and families fleeing violence, persecution and dire living conditions. Migrants and refugees often play a significant role in their host country's economy, if and when appropriate channels for integration are provided. Whilst they may be often perceived narrowly as filling labour gaps or shortages, many contribute to innovation and economic growth. Finding effective ways of welcoming and supporting displaced individuals and families or those on the move seeking a better or more secure life in other countries is highly contested in the UK, Europe and internationally.

The impact of migrant, refugee and asylum seekers inequality is illustrated through a recent case study drawing on the unfolding of contentious British government policies. For example, in April 2022, it was announced by the Home Secretary "...anyone entering the UK illegally" after 1st January 2022 could be sent to Rwanda", with no limit on numbers (BBC, 2023). In June 2023, the Court of Appeal overturned an earlier ruling by the High Court that the plan was unlawful. The judges ruled that the east African nation is not a safe third country because of "deficiencies" in the asylum system which mean that some claimants could be sent back to their home countries, where they might face persecution. The battle between government and the legal system continues. The High Court ruling indicated the Rwanda policy breaches Article 3 of the European Convention on Human Rights (European Convention, 1950), which prohibits torture and inhuman treatment. It was not a unanimous decision. Two judges agreed to reverse the High Court decision but a third did not. A High Court challenge led by government continues.

In contrast, after an unprecedented bombardment of missiles from Hamas, a pro-Palestinian militant organisation that has dominated Gaza since 2005, Israel formally declared war on Gaza and warned Palestinian nationals to evacuate the area. The United Nations (2023) reported the escalating conflict has displaced hundreds of thousands of people. In Afghanistan, more than 1.6 million Afghans have fled the country since 2021, bringing the total number of Afghans in neighbouring countries to 8.2 million – accounting for one of the largest protracted refugee situations in the world (UN Refugee Agency, 2023). While addressing the complexities of critical factors influencing and driving migration, this is a major global challenge. Therefore, taking a proactive, human-centred, and empathic approach is essential for a more inclusive, prosperous and secure global future.

Implications for policymaking

Earlier, the International Association for Vocation and Educational Guidance (IAEVG, 2015) Communiqué on Educational and Career Guidance for Displaced Migrants indicated that this topic is of or should be a worldwide issue of concern that impacts the lives of individuals, families, communities and countries, and emphasises the importance of bringing attention to advocacy services such as career guidance and counselling to support educational and vocational integration in countries of settlement. The IAEVG also highlights the critical role of policymakers, professional bodies, practitioners and employers in this regard.

A Joint Statement by the European Commission and European Social and Economic Partners "Leveraging the European Partnership for Integration to support the labour market integration of refugees, including people fleeing Russia's war of aggression against Ukraine and other third-country nationals" (EC, 2022) states: "...challenges include providing adequate information to people about their rights, ensuring equal opportunities and access to the labour market; ensuring access to childcare and education, in particular in local schools; providing access to essential services in line with the European Pillar of Social Rights; housing and ensuring language and other training, as appropriate. In addition, the uncertainty over how long refugees from Ukraine will stay in the EU makes planning difficult for all involved and calls for flexible approaches." These partners recognise the urgent need for skills assessment, recognition of qualifications, and job vacancy matching. Career guidance and counselling in this context becomes a critical success factor, as highlighted by co-authors in this book

Moreover, in these extraordinary times, career guidance and counselling services are needed to help people better understand how their surroundings (past and present) shape and influence their life, relationships, decisions, and learning and work opportunities. A holistic perspective provides a foundation for migrants, refugees and asylum seekers to reflect on what they are going through. In addition to providing information and support within educational, training and career development domains, the well-being and collective well-being requires attention by policymakers and practitioners. Therefore, how to support migrants, refugees and asylum seekers to move on for their collective well-being and effective and sustainable labour market integration requires skilful practitioners and training and support in this regard.

Career guidance and counselling services are multi-faceted and must be tailored to meet the unique needs of individuals, families and whole communities who are facing the disruption of fleeing from their home countries. Of primary consideration are services to help migrants achieve a sense of stability and security in the context of a new country, while often navigating major differences in the cultural contexts of education and employment. Those who are vulnerable and disadvantaged often have less confidence. Career guidance and counselling practitioners have roles to play in bringing attention to the issues faced by displaced migrants and in advocating for service provision. Such services could involve working with the local immigrant community and their leaders to identify needs and relevant services, working with school personnel to ease the educational transitions of children and youth, and services to support adults to engage in new learning systems and improving their qualifications to support their re-entry to employment systems.

On an individual level, career guidance and counselling interventions can support migrants to identify their skills, increase their confidence and sense of hope for the future. It also identify training needs, where appropriate, to increase employability and provide the active steps that can be taken towards securing employment stability. Skilful practitioners can help displaced persons to identity key community resources and to participate on interdisciplinary teams that offer a comprehensive approach to educational and vocational support leading to their positive well-being through meaningful engagement with educational and employment systems. Overall, a dynamic suite of approaches and tools are required to meet the diversity of individuals and their unique set of circumstances

Implications for practice

When career guidance and counselling practitioners begin their careers, they need to develop skills to work in a multitude of environments, which offer opportunities to flex their skills with various clients. A challenging but essential part of developing counselling expertise to with work with clients from varied cultures is looking inward and examining one's own biases and privilege. Multicultural therapists must be self-aware and examine how their upbringing and backgrounds influence the way they treat their clients. It is vital that practitioners then learn how to balance those tendencies with greater awareness and perspective, approaching each client with sensitivity.

Bimrose, Mc Mahon and Watson (2015) also emphasise the need for career theory, research, policy and practice to adapt to cultural and contextual differences amongst potential clients and consumers of careers support services in both developed and developing countries. They argue that the theoretical approaches that have emerged from Western economies need to be broadened significantly to take account of more global perspectives.

Future research

We conclude by outlining a number of implications for future research on this topic. For example:

- There is insufficient empirical research on migrants' identity transformation and their lived experiences in new community settings.
- There is a requirement for deeper understanding of migrants' own use of, and preferences for, different types of media. This is particularly important for understanding how and to what extent online information, advice and guidance or counselling sources can shape and influence perceptions.
- There are gaps in the literature on migrants' children and their career-related learning from an early age.
- There is scope to use the notion of migrants' identity and transitions as a focal point for both Western and Eastern scholarly debates that move beyond established academic boundaries with more methodological approaches and meta-analyses drawn from research and practice.
- There have been few substantive studies that have included cost-benefit analysis or use of big data sets to improve policymakers' understanding of the economic benefits in investing in programmes targeted at migrants, asylum seekers and/or refugees.
- Longitudinal studies are helpful to understand the life patterns of migrants and how they grow and develop throughout the life-course.
- There is an urgent need to develop culturally resonant training, tools and techniques to address the developmental needs of migrants.

In developing this work, we need greater attention to be given to actions for impact that put individuals and families at the heart of the process. As Maya Angelou said "*I have learnt that people will forget what you said, people will forget what you did, but people will not forget how you made them feel.*" Doing good work can be difficult at times. Community attachment, dedication and a sense of belonging should be there as an opportunity for all. Through greater cooperation, compassion and forward-thinking policies, nations can turn the narrative around and recognise more widely that migrants are people (not statistics) who have talents and assets rather than liabilities, and if given the chance can ultimately help build stronger and more resilient societies.

References

BBC. (2023). What is the UK's plan to send asylum seekers to Rwanda?, 12th July 2023. Retrieved from: www.bbc.co.uk/news/explainers-61782866

Berry, J. W. (2006). Acculturative stress. In P. T. P. Wong & L. C. J. Wong (Eds.), *Handbook of Multicultural Perspectives on Stress and Coping* (pp. 287–298). Spring Publications. https://doi.org/10.1007/0-387-26238-5_12

Bimrose, J., Mc Mahon, M., & Watson, M. (2015). *Epilogue in Women's Career Development Throughout the Lifespan: An International exploration* (p. 263). Routledge.

European Training Foundation, Organisation for Economic Cooperation and Development., International Labour Organisation, European Centre for the Development of Vocational Training (Cedefop), & the United Nations Educational, Scientific and Cultural Organization (UNESC). (2021). Investing in career guidance: Revised Edition 2021. www.etf.europa.eu/en/publications-and-resources/publications/investing-career-guidance

European Convention. (1950). The European Convention on Human Rights. https://www.echr.coe.int/documents/d/echr/Convention_ENG

European Council. (2022). A Joint Statement by the European Commission and European Social and Economic Partners "Leveraging the European Partnership for Integration to support the labour market integration of refugees, including people fleeing Russia's war of aggression against Ukraine and other third-country nationals". 19th December 2022. Retrieved from: https://etuc.org/en/document/joint-statement-european-commission-and-economic-and-social-partners-renewal-european#:~:text=On%2019%20December%202022%2C%20under%20the%20European%20Partnership,the%20EU%20labour%20market%20with%20a%20joint%20statement

IAEVG. (2015). Communiqué on Educational and Career Guidance for Displaced Migrants Tsukuba, Japan, 2015.

Mauldin, J. (2018). The Age of Change Is Coming, and These Tech Trends Will Drive Economic Growth. *Forbes*, 29 August – Retrieved from: www.forbes.com/sites/johnmauldin/2018/08/29/the-age-of-change-is-comingand-these-tech-trends-will-drive-the-next-decades-economic-growth/#6e78467131fd

MIDEQ. (2023). Migration Corridors, Centre for Trust, Peace and Social Relations, Coventry University. Retrieved from: www.mideq.org/en/migration-corridors/, October 2023.

Potochnick, S. R., & Perreira, K. M. (2010). Depression and anxiety among first-generation immigrant Latino youth: key correlates and implications for future research. *Journal of Nervous and Mental Disease.* Jul;198(7):4 70–477. https://pubmed.ncbi.nlm.nih.gov/20611049/

Rogers-Sirin, L., Ryce, P., & Sirin, S. R. (2014). Acculturation, acculturative stress, and cultural mismatch and their influences on immigrant children and adolescents' well-being. In R. Dimitrova, M. Bender, & F. van de Vijver (Eds.), *Global Perspectives on Well-Being in Immigrant Families* (pp. 11–30). Springer. https://doi.org/10.1007/978-1-4614-9129-3_2

Selcuk, R. S., Esther, J. S., Clare, C., & Elysia, C. (2020). The antiimmigrant sentiment and its impact on immigrant families. In W. Kim Halford & Fons van de Vijver (Eds.), *Cross-Cultural Family Research and Practice* (pp. 415–436). Elsevier.

United Nations. (2023). World News in Brief: Displacement in Gaza and Israel, Afghan Earthquake Response, 9th October 2023. Retrieved from: https://news.un.org/en/story/2023/10/1142077

United Nations Refugee Agency. (2023). Afghanistan Refugee Crisis Explained, USA for UNHCR, The United Nations Refugee Agency, July 2023. Retrieved from: www.unrefugees.org/news/afghanistan-refugee-crisis-explained/

Index

Page numbers in **bold** refer to tables and those in *italic* refer to figures.